KEATS AND EMBARRASSMENT

CHRISTOPHER RICKS

Keats and Embarrassment

OXFORD
AT THE CLARENDON PRESS
1974

Oxford University Press, Ely House, London W. 1

GLASGOW NEW YORK TORONTO MELBOURNE WELLINGTON
CAPE TOWN IBADAN NAIROBI DAR ES SALAAM LUSAKA ADDIS ABABA
DELHI BOMBAY CALCUTTA MADRAS KARACHI LAHORE DACCA
KUALA LUMPUR SINGAPORE HONG KONG TOKYO

ISBN 0 19 812055 9

L.C.# 74-168918

© *Oxford University Press 1974*

*Printed in Great Britain
at the University Press, Oxford
by Vivian Ridler
Printer to the University*

PREFATORY NOTE

KEATS'S poems are quoted from *The Poetical Works of John Keats*, edited by H. W. Garrod (The Clarendon Press: 2nd edn., 1958); and his letters from *The Letters of John Keats 1814–1821*, edited by Hyder Edward Rollins (Harvard University Press: 1958), though I have not reproduced Keats's cancellations and I have on occasion moved up into the text, within square brackets, an explanatory word from Rollins's footnotes.

Permission to use copyright material is gratefully acknowledged as follows: to Mrs. Laura Huxley and Chatto & Windus Ltd. for Aldous Huxley's 'Frascati's' from *Leda* (1920); to Laurence Pollinger Ltd. and New Directions Publishing Corporation for Denise Levertov's 'Second Didactic Poem' from *The Sorrow Dance* (Jonathan Cape Ltd. and New Directions Publishing Corporation, 1967). © 1966 by Denise Levertov Goodman; to the Philosophical Library Inc. for Merrill Moore's sonnet 'Eyes in Libraries'.

I am grateful to Dame Helen Gardner and to Mr. Neil Hertz; also to the Provost of University College London, Lord Annan, for the invitation to deliver in 1973 the Lord Northcliffe Lectures on Literature, these forming part of this book.

C. B. R.

CONTENTS

I

INTRODUCTORY

LET me set down three propositions. First, that embarrassment is very important in life. Second, that one of the things for which we value art is that it helps us to deal with embarrassment, not by abolishing or ignoring it, but by recognizing, refining, and putting it to good human purposes; art, in its unique combination of the private and the public, offers us a unique kind of human relationship freed from the possibility, which is incident to other human relationships, of an embarrassment that clogs, paralyses, or coarsens. Third, that Keats as a man and a poet was especially sensitive to, and morally intelligent about, embarrassment; that the particular direction of his insight and human concern here is to insist upon raising the matter of embarrassability (whereas some other writings and people furnish a different kind of principled relief for us, by means of the cool tactful pretence that the possibility of embarrassment does not arise when we are in their company). I should stress that the attempt is not in any way to search out Keats's psyche, but to get closer to a sense of his special goodness as a man and as a poet; to see the shape of his imagination, and the truth of it. I am aware that this constitutes no kind of biography (but then there have recently been three invaluable biographies, by Walter Jackson Bate, Aileen Ward, and Robert Gittings), and that there are many essential kinds of literary criticism not at all attempted here. But without at all lessening the achievement of Keats's poetry there is a good deal in T. S. Eliot's bringing together Keats, Goethe, and Baudelaire as 'men who are important first because they are human prototypes of new experience, and only second because they are poets'.[1]

Embarrassment is subtle and pervasive in its constraints and

---

[1] *The Criterion*, ix (1930), 358.

pressures. We should value it for this, as does Erving Goffman, the best of the social psychologists who have pondered it:

By showing embarrassment when he can be neither of two people, the individual leaves open the possibility that in the future he may effectively be either. His role in the current interaction may be sacrificed, and even the encounter itself, but he demonstrates that, while he cannot present a substainable and coherent self on this occasion, he is at least disturbed by the fact and may prove worthy at another time. To this extent, embarrassment is not an irrational impulse breaking through socially prescribed behaviour but part of this orderly behaviour itself. Flusterings are an extreme example of that important class of acts which are usually quite spontaneous and yet no less required and obligatory than ones self-consciously performed.[1]

But we should be anxious about it too, since there is no power which society rightly possesses which society will not abuse. It can clearly be a good or a bad thing that, as Dr. Johnson observed, 'No man finds in himself any inclination to attack or oppose him who confesses his superiority by blushing in his presence' (*The Rambler*, No. 159). Propitiation should be neither blankly spurned nor blankly propitiated. From a different viewpoint, the people who pass by on the other side do so because it is somehow embarrassing to get caught up in all that; the unfortunate who collapses in a railway station needs for his Good Samaritan someone undeterred by the small hot pricklings of embarrassment.

The hot flush of embarrassment rises with special frequency and centrality in the nineteenth century. In this it resembles that other hot flush, of indignation. Indignation is a feeling particularly strongly incited and thought about in nineteenth-century literature. This is partly because of what it is proper to feel about the

---

[1] 'Embarrassment and Social Organization', *American Journal of Sociology*, lxii (1956), 264–75; *Interaction Ritual* (1967; 1972 edn., p. 111). See also André Modigliani, 'Embarrassment and Embarrassability', *Sociometry*, xxxi (1968), and 'Embarrassment, Facework, and Eye Contact: Testing a Theory of Embarrassment', *Journal of Personality and Social Psychology*, xvii (1971). On embarrassment as a socializing force, see Edward Gross and Gregory P. Stone, 'Embarrassment and the Analysis of Role Requirements', *American Journal of Sociology*, lxx (1964). On the psychology and psychiatry of embarrassment, see Jerome M. Sattler, *A Theoretical, Developmental, and Clinical Investigation of Embarrassment*, Genetic Psychology Monographs, lxxi (1965).

cruelties visited upon children, as contrasted, say, with those visited upon King Lear; he is so much larger than we are that to feel indignation on his behalf would be to feel something too small, too open to condescension; pity and terror are for Lear, whereas for the Fanny of *Mansfield Park*, the David of the opening chapters of *David Copperfield*, and the Jane of the opening of *Jane Eyre*, indignation is the deep true feeling.

Indignation stands interestingly to embarrassment; the one hot flush drives out the other, as fire fire, so that a common way of staving off the embarrassment one would otherwise feel is by inciting oneself to indignation. One does this when mildly wronged (the wrong change, say) and obliged to attract attention in public to get things put right; the smallish indignation gets factitiously stoked because you will not be ridden by embarrassment once you are hotly riding indignation. Goffman brings together the two words, but not explicitly the two impulses: 'The expectations relevant to embarrassment are moral, then, but embarrassment does not arise from the breach of *any* moral expectation, for some infractions give rise to resolute moral indignation and no uneasiness at all.'[1] Likewise it was to be expected that a man like Keats, so honourably alive to embarrassment, should also have been notably moved to generous indignation: 'He was pleased with every thing that occurred in the ordinary mode of life, & a cloud never passed over his face, except of indignation at the wrongs of others. . . . But if any act of wrong or oppression, of fraud or falsehood, was the topic, he rose into sudden & animated indignation.'[2]

The word 'embarrassment' in our modern sense—'constrained feeling or manner arising from bashfulness or timidity'—found itself called for at the end of the eighteenth century (the *O.E.D.* gives 1774, Burke). As for the adjective 'embarrassed' in our sense, apart from dubious instances in 1683 and 1761 (dubious in that they may mostly represent perplexed and confused rather than constrained and bashful), the first instance comes from the writer whom one would have suspected of having need for it: Sterne. 'As much

---

[1] *Interaction Ritual*, p. 105.
[2] Benjamin Bailey to R. M. Milnes, 7 May 1849; *The Keats Circle*, ed. Hyder Edward Rollins (2nd edn., 1965), ii. 273-4.

embarrassed as . . . the lady could be herself' (*A Sentimental Journey*, 1768). By the end of the nineteenth century it had become an ordinary handle to take hold of the bundle, as when Henry James entitles a volume of stories *Embarrassments* (1896).[1] The point is not, of course, that nobody previously blushed, but that blushing and embarrassment came to be thought of as crucial to a great many social and moral matters. In 1839 Thomas H. Burgess published his rich and various book on *The Physiology or Mechanism of Blushing; Illustrative of the Influence of Mental Emotion on the Capillary Circulation; With a General View of the Sympathies, and the Organic Relations of those Structures with which they seem to be Connected.*

Podsnap is, after all, a very nineteenth-century figure:

The question about everything was, would it bring a blush into the cheek of the young person? And the inconvenience of the young person was, that, according to Mr. Podsnap, she seemed always liable to burst into blushes when there was no need at all. There appeared to be no line of demarcation between the young person's excessive innocence, and another person's guiltiest knowledge. (*Our Mutual Friend*, Chapter 11.)

Yet Podsnap, though an ass, is no fool. He was right to sense that the complex of feelings about the young person (so important to the nineteenth century) was at one with the complex of feelings about blushes, blushes to which indeed young persons are markedly prone. For like much else in Romanticism, the young person and the blush both embody paradoxes about innocence and guilt, a disconcerting mixed feeling very different from the old clarity of demarcation. Ruskin was no Podsnap, but he too was moved by this, as in the paradox of blood and iron: 'Is it not strange to find this stern and strong metal mingled so delicately in our human life that we cannot even blush without its help? Think of it, my fair and gentle hearers; how terrible the alternative—sometimes you have actually no choice but to be brazen-faced or iron-faced'.[2] Ruskin was moved, moreover, to make the highest claim for a blush's beauty: 'All good colour is gradated. A blush rose (or, better still, a blush itself,) is

---

[1] *The Spectator*, Aug. 1896, said: 'Really these stories are often *Embarrassments* in a sense other than that intended by their author.'

[2] *The Two Paths* (1859); *Works*, ed. E. T. Cook and A. Wedderburn, xvi. 384.

the type of rightness in arrangement of pure hue.'[1] The sentiment seems to me a very nineteenth-century one. Perhaps a history of cosmetics—and in particular of rouge—would show the changing attitudes to the blush. Dr. Burgess in 1839 (p. 124) quotes Bichât's distinction between a true blush, which is unfeignable, and other emotions: 'Anger, joy, &c, may be imitated by frowning, by laughing, &c; *but it is the* ROUGE *by which the actress represents modesty and innocence*; let it be wiped off, and the paleness of fear and terror instantly appears.'

Is embarrassment not only a nineteenth-century sentiment but a narrowly English one? There is indeed something very English about the great importance accorded to embarrassment, and this is part of that deep Englishness of Keats in which he delighted and which is so vital and honourable. But to say this is not to concede that the preoccupation with embarrassment is therefore a parochialism or a quirk or a disability. It has always been part of the Englishman's objection to foreigners that they are 'brazen-faced', unembarrassable, and therefore untrustworthy. Especially the French. What the Spaniards said of the South American Indians, the English might say of the French: How can those be trusted, who know not how to blush? What was in the one case false physiology (research into the blushing of the dark-skinned races was a nineteenth-century preoccupation) might in the other be true philology. How can you trust a people whose very language does its best to conceal the existence of the blush? *Rougir* does not in itself offer any distinction between a blush and a flush. Robert's *Dictionnaire* shows of course that a context, strong enough virtually to be a story, can establish the distinction: '*Spécialt*. Rougir de pudeur. *Ne rougir de rien*. V. Impudent. *Des peintures lubriques qui feraient rougir des capitaines de dragons. Fig.* Éprouver un sentiment de culpabilité, de honte, de confusion.' As that last list suggests, the French *embarras* does not exist to effect the work done by the English 'embarrassment'; the French does indeed exist—'État de celui qui . . . éprouve une sorte de malaise pour agir ou parler. V. Confusion, émotion, gaucherie, gêne, honte, malaise, timidité, trouble'—but *embarras* as embarrassment neither rules those synonyms nor rules the many

---

[1] *The Two Paths*; *Works*, xvi. 424.

senses of *embarras* as the English 'embarrassment' now does. There are similar problems with the translatability of 'self-consciousness'. But the difference between *rougir* and 'blush' is the most to the point. Nor is this a mere chauvinism. For even if we were to grant that the total equation that would compare one culture or language with another is too multifarious to be calculable, it could still be true that the differences between cultures are at some particular points assessable. '—They order, said I, this matter better in France—.' More specifically, one could suggest that English life and literature have had the advantages and disadvantages of embarrassability, and that the French have had the advantages and disadvantages of unembarrassability. The falsities of embarrassability, then, are by a natural paradox an especially rich field for the English writers: Dickens on Podsnap. The falsities of unembarrassability, by the same token, are ripe for the French writer. No novel has ever been as unremittingly concerned with embarrassment as *Les Liaisons dangereuses*; no English novel, perhaps, would ever have been able to be so subtly and inwardly appalled by the ingenious deceptions and self-deceptions of unembarrassability. Mme de Merteuil ends a letter to Valmont: 'Adieu, Vicomte; bon soir et bon succès: mais, pour Dieu, avancez donc. Songez que si vous n'avez pas cette femme, les autres rougiront de vous avoir eu' (XX). It may be that nobody but the French would speak so to each other, but then nobody but a French writer would so unerringly and variously capture their propensity to do so. In this as in so much else, Byron is Keats's mighty opposite; the English have long felt, not only that the French overestimate Byron, and esteem him for the wrong things, but also that there is something a bit too French about Byron himself. How characteristic are those unheated words imported from French into English which were so endlessly necessary to Byron in his letters: 'sang froid' and (a word which the Englishman hardly knows how to pronounce) 'nonchalant'. Keats's true form of a comforting nonchalance, different from Byron's which has its own truth, is achieved when he explicitly disclaims a false comfortable kind: 'I should, in duty, endeavour to write you a Letter with a comfortable nonchalance, but how can I do so when you are in so perplexing a situation, and I not able to help you out of it.'[1] It will be right to return to Byron whose high achievement wonderfully criticizes and is criticized by Keats's; for the moment, one could suggest that in the end Byron was precluded from being as great a writer as his contemporary Stendhal because Byron's language and culture made it perilously easy for him to treat as mere affectation certain matters—or certain styles—of embarrassability and unembarrassability about which Stendhal was obliged to be in deadly earnest.

In 1897 blushing was studied in 120 cases, and the general symptoms listed:

Tremors near the waist, weakness in the limbs, pressure, trembling, warmth, weight or beating in the chest, warm wave from feet upward, quivering of heart, stoppage and then rapid beating of heart, coldness all over followed by heat, dizziness, tingling of toes and fingers, numbness, something rising in throat, smarting of eyes, singing in ears, prickling sensations of face, and pressure inside head.[2]

It sounds like a list of the sensations that are alive in Keats's poems, poems which are full of blushes—often rhyming with flushes, from which a rhyme (when attentive and not slovenly) asks us to distinguish them. Dr. F. R. Leavis has spoken of the crucial critical question as 'the relation between Keats's sensuousness and his seriousness';[3] the blushes are intimately part of his sensuousness, and I believe that they are of great importance to an understanding of his seriousness. The work of criticism which is especially liberating in all this is John Bayley's 'Keats and Reality' (*Proceedings of the British Academy*, 1962). Mr. Bayley argued that Keats's genius was essentially 'unmisgiving'—the word was Leigh Hunt's, and Mr. Bayley held that the influence of Hunt was truly benign; the central Keats is the rich poet of *Endymion* and 'The Eve of St. Agnes', rather than the sombre mature poet (strained and against the grain)

---

[1] To George and Georgiana Keats, 12 Nov. 1819; *The Letters of John Keats 1814–1821*, ed. Hyder Edward Rollins (1958), ii. 229.
[2] Havelock Ellis, *The Evolution of Modesty* (1910), III (*Studies in the Psychology of Sex*).
[3] *Revaluation* (1936), p. 272.

of, say, *The Fall of Hyperion*. Keats's art at its best risks vulgarity:
'It turns what might appear mean and embarrassing into what is
rich and *disconcerting*.'

Yet I think that Mr. Bayley did an injustice both to Keats and
to his own apprehension when he introduced the embarrassing only
to have it simply disadvantageous and so simply transmutable;
I do not think that *disconcerting* is quite the antithesis to *embarrassing*
that Mr. Bayley's prose pretends, or that italicizing it will do the
trick, or that Keats's art does exactly this with the embarrassing.
Take a passage which does indeed epitomize the Keats whom Mr.
Bayley rightly admires so much and about which he says the
felicitous thing.

> Perhaps, the trembling knee
> And frantic gape of lonely Niobe,
> Poor, lonely Niobe! when her lovely young
> Were dead and gone, and her caressing tongue
> Lay a lost thing upon her paly lip,
> And very, very, deadliness did nip
> Her motherly cheeks.
>
> (*Endymion*, I. 337–43)

Mr. Bayley contrasts this with the grief of Moneta in *The Fall of
Hyperion*:

> Then saw I a wan face,
> Not pin'd by human sorrows, but bright blanch'd
> By an immortal sickness which kills not;
> It works a constant change, which happy death
> Can put no end to; deathwards progressing
> To no death was that visage; it had pass'd
> The lily and the snow; and beyond these
> I must not think now, though I saw that face—
> But for her eyes I should have fled away.
>
> (I. 256–64)

Mr. Bayley prefers the art which created the grief of Niobe:

The words here are 'unmisgiving' and alive (compare the potent
word *gape* with *wan* and *blanch'd*). This is the real anguish of the
human heart.... The contrast between caressing, with its firm sexual

meaning, and the terrible disregard for itself of this face in torment, would be almost too painful, were it not that the intensity of the image 'causes all disagreeables to evaporate'.

But the power and humanity of these strange lines about Niobe is not simply or solely a matter of their presenting a real anguish, and we need to ask just what 'almost too painful' means here. What animates the lines is a particular recognition about an abandonment to grief such as Niobe's: that it is embarrassing. Here is the physicality of a grief manifest in 'the trembling knee / And frantic gape'; what makes the lines disconcerting indeed is the candour with which they raise a matter that a more grandly tragic manner may be prone to forget: that a great impediment to our full sympathy with frantic grief is its being embarrassing to contemplate, especially in its physical distortion. The tear-swollen child will often get less and less sympathy as it needs more and more; Niobe, whose children have all been killed, is reduced to the paroxysm of a child. Keats's lines seem to me to be intimating not just a sense of anguish but a recognition of this particular dismaying unignorable thing about the way in which we are liable to gaze upon anguish; as in Keats's erotic poetry (which comes to mind too for the reasons that Mr. Bayley gives), the sense not just that something is happening but that something is being watched is an important giver of depth. But the value of the lines—morally and artistically—is not a matter only of their recognizing a challenging human fact, that the embarrassingness of acute grief makes it hard for us to evince a full sympathy, but is also a matter of Keats's showing us that though hard it can be done. For his lines not only do not avert their eyes from the mere gape (always fascinating in its way), they do not look upon it with distaste or thwarted sympathy either; they embody a generosity that can accommodate a truthful recognition (and not be mesmerized), evoked through the repetitions which are like those of grief itself and so are in companionship with grief ('lonely Niobe, / Poor, lonely Niobe', 'very, very'); evoked too in the simple dignity of 'Her motherly cheeks'.

I think, then, that Mr. Bayley was rather too eager to see the embarrassing in Keats give way to something nobler, whereas the nobility of Keats (the man and the poet) is very much a matter of his not flinching from embarrassment while at the same time thinking it always inextricably involved in important moral concerns. But certainly the word 'embarrass' is a natural one for the critic of Keats; Lionel Trilling was moved by his own summary of 'Sleep and Poetry' to what is one of the shortest paragraphs he has ever written, embarrassedly laconic: 'Such doctrine from a great poet puzzles and embarrasses us. It is, we say, the essence of Philistinism.'[1]

Keats's Preface to *Endymion* announced his regret at publishing it and his wish respectfully 'to conciliate men who are competent to look, and who do look with a zealous eye, to the honour of English literature':

The imagination of a boy is healthy, and the mature imagination of a man is healthy; but there is a space of life between, in which the soul is in a ferment, the character undecided, the way of life uncertain, the ambition thick-sighted: thence proceeds mawkishness, and all the thousand bitters which those men I speak of must necessarily taste in going over the following pages.

It is a vivid and memorable sigh—but it is most convincing as a sigh, and not as a statement that should be altogether believed. That it should have been so widely believed is hardly surprising; it sweeps away some troublesome matters and it proffers a reassuring line of demarcation. Moreover, to speak harshly of this 'space of life between' boyhood and manhood which we should now call adolescence is sure to win approval; the boy and the man concur, for different reasons, in contemptuous rejection of the adolescent, and the adolescent is especially liable to contemptuous self-rejection. So all are gratified by Keats's harshness. Yet there is something very improbable about there being a whole phase of life which embodies nothing but disadvantage; one would have thought it more likely that the imagination of a boy and of a man each possessed a particular vantage-point, clarifying some things about life and obfuscating others (without the differences merely coming to six of one and half a dozen of the other); and that the healthy and

---

[1] 'The Fate of Pleasure', *Partisan Review* (1963); *Beyond Culture* (1966), p. 68.

the unhealthy must be incident to any space of life. The more open way to come at it is to ask: along with the disabilities and mawkishness of adolescence, what truths about life is the adolescent better stationed to see than either the boy or the man?

Keats was embarrassed by *Endymion* and by his self-inflicted obligation to dissociate himself from the poem even while publishing it (such conflicting impulses are endemic in embarrassment). The original preface which he drafted[1] was lamentably ill judged; it took the one line that his temperament and his honesty rendered altogether unconvincing, the line that he was not really embarrassed at all:

It has been too much the fashion of late to consider men biggotted and adicted to every word that may chance to escape their lips: now I here declare that I have not any particular affection for any particular phrase, word or letter in the whole affair. I have written to please myself and in hopes to please others, and for a love of fame; if I neither please myself, nor others nor get fame, of what consequence is Phraseology?

Byron was a man and a writer who could use such lordliness in order to discover and enforce truths about himself and others, but Keats was not; and even the published Preface, revised from this one at his friends' insistence, cannot escape the embarrassment inherent in his predicament. That the Preface touches upon matters of the deepest concern to him is clear from the central importance which it gives to the mawkish, always a word that evinces strong thinking and feeling in Keats; but that it is flinching away from these very matters is betrayed by the singular inappropriateness of the word 'bitters': 'thence proceeds mawkishness, and all the thousand bitters which those men I speak of must necessarily taste in going over the following pages.' For if there were ever a poem which adds, again and again, sweets to the sweet, it is *Endymion*.

The case for a great deal that is best in Keats is the case for that space of life, adolescence; or rather for a recognition and incorporation of those insights into life which may be more accessible to a perceptive adolescent than to others. There are too, as is well

---

[1] Garrod's Oxford English Texts edition of the poems reproduces it on pp. xciii–xciv.

known of Keats, the insights of infantility (and what disconcerts the boy and the man about the adolescent is his affinity with the infantile). Keats's friend Woodhouse saw that this was a vulnerability: 'And shall we not excuse the errors, the luxuriances of youth? are we to expect that poets are to be given to the world, as our first parents were, in a state of maturity? are they to have no season of Childhood?'[1] But Woodhouse was wrong to put it so defensively, and Keats's antagonists were right to think that what was at stake was more radical than youthful inexperience. For a particular strength of Keats is the implication that the youthful, the luxuriant, the immature, can be, not just excusable errors, but vantage-points.

Nor is it true that there is nothing which adolescents are particularly good at: they are particularly good at blushing. What they know about, and can help us to know about, is embarrassability.

Endymion comes upon Adonis sleeping:

> Sideway his face repos'd
> On one white arm, and tenderly unclos'd,
> By tenderest pressure, a faint damask mouth
> To slumbery pout; just as the morning south
> Disparts a dew-lipp'd rose.
>
> (*Endymion*, II. 403–7)

The tenderest pressure of the lines themselves is devoted to intimations of embarrassment; so it is as a relief from embarrassment that this is made explicit—nine lines later, with the coolness that shades a blush within the pathetic fallacy: 'The creeper, mellowing for an autumn blush' (Keats's manuscript version had stressed the reciprocity of this blush: 'The creeper, blushing deep at Autumn's blush'). Then, a further twelve lines later, out to the human watcher:

> At these enchantments, and yet many more,
> The breathless Latmian wonder'd o'er and o'er;
> Until, impatient in embarrassment,
> He forthright pass'd . . .

[1] To Mary Frogley, 23 Oct. 1818; i. 384.

The embarrassment is something which the reader is to share with Endymion, and it is 'slumbery pout' which tenderly calls it forth. What is embarrassing about watching somebody asleep is their no longer having command of their features; we feel an unfair advantage in seeing them so. The weight of Adonis's flesh is such as gently to force his mouth into a pout—or rather into what would be a pout if he were awake. The word 'pout' insists that we recognize the faint tremor of distaste which we cannot but feel at the simple physicality, the weight of flesh; but 'slumbery' has already in a sense neutralized this faint distaste, since the feeling is thus made as unjust as it would be to think of a man asleep as indeed pouting. What Keats sees is that it is not necessarily or more importantly the physicality of ugliness which can embarrass, but the physicality of beauty; the weight of Adonis's head is not gross, and yet even it includes this possibility of arousing distaste, and not to recognize this is not to recognize what a full human generosity is. Keats's insight here seems to me to spring from the most deeply ordinary things in life: that we are embarrassed either to sleep in public or to watch the sleeping, for instance in a train. In 'The Biological Significance of Blushing and Shame', John T. MacCurdy —who argues that embarrassment is primitively connected with defencelessness—remarks that 'almost everyone is ashamed of falling asleep inadvertently and usually protests that he has been awake all the time, and those of the upper classes object to sleeping at all in anything but a private room.'[1] Defencelessness, trust, the relinquishment of conscious control, the frankest physicality: it is this complex of feelings which makes it natural and invigorating that it should be love which, here as elsewhere, makes embarrassment needless, unthinkable. One reason why it is so lovely to watch your baby or child sleeping is that it is love which makes it feel altogether proper to watch somebody sleeping without any possibility of embarrassment on either side should he awake. The sleeping Adonis is like a child as well as like a lover. But then lovers can watch over each other sleeping—can, in that phrase which like many another euphemism expresses a deep truth, 'sleep together'. Byron first ascends into rueful comedy from the infant and the child

[1] *British Journal of Psychology*, xxi (1930).

to the miser, and then sinks deep into chastened recognition when
he contemplates this loving contemplation:

> An infant when it gazes on a light,
>   A child the moment when it drains the breast,
> A devotee when soars the Host in sight,
>   An Arab with a stranger for a guest,
> A sailor when the prize has struck in fight,
>   A miser filling his most hoarded chest
> Feel rapture, but not such true joy are reaping
> As they who watch o'er what they love while sleeping.
>
> For there it lies so tranquil, so beloved;
>   All that it hath of life with us is living,
> So gentle, stirless, helpless, and unmoved,
>   And all unconscious of the joy 'tis giving.
> All it hath felt, inflicted, passed, and proved,
>   Hushed into depths beyond the watcher's diving,
> There lies the thing we love with all its errors
> And all its charms, like death without its terrors.
>
> (Don Juan, Canto II. 196–7)

Death without its terrors, or life without its embarrassments. What
Keats's lines achieve is the sense that only his parent or his lover
could look without tremor upon Adonis sleeping, and yet that only
the mean-spirited would find embarrassment glowing into heat-
stroke or cooling into distaste. The particular tremor created by
'slumbery pout' is a working specifically of language upon us, and
not possible to any other medium; so that when Ian Jack[1] says of
Poussin's 'Echo and Narcissus' that 'the face of Narcissus is very
much as Keats describes that of Adonis, with a "slumbery pout" ',
I am moved to a sense of how different a thing a picture is from a
poem; 'pout' introduces a notion of motivation (of using one's
features to signal something) which 'slumbery' rescinds even before
it gets said, and I cannot see that this particular effect can be
achieved through the medium of paint—the picture can show the
features forming what might be a pout, but for us to construe the

---

[1] *Keats and the Mirror of Art* (1967), p. 157.

features as such is quite different from the move which language can make here, of calling it a pout but ripely cancelling that in advance without striking it from the record. Paint cannot use negatives, or oxymorons, in the same way as language can. This matters above all because of the particular ways in which language —the word for a thing, and not necessarily the thing itself—can embarrass.

A traditional objection to all this would be to say that what Keats manifests is not a sensitivity to embarrassment but an insensitivity in the direction of prurience. Prurience, pruriency, and prurient come fully into their modern meaning (from 'itching') in the eighteenth century. The *O.E.D.* definitions are markedly unsatisfactory. Pruriency: 'liking for or tendency towards impure or lascivious thought'. Prurient: 'given to the indulgence of lewd ideas; impure-minded; characterized by lasciviousness of thought or mind.' I should have thought that someone's mind could easily be impure, lewd, or lascivious without being prurient, and that even 'given to the indulgence of lewd ideas' needs to say more about the nature of the indulgence; the prurient is characterized by a particular attitude which it adopts towards its own impure imaginings, an attitude of cherishing, fondling, or slyly watching. Like that other accusation which indicts the attitude with which a man contemplates his own thoughts, the accusation of complacency, prurience is an accusation not only very difficult to defend oneself against but also especially likely to rebound, since the accuser himself is up to some contemplation or other. Thus when C. S. Lewis speaks of Satan (at *Paradise Lost*, IV. 492–511, presumably) as 'leering and writhing with prurience',[1] and when Milton's lines are seen to give no more warrant for 'writhing' than the words 'aside' and 'askance', one may legitimately wonder whether the watching Satan has not momentarily possessed his watching critic.

Blackwood's in January 1826 similarly indulged its imagination in accusing Keats: 'He outhunted Hunt in a species of emasculated pruriency, that . . . looks as if it were the product of some imaginative Eunuch's muse within the melancholy inspiration of the

[1] *A Preface to Paradise Lost* (1942), p. 97.

Haram.'[1] It had, eight years earlier, deplored 'the following prurient and vulgar lines' (I add the three lines introductory):

> Add too, the sweetness
> Of thy honied voice; the neatness
> Of thine ankle lightly turn'd:
> With those beauties, scarce discern'd,
> Kept with such sweet privacy,
> That they seldom meet the eye
> Of the little loves that fly
> Round about with eager pry.
>
> ('To **', 'Hadst thou liv'd')

The lines are very early, very minor Keats, but they are not mindless. The train of thought is from her voice, which can be heard but not seen; then to her ankle flickeringly seen perhaps; then to her breasts, 'those beauties, scarce discern'd'. The lines contemplate not just her clothed breasts but the little loves that try to contemplate them; Keats is engaging, albeit timorously, with a paradox of the private and the public that was always to matter to him and which is patently implicated in embarrassment (as breasts very much are). The contemplations of art are at once very public and very private; Keats enforces this partly by his use of 'pry', a word which he wishes to redeem from the merely inquisitive or prurient. 'Eager' is to put an edge on it. Keats has many other characteristic uses of 'pry', its impulse checked or refined: for instance, by 'aloof' in one direction (scruple), in 'In leafy quiet: where to pry, aloof, . . .' ('To G. F. Mathew', 47); or by 'stare' in another direction (openness), in 'So that we look around with prying stare' ('Sleep and Poetry', 32); or by 'earnestly' in another direction (gravity):

> Who gathering round the altar, seemed to pry
> Earnestly round as wishing to espy
> Some folk of holiday . . .
>
> (*Endymion*, I. 111–13)

This last example takes us back to the earlier one because of its rhyme; to rhyme *pry* with *espy* is to proffer a brisk little contrast. The earlier sequence of rhymes was more concerned with paradox

---

[1] *Keats: the Critical Heritage*, ed. G. M. Matthews (1971), p. 35.

than with simple contrast; *privacy*, *eye*, *fly*, *pry*: the four are suggestive in their interrelationships (*eye* contrasting with *privacy* but at
one with *pry*; *fly* perhaps seeking *privacy* to escape *pry* and *eye*), and
particularly *privacy* and *pry*. Not only are they directly at odds in
meaning, but amusingly not so in form; *pry* is after all a word for
which *privacy* finds room within itself. Keats was fond of using such
rhyme-words as 'privacy' in order to tease out these paradoxes of
the public and the private in love and art; see how delicately the
ideas are led by and held by the rhyme-words in these enchanting
lines from 'The Eve of St. Agnes' about seeing while unseen:
Porphyro's thought has paced ahead,

> Which was, to lead him, in close secrecy,
> Even to Madeline's chamber, and there hide
> Him in a closet, of such privacy
> That he might see her beauty unespied,
> And win perhaps that night a peerless bride,
> While legion'd fairies pac'd the coverlet,
> And pale enchantment held her sleepy-eyed.
>
> (XIX)

It is characteristic of Keats, a man whose imagination was so moved
to fine phrases by the thought of a lover looking, that he should have
said 'I look upon fine Phrases like a Lover'. He did not just mean that
he loved fine phrases. Moreover, the remark itself is part of that
serene continuity which, in the respectful affection of one of Keats's
letters, links all to which he is loyal: friendship, fine writers, himself, the happiness of his friends (and the news of it received from
another friend), and the simply actual (from his own love of fine
phrases to Bailey's love of his newly wedded wife):

I am convinced more and more every day that (excepting the human
friend Philosopher) a fine writer is the most genuine Being in the
World—Shakspeare and the paradise Lost every day become greater
wonders to me—I look upon fine Phrases like a Lover—I was glad
to see, by a Passage in one of Brown's Letters some time ago from the
north that you were in such good Spirits—Since that you have been
married and in congra[tu]lating you I wish you every continuance
of them—Present my Respects to Mrs Bailey. This sounds oddly to
me, and I dare say I do it awkwardly enough: but I suppose by this

time it is nothing new to you—Brown's remembrances to you—As far as I know we shall remain at Winchester for a goodish while—
Ever your sincere friend
John Keats.[1]

To be able to hold such different acts of sympathy, without any slight to each other, within such flowing generosity is characteristic of Keats; and so too is his tacit feeling that it would be presumptuous of him to speak effortlessly of 'Mrs Bailey' and not be explicit about the faint feeling of oddity and embarrassment natural to doing so. Yet in acknowledging the small sense of awkwardness (a proper feeling—there would be something wrong with anyone who felt no such awkwardness or constraint when a good friend marries someone whom he does not know and he wishes to send sincere good wishes to this new intimate stranger), Keats not only frees himself from the awkwardness but frees the friend too. 'Present my respects to Mrs Bailey. This sounds oddly to me, and I dare say I do it awkwardly enough . . .' But Keats is truly never less awkward (his indispensable word in matters of embarrassment) than when he truly acknowledges that he momentarily feels so. His tact, his delicacy of apprehension for the feelings of others, is at one with the delicacy with which he apprehends his own feelings, those of a 'most genuine Being'.

<hr>

[1] To Benjamin Bailey, 14 Aug. 1819; ii. 139–40.

II

KEATS AND BLUSHING

THOMAS BURGESS in 1839 began *The Physiology or Mechanism of Blushing* with a passionate determination not to be thought trivial:

Who has not observed the beautiful and interesting phenomenon of BLUSHING? Who indeed has not had it exemplified in his own person, either from timidity during the modest and sensitive days of boyhood, or from the conscious feeling of having erred in maturer years? When we see the cheek of an individual suffused with a blush in society, immediately our sympathy is excited towards him; we feel as if we were ourselves concerned, and yet we know not why. The condition by which the emotion thus proclaimed is excited, viz., extreme sensibility, the innate modesty and timidity which are the general concomitants of youth, enlist our feelings in favour of the party, appeal to our better nature, and secure that sympathy, which we ourselves may have claimed from others on similar occasions.

There are some, perhaps, who may be inclined to smile at the subject of this Essay. But if these individuals will but reflect on the wonderful mechanism of their being; if they remember that there is not a function, even the simplest, carried on in the economy of man, which is not in the most perfect harmony with all the others, and suggest to themselves that there is a physiology of the mind as well as of the body, perhaps they may be inclined to excuse me for contemplating with wonder and admiration the beautiful illustration of one among the moral laws of nature.

No poet knew more intimately than Keats that 'there is a physiology of the mind as well as of the body'.

In *John Keats's Dream of Truth*, John Jones has a richly evocative account of what a blush can mean in Keats. He contrasts the false and the true:

My scorn for the goddess's notion of atoning for her sexual pleasure 'by some coward blushes' [*Endymion*, II. 788] was at bottom directed

against its mental emptiness; the cheapness of her shame, certainly
there and offensive, is undercut by its incredibility. This sort of
blushing Keats can never substantiate. But there is another sort, the
sort of

> that cheek so fair and smooth;
> O let it blush so ever! let it soothe
> My madness! let it mantle rosy-warm
> With the tinge of love,
>
> [IV. 311–15]

which proves the object ripe for tasting. This blushing unmental
proof, while it reaches forward to possess, has a way of respecting the
object's freedom. In urging 'let it mantle rosy-warm' Keats apprehends something alive on its own, self-charged, a separate and secret
centre. He is appealing to the same imagined hidden source as when
he asks the rose to 'glow intense and warm the air'. This life-fostering
fancy of his spills over into the many attempts to guess admiringly
not just at phases of other lives but at their latent principles; and
then to transpose his conclusions into language which the snailhorn
understands. Blushing joins with glowing and flushing, with smothering and stifling and obscure inner pressures, with floating and heavi-
ness and aching and languor—a central knot of conditions which
hover on the verge of namelessness, all hard worked by him and all
striving to mature an account of how one feels into a revelation of
what one is.[1]

As imaginative criticism (to which I am very much indebted), this
is so good that some may wonder why anything more needs to be
said about blushing. I believe that it needs to be taken in two other
directions; Mr. Jones, though he is excellent on blushing as a sensation and as an imagining of life, makes no claim either to any
consideration of blushing and embarrassment as a moral and social
matter (involved in friendship and love) or to any consideration of
the relationship here of Keats as a poet to Keats the man, the man
whose letters are to many of us the greatest letters we have ever
read.

'The Poet as Hero: Keats in His Letters':[2] Keats was a hero, as
Lionel Trilling subtly and openly argued. Yet Keats's sense that

---

[1] (1969), p. 144. For the 'snailhorn', see p. 30 below.
[2] Introduction to *The Selected Letters of John Keats* (1951); *The Opposing Self* (1955).

difficulties must be faced and can be strengthening incorporates a
humane acknowledgement that there need be nothing dishonour-
able about a 'refuge': 'I must think that difficulties nerve the Spirit
of a Man—they make our Prime Objects a Refuge as well as a
Passion.'[1] Among the 'disagreeables' (Keats's word) of life, among
the difficulties which should nerve a man, was the ordinary human
fact of embarrassment.

Keats wrote to his friend John Hamilton Reynolds:

My dear Reynolds.
    It is an awful while since you have heard from me—I hope I may
not be punished, when I see you well, and so anxious as you always
are for me, with the remembrance of my so seldom writing when you
were so horribly confined—the most unhappy hours in our lives are
those in which we recollect times past to our own blushing—If we
are immortal that must be the Hell—[2]

Those last words are not a mere figure of speech; Keats is embarrassed and ashamed (not the same) for his neglect of Reynolds,
especially given Reynolds's ill health; and again it is not only candour, but also a sense of the nature of embarrassment and its
reciprocity, which makes him begin his letter by speaking openly
of blushing. I cannot think of any other great writer who has
thought that if Hell exists it will be an eternity of blushing.

Blushing in Hell, rather than in Purgatory, is morally complicated
by the fact that a blush may be an acknowledgement of error;
blushing in Heaven offers a mirror-image of the same complication.
It has long been felt that we cannot imagine either the goodness or
the livingness of gods and angels unless somehow we can imagine
them blushing, despite the fact that the blush would have seemed
to be a concomitant of the Fall. It is characteristic of Milton's
courage and humanity that in insisting that sexual intercourse pre-
ceded the Fall he should also have asked us to imagine the full
innocence of a prelapsarian blush:

> To the Nuptial Bowre
> I led her blushing like the Morn
> (*Paradise Lost*, VIII. 510–11)

---

[1] To B. R. Haydon, 10–11 May 1817; i. 141.   [2] 27 Apr. 1818; i. 273.

C. S. Lewis found this blush embarrassing,[1] but the glory of it is the deep tact of Milton's wording: first, in that though 'blushing like the Morn' mostly attaches to 'her', the syntax is such that some tender possibility is left open that Adam too is blushing (more faintly, since the attachment of the words is fainter); second, in the felicity of the pathetic fallacy. For 'blushing like the Morn', so boldly natural and commonplace a comparison (as natural and commonplace and fine as the morn itself), confers this simple naturalness upon the blush itself—the naturalness not just of the morn but of the very comparison; and the innocence of morn (there at the morn of life too) glows into the innocence of the blush. A hundred lines later we learn that what is good enough for Adam and Eve is good enough for Raphael:

> Love not the heav'nly Spirits, and how thir Love
> Express they, by looks onely, or do they mix
> Irradiance, virtual or immediate touch?
>   To whom the Angel with a smile that glow'd
> Celestial rosie red, Loves proper hue,
> Answer'd. Let it suffice thee that thou know'st
> Us happie, and without Love no happiness.
>
> (VIII. 615–21)

This courts ridiculousness, but as often in Milton (and in the Wordsworth whom Milton animated) the possibility of the ridiculous is part of the amplitude of his poetry. Empson bluffly paraphrases: Adam 'says in effect, "Come now, what do you know about this? Have you got any sex?" and Milton to his eternal credit makes the angel blush'.[2] I like *eternal* there; but what matters is to see that it is to the poem's credit as well as Milton's, and that the

---

[1] *A Preface to Paradise Lost*, pp. 118–20.

[2] *Milton's God* (revised edn., 1965), p. 105. Compare pp. 106–7: 'He may simply have had unexpected feelings about blushes. While at school I was made to read *Ecce Homo* by Sir John Seeley (1866), a life of Jesus which explains that, when he was confronted with the woman taken in adultery and wrote with his finger in the sand, he was merely doodling to hide his blushes; then the book makes some arch comments on his sexual innocence, as if by Barrie about Peter Pan. I thought this in such bad taste as to be positively blasphemous, which rather surprised me as I did not believe in the religion. Milton says in the poem that the rosy red of the angel is love's proper hue, so perhaps he did, in a Victorian manner, regard other people's blushes as a source of keen though blameless sexual pleasure.'

credit is a complicated one since it involves the complexities of guilt and innocence in blushing and embarrassment.

Keats nowhere imagines such full grandeur for the blush of god or angel. But his sense of the importance of blushing to our apprehension of others did not permit him to shirk this strange humanizing of the classical gods, whose superiority to humans seems less a matter of a finer spirituality than a more candid recognition of physicality.

> Ah, what a world of love was at her feet!
> So Hermes thought, and a celestial heat
> Burnt from his winged heels to either ear,
> That from a whiteness, as the lily clear,
> Blush'd into roses 'mid his golden hair,
> Fallen in jealous curls about his shoulders bare.
>
> (*Lamia*, I. 21–6)

This was indebted to Raphael's blush, as the coming together ot *love*, *celestial*, and *roses* in this blush suggests; and the best stroke— 'jealous curls'—is pure Milton in the way it enforces innocence by using a word which in its ordinary contexts would insist upon guilt; like Eve's 'wanton ringlets', Mercury's 'jealous curls' are wonderfully pure, 'clear', not jealous a bit. The largeness of mood is true to Keats, as is the winged movement by which the imagination converts the metaphor of 'at her feet' to the literal wings of Mercury at his feet (literal but magical). All the variety of impulse in the lines comes finally to rest in the word 'bare'.

John Jones deplored the 'imbecile morality'[1] of the goddess's adjuration to Endymion:

> I love thee, youth, more than I can conceive;
> And so long absence from thee doth bereave
> My soul of any rest: yet must I hence:
> Yet, can I not to starry eminence
> Uplift thee; nor for very shame can own
> Myself to thee. Ah, dearest, do not groan
> Or thou wilt force me from this secrecy,
> And I must blush in heaven. O that I

---

[1] *John Keats's Dream of Truth*, p. 139.

Had done 't already; that the dreadful smiles
At my lost brightness, my impassion'd wiles,
Had waned from Olympus' solemn height,
And from all serious Gods; that our delight
Was quite forgotten, save of us alone!
And wherefore so ashamed? 'Tis but to atone
For endless pleasure, by some coward blushes:
(*Endymion*, II. 774–88)

This is not very vivid or precise, one might agree, but imbecility is too harsh an accusation, and moreover the human point is precisely that this is indeed a pother—that there is a strange and pathetic disparity between the fleeting coward blushes and the endless pleasure, between the small fear of blushing and the large sacrifices which men, and even goddesses, will make to avert that fear. Embarrassment can be an antagonist whom even love may sometimes succumb to fearing: this seems to me perceptive and seldom said. It is not only those who suffer from ereutophobia, a morbid propensity to blush or to fear blushing, who should acknowledge this. The difference is the size of the self-recognition in Keats, and this has its bearing on the odd relationship of embarrassability to empathy. The hypothesis of the social psychologist Modigliani[1] was that a person of empathy would be especially embarrassable, yet in the event the experiment contradicted the hypothesis. The weak correlation between empathy and embarrassability is an interesting finding, especially in its bearing on Keats, acute to embarrassment and probably more widely and subtly gifted with powers of empathy than any other English poet.[2] Being embarrassable is not, after all, the same as recognizing the possibility of embarrassment; the heat of Keats's empathy (his special gift for beauty and truth) is such as to evaporate this disagreeable. At the least I think it matters that empathy is of such importance both to Keats and to the student of embarrassment—as, of course, is identity. As Goffman says, 'In all these settings the same fundamental thing occurs: the expressive facts at hand threaten or discredit the assumptions a participant finds he has

---

[1] 'Embarrassment and Embarrassability', *Sociometry*, xxxi (1968).
[2] Bate's *John Keats* is especially illuminating on this.

projected about his identity.'[1] Keats was especially sensitive to anything which threatened or discredited identity (his and others'), and he was especially audacious in believing that the healthy strength of a sense of identity depends paradoxically upon the risk and openness and not upon self-protection; depends upon risking the absence of identity rather than upon guarding the circumscription of one's identity:

> several things dovetailed in my mind, & at once it struck me, what quality went to form a Man of Achievement especially in Literature & which Shakespeare possessed so enormously—I mean *Negative Capability*, that is when man is capable of being in uncertainties, Mysteries, doubts, without any irritable reaching after fact & reason—

> A Poet is the most unpoetical of any thing in existence; because he has no Identity—

> ... That Dilke was a Man who cannot feel he has a personal identity unless he has made up his Mind about every thing.[2]

Keats's imagination is alive to embarrassment, so that a slack piece of writing will suddenly tauten in coming near his heart:

> Lo! how they murmur, laugh, and smile, and weep:
> Some with upholden hand and mouth severe;
> Some with their faces muffled to the ear
> Between their arms; some, clear in youthful bloom,
> Go glad and smilingly athwart the gloom;
>   ('Sleep and Poetry', 142–6)

The embarrassed ones are beautifully seen and sympathized with:

> Some with their faces muffled to the ear
> Between their arms;

the effect is at once richly expressive and richly emblematic, like an Elizabethan gesture or posture (melancholy pulling its hat down over its brows), or like the art of Massine which T. S. Eliot so

---

[1] *Interaction Ritual*, pp. 107–8.
[2] Respectively, to George and Tom Keats, 21, 27 (?) Dec. 1817, i. 193; to Richard Woodhouse, 27 Oct. 1818, i. 387; to George and Georgiana Keats, 24 Sept. 1819, ii. 213.

admired: 'The difference between the conventional gesture of the ordinary stage, which is supposed to *express* emotion, and the abstract gesture of Massine, which *symbolises* emotion, is enormous.'[1] In Keats's lines, though, the expressive and the symbolic are both alive. 'Their faces . . . the ear . . . their arms': the effect of acute embarrassment as a physical discomposure, dislocation, has seldom been better caught; it is there in the odd effect of the singular ('to the ear'), and in the muffled but oppressive movement through the prepositions ('with . . . to . . . between'). The difference in quality (perception and phrasing) between this line and a half and those around could hardly be greater. 'Lo! how they murmur, laugh, and smile, and weep': this does nothing to earn the right to say 'Lo!', since it shows and feels nothing of what it is to murmur, laugh, smile, or weep. 'Some with upholden hand and mouth severe': this ventures upon prose and natural sculpture, often a true source of power in Keats but here without immediacy (upholden just how? severe as doing just what to the mouth?). Then in the following lines, the faces that are offered as seen—'clear in youthful bloom' and going 'smilingly'—are not seen or felt with anything of the immediacy which is so moving in those muffled faces not to be seen. I think that John Jones is muffling one important implication of this passage—while clarifying others—when he finds it all equally valuable evidence of Keats's sense of the disconcerting and thrilling autonomy of the parts of the body: 'Staring eyes, parted lips, "upholden hand and mouth severe" situations, are already familiar because they recall the phenomenon of dispersal in which Keats's human theme of the moment—fear, anger, love—gets carried into the body's separate parts.'[2]

Dr. Burgess in 1839 began the first chapter of *The Physiology or Mechanism of Blushing* with a confident relating of the public-private communication which is blushing to that which is poetry. 'Blushing may be styled the poetry of the Soul!' When Burgess (p. 173) says of blushing that '*it is the lava of the heart produced by an eruption of feeling*', we may recall Byron's saying that 'poetry is the lava of the imagination whose eruption prevents an earthquake'.[3]

---

[1] *The Criterion*, i (1923), 305.   [2] *John Keats's Dream of Truth*, p. 159.
[3] 10 Nov. 1813; *Letters and Journals*, ed. R. E. Prothero, iii. 405.

The body's separate parts—and yet their vital interdependency, or in the words of Burgess's title '. . . the Sympathies, and the Organic Relations of Those Structures with which They Seem to be Connected'—are the concern of the medical man, and in starting upon a medical career Keats joined the profession which has a more intimate relation with embarrassment than any other. There is no other profession which makes upon its practitioner so central and total a demand that he—or she—not be embarrassed; the embarrassed doctor or surgeon or psychiatrist would not be able to do his job (and not only because of the effect of his embarrassment upon the patient), whereas a chemist, an architect, or a librarian need only prefer not to be embarrassed. Again there is no other profession (not even the lawyer) which so combines the most intensely private and the most intensely public; this creates something of a counterpart to art such as has long made the medical profession of special interest to art (from the Victorian novels' preoccupation with the doctor,[1] through *Doctor Zhivago*, which is alive to the affinity of doctor to poet, down to Dr. Finlay). So it is not surprising that the doctor should be a special target for the ereutophobe: 'She constantly visited every possible variety of physician, would undress for examination with an almost conscious pleasure (the doctor serving to relieve her guilt feelings), and repeatedly exposed herself elsewhere "innocently" to attack, admitting that she was playing with fire.'[2]

At the other extreme from the ereutophobe who yet longs to be stared at, and who plays with fire, her cheeks on fire, is the human being whose utter imperviousness to anybody's stare challenges our sense even of what it is to be human. I am thinking of a very famous and magnificent passage in Keats's letters. He wrote to Reynolds: 'The short stay we made in Ireland has left few remembrances— but an old woman in a dog-kennel Sedan with a pipe in her Mouth, is what I can never forget—I wish I may be able to give you an idea of her.'[3] A few days earlier he had done his best:

On our return from Bellfast we met a Sadan—the Duchess of Dunghill

---

[1] See Mrs. Leavis's excellent discussion of this in *Dickens the Novelist* (1970).
[2] Edmund Bergler, 'A New Approach to the Therapy of Erythrophobia', *Psychoanalytic Quarterly*, xiii (1944).   [3] 13 July 1818; i. 326.

—It is no laughing matter tho—Imagine the worst dog kennel you ever saw placed upon two poles from a mouldy fencing—In such a wretched thing sat a squalid old Woman squat like an ape half starved from a scarcity of Buiscuit in its passage from Madagascar to the cape,—with a pipe in her mouth and looking out with a round-eyed skinny lidded, inanity—with a sort of horizontal idiotic movement of her head—squab and lean she sat and puff'd out the smoke while two ragged tattered Girls carried her along—What a thing would be a history of her Life and sensations.[1]

It is a superb moment of imagination precisely because it finds itself confronted by the unimaginable: life and sensations from which even Keats's extraordinary powers of empathy are excluded. Yet his sympathy is not precluded, and his cry here—'What a thing would be a history of her Life and sensations'—is one that might have spurred Dickens in Keats's century or Beckett in ours. The impossibility of conceiving of an inner life for this extraordinary old woman is a counterpart in terms of an individual to the impossibility of conceiving of an Ireland free of misery; only half a dozen lines earlier Keats had written: 'What a tremendous difficulty is the improvement of the condition of such people—I cannot conceive how a mind "with child" of Philanthropy could gra[s]p at possibility—with me it is absolute despair.' As so often in Keats, 'conceive' there really does imagine bringing something towards birth; but the old woman's life and sensations are truly conceived of as inconceivable. Yet it is important to see that it is the grandeur of her ridiculousness which makes her so; 'It is no laughing matter tho', because it would be inanity to laugh at someone who could not be imagined as capable of being moved to or by laughter. The grandeur of her ridiculousness is a matter of its imperviousness to any sense of the ridiculous; and though there is much more to Keats's vision of the old woman than can be harnessed to anything that has to do with embarrassment, the passage is among other things an evocation of the unembarrassable. The total imperviousness and unembarrassability of the old woman precipitate in Keats the awed humanity of a great anthropologist, another profession

---

[1] To Tom Keats, 9 July 1818; i. 321–2.

which cannot afford to have any time for embarrassment and which
therefore needs to be all the more alert to it.

We can approach another aspect of embarrassment if we recall
that one of its meanings is financial. In May and June 1817 Keats
wrote twice to his publishers, Taylor and Hessey, the first time
acknowledging their advance of £20 and the second time asking for
a further £30. Both must be quoted in full.

My dear Sirs,
  I am extremely indebted to you for your liberality in the Shape of
manufactu[r]ed rag value £20 and shall immediately proceed to destroy
some of the Minor Heads of that spr[i]ng-headed Hydra the Dun—
To conquer which the knight need have no Sword. Shield Cuirass
Cuisses Herbadgeon spear Casque, Greves, Pauldrons Spurs Chevron
or any other scaly commodity: but he need only take the Bank Note of
Faith and Cash of Salvation, and set out against the Monster invoking
the aid of no Archimago or Urganda—and finger me the Paper light
as the Sybils Leaves in Virgil whereat the Fiend skulks off with his
tail between his Legs. Touch him with this enchanted Paper and he
whips you his head away as fast as a Snail's Horn—but then the
horrid Propensity he has to put it up again has discouraged many
very valliant Knights—He is such a never ending still beginning sort
of a Body—like my Landlady of the Bell—I should conjecture that the
very Spright that the "g[r]een sour ringlets makes hereof the Ewe
not bites" had manufactured it of the dew fallen on said sour ringlets
—I think I could make a nice little Alegorical Poem called "the Dun"
Where we wold have the Castle of Carelessness—the Draw Bridge of
Credit—Sir Novelty Fashion's expedition against the City of Taylors
—&c &c—— I went day by day at my Poem for a Month at the end
of which time the other day I found my Brain so over-wrought that
I had neither Rhyme nor reason in it—so was obliged to give up for
a few days—I hope soon to be able to resume my Work—I have
endeavoured to do so once or twice but to no Purpose—instead of
Poetry I have a swimming in my head—And feel all the effects of a
Mental Debauch—lowness of Spirits—anxiety to go on without the
power to do so which does not at all tend to my ultimate Progression—
However tomorrow I will begin my next Month—This Evening I go
to Cantrerbury—having got tired of Margate—I was not right in my
head when I came—At Cant^y I hope the Remembrance of Chaucer
will set me forward like a Billiard-Ball—I am gald [glad] to hear of M^r

T's health and of the Wellfare of the In-town-stayers" and think
Reynolds will like his trip—I have some idea of seeing the Continent
some time in the summer—
    In repeating how sensible I am of your kindness I remain
                        Your Obedient Servt and Friend
                                John Keats—
I shall be very happy to hear any little intelligence in the literary or
friendly way when you have time to scribble.—[1]

It is, naturally enough, an embarrassed letter, as is clear from its
elaborate whimsy. But even here the movements of embarrassment
are active and effectual as well as shrinking; notice the fertility of
mind and language with which Keats spins his Spenserian allegory,
adapts his Biblical terminology, deploys his literary allusions, and
unfolds his jokes: these are all doubly to the point, since not only
do they reassure his own embarrassment they also reassure Taylor
and Hessey; the verbal vitality, the literary gifts, are such as to
reassure the publishers who in this very letter are having to be told
that 'I hope soon to be able to resume my Work—I have endeavoured to do so once or twice but to no Purpose'. So it is not
surprising that this ordinary situation of embarrassment should
have involved him in so many of the preoccupations that are pure
Keats: the shrinking 'Snail's Horn' which he revered from *Venus
and Adonis* and which served him again and again for his deep concerns ('that trembling delicate and snail-horn perception of
Beauty');[2] his own writing and the mysterious baulkings of it; the
way in which a metaphor moves naturally and simply into the
literal ('anxiety to go on without the Power to do so which does not
at all tend to my ultimate Progression. . . . This Evening I go to
Cantrerbury') and then back into metaphor ('set me forward like
a Billiard-Ball'—that billiard-ball will set itself forward in another
invigorating appearance elsewhere in Keats);[3] the animating delight
in Chaucer. All of these rise naturally to Keats's pen when he is
writing with a consciousness of the embarrassing.

    The other letter to Taylor and Hessey has the more embarrassing
purpose of asking and not just acknowledging. Its metaphor is an

---

[1] 16 May 1817; i. 145–7.   [2] To Haydon, 8 Apr. 1818; i. 265.
[3] See p. 149.

intelligent protection against embarrassment, in being whimsical, in being extreme, and in being itself a way of speaking which could embarrass the maidenish.

My dear Sirs,
  I must endeavor to lose my Maidenhead with respect to money Matters as soon as possible—and I will to—so here goes—A Couple of Duns that I thought would be silent till the beginning, at least, of next Month (when I am certain to be on my legs for certain sure) have opened upon me with a cry most "untunable" never did you hear such un "gallant chiding"
  Now you must know I am not desolate but have thank God 25 good Notes in my fob—but then you know I laid them by to write with and would stand at Bay a fortnight ere they should grab me— In a Month's time I must pay—but it would relieve my Mind if I owed you instead of these Pelican duns.
  I am affraid you will say I have "wound about with circumstance" when I should have asked plainly—However as I said I am a little maidenish or so—and I feel my virginity come strong upon me—the while I request the loan of a £20 and a £10—which if you would enclose to me I would acknowledge and save myself a hot forehead— I am sure you are confident in my responsibility—and in the sense [of] squareness that is always in me—
                          Your obliged friend
                          John Keats—[1]

The squareness is patent, not least in the true urging that it is in Taylor and Hessey's interests that Keats should indeed not spend on his duns, but on time for writing, the money he already has. But what is memorable and acute is the way in which the 'maidenhead' figure of speech is so much more than a jocularity. (Even 'these Pelican duns'—Lear's 'those pelican daughters'—takes its place within the figure.) The relation of embarrassment to sexual feelings and to creativity is strongly intimated; moreover if Taylor and Hessey will send the money, he will be able to acknowledge it in writing 'and save myself a hot forehead'. Not only does this recognize the way in which the written word protects us against embarrassment, and the way in which this will be good for them as

[1] 10 June 1817; i. 147–8.

well as him (they will save themselves Keats's hot forehead—
embarrassment is embarrassing); it recognizes too the erotic
creativity of a blush. For Keats is pre-eminently the poet of the hot
forehead, a forehead of conceptions and often of erotic conceptions.
Yet what stabilizes and controls the maidenhead metaphor is its
being subservient to a different love: 'Your obliged friend' is a
conclusion which has been authenticated by the literary allusion
with which Keats speaks plainly of not having perhaps spoken
plainly enough: 'I am affraid you will say I have "wound about
with circumstance" when I should have asked plainly.' For it is
Antonio who urges Bassanio not to be embarrassed in his request:

> You know me well, and herein spend but time
> To wind about my love with circumstance;
> And out of doubt you do me now more wrong
> In making question of my uttermost
> Than if you had made waste of all I have . . .
> (*The Merchant of Venice*, I. i. 153–7)

'Your obliged friend': Keats preferred the embarrassment of knowing to whom he was obliged. He chafed when he received £25 from
'Mr. P. Fenbank' (probably a joking pseudonym). His reaction
brought together all the proper reactions: that it would have been
churlish of him to refuse it; that he could not help feeling a little
galled; that he did his best to find out the donor; and that he did not
know quite what he would do should he ever meet him. We should
say of his reaction, 'all very proper'. 'I tu[r]n'd over and found a
£25-note—Now this appears to me all very proper—if I had refused
it—I should have behaved in a very bragadochio dunderheaded
manner—and yet the present galls me a little. and I do not know
whether I shall not return it if I ever meet with the donor—after
whom to no purpose I have written—'[1]

Haydon recorded in his diary, 7 April 1817: 'Keats said to me today
as we were walking along "Byron, Scott, Southey, & Shelley think
they are to lead the age, but [*the rest of the sentence, consisting probably
of eight or ten words, has been erased*]." This was said with all the con-

---

[1] To George and Georgiana Keats, 29 (?) Dec. 1818; ii. 17.

sciousness of Genius; his face reddened.'[1] Keats's face was to matter to Haydon because the painter wished it to figure, along with Wordsworth's, in his *Christ's Entry into Jerusalem*; Keats's letter to Haydon succeeds in complimenting him without being self-complimentary by means of another of those good-humoured juxtapositions of the literal and the casually metaphorical: 'I am glad you are hard at Work—'t will now soon be done—I long to see Wordsworth's as well as to have mine in: but I would rather not show my face in Town till the end of the Year—'[2]

Horace Smith, long after Keats was dead, recollected that 'his manner was shy and embarrassed';[3] Keats himself had relished Smith's poem 'Nehemiah Muggs', and one of the passages which he transcribed[4] was this evocation of embarrassed timorousness:

> He shudder'd & withdrew his eye
> Perk'd up his head some inches higher
> Drew his chair nearer to the fire
> And hummed as if he would have said
> Pooh! Nonsense! damme! who's afraid[5]
> Or sought by bustling up his frame
> To make his courage do the same
> Thus would some blushing trembling Elves
> Conceal their terrors from themselves
> By their own cheering wax the bolder
> And pat themselves upon the shoulder

Keats was not one to pat himself upon the shoulder—especially did he not pride himself upon his physical self, and perhaps one of the things he liked about Smith's poem was the good humour with which it used phrases like 'Perk'd up his head some inches higher' and 'bustling up his frame'. For there can be no doubt that Keats felt very strongly about his height (5 ft. $\frac{3}{4}$ in.), and that this mattered most to him, and was an embarrassment more than superficial, because of love and desire. His poem 'Had I a man's fair

---

[1] *The Diary of Benjamin Robert Haydon*, ed. Willard Bissell Pope, ii (1960), 106–7.
[2] 11 May 1817; i. 143.
[3] Robert Gittings, *John Keats* (1968), p. 107 n.
[4] To George and Tom Keats, 14(?) Feb. 1818; i. 229.
[5] Hyder Rollins notes that Keats twice quotes this line in his letters (i. 214 and i. 246).

form' was glossed by his friend Woodhouse: 'the author has an idea that the diminutiveness of his size makes him contemptible and that no woman can like a man of small stature.'[1] Even to Fanny Brawne, Keats was to write: 'Upon my soul I cannot say what you could like me for. I do not think myself a fright any more than I do M^r A Mr B. and M^r C—yet if I were a woman I should not like A—B. C. But enough of this—'[2] That last proper impatience with himself lets him bustle up his frame in a good spirit. Even to his friends he could not write without a tinge of bitterness, as when a word like 'stunted' brings with it more of a crackle than the context can quite accommodate, in a letter to the Misses Jeffrey: 'I wish you were here a little while—but lauk we havent got any female friend in the house—Tom is taken for a Madman and I being somewhat stunted am taken for nothing—.'[3] Or there is the fuse of thought, in a letter to Fanny Brawne, which ignites the supplicating humbleness of his being on his knees so that it flares into his physical self-doubts:

If you should ever feel for Man at the first sight what I did for you, I am lost. Yet I should not quarrel with you, but hate myself if such a thing were to happen—only I should burst if the thing were not as fine as a Man as you are as a Woman. Perhaps I am too vehement, then fancy me on my knees, especially when I mention a part of you Letter which hurt me; you say speaking of Mr. Severn "but you must be satisfied in knowing that I admired you much more than your friend." My dear love, I cannot believe there ever was or ever could be any thing to admire in me especially as far as sight goes—I cannot be admired, I am not a thing to be admired.[4]

One of the things which make Keats's letters to his brother George and his sister-in-law Georgiana the most fully loving of all his letters is that they can accommodate with perfect good humour his jokes about his height. Partly this may be because Georgiana was at once a woman of whom he was very fond (yet not a blood-relation) and a woman whom he was altogether precluded from wooing—there is a lovely relaxation about the way in which his

---

[1] Woodhouse; quoted by Robert Gittings, *John Keats*, p. 58.
[2] 5–6 Aug. 1819; ii. 137.   [3] 4 June 1818; i. 291.
[4] 25 July 1819; ii. 132–3.

letters flirt with her. But mostly it is just that he loved George and Georgiana so much that embarrassment about his height was out of the question—and the right way to show this was by mock-ruefulness. I think it central to Keats's moral imagination that he should have felt as he did, not proclaiming to himself that of course it did not matter a bit that he was five foot tall, but rightly seeing that thanks to love it did not matter a bit. The perfect occasion manifesting this grateful ease is Georgiana's baby:

I admire the exact admeasurement of my niece in your Mother's letter—O the little span long elf—I am not in the least judge of the proper weight and size of an infant. Never trouble yourselves about that: she is sure to be a fine woman—Let her have only delicate nails both on hands and feet and teeth as small as a May-fly's. who will live you his life on a square inch of oak-leaf.[1]

I must not forget to mention that your mother show'd me the lock of hair—'t is of a very dark colour for so young a creature. When it is two feet in length I shall not stand a barley corn higher. That's not fair—one ought to go on growing as well as others—[2]

Another letter to George and Georgiana makes clear the strength of his feeling as well as the cluster of his feelings. It begins with a characteristic verbal germination from 'shrunk from':

I have not seen Mr Lewis lately for I have shrunk from going up the hill—Mr Lewis went a few morning[s] ago to town with Mrs Brawne they talked about me—and I heard that Mr L Said a thing I am not at all contented with—Says he 'O, he is quite the little Poet' now this is abominable—you might as well say Buonaparte is quite the little Soldier—You see what it is to be under six foot and not a lord—There is a long fuzz to day in the examiner about a young Man who delighted a young woman with a Valentine—I think it must be Ollier's. Brown and I are thinking of passing the summer at Brussels if we do we shall go about the first day of May—We ie Brown and I sit opposite one another all day authorizing (N.B. an s instead of a z would give a different meaning) He is at present writing a Story of an old Woman who lived in a forest and to whom the Devil or one [of] his Aid de feus came one night very late and in disguise—[3]

---

[1] 18 Sept. 1819; ii. 189.   [2] 24 Sept. 1819; ii. 213.   [3] 14 Feb. 1819; ii. 61.

Then into an astonishing *Zuleika Dobson*-like tale of how an old lady becomes irresistibly beautiful:

evey one falls in love with her—from the Prince to the Blacksmith. A young gentleman on his way to the church to be married leaves his unfortunate Bride and follows this nonsuch—A whole regiment of soldiers are smitten at once and follow her—A whole convent of Monks in corpus christi procession join the Soldiers—The Mayor and Corporation follow the same road—Old and young, deaf and dumb—all but the blind are smitten and form an immense concourse of people who—what Brown will do with them I know not—The devil himself falls in love with her flies away with her to a desert place—in consequence of which she lays an infinite number of Eggs—

What is significant is the sequence which goes from 'O, he is quite the little Poet', through the 'young Man who delighted a young woman with a Valentine', to authorship and Brown's story of the magically irresistible beauty. For in choosing to be a poet—to be supremely a writer and reader—Keats chose a way of life which made differences of height least noticeable; and he knew too that 'authorizing' had its own relationship to beauty and to love's imaginings. In bringing together his own height, Mrs. Brawne, a young man's valentine, authorship, and a fabulous tale, he is sketching a cluster of feelings which begin in embarrassment, a commonplace matter but really not a simple one.

Just as the impalpable subjective world of the creative imagination and its beauty can create its own liberation from embarrassment, so too can the palpable objective world of nature and its beauty. There is no discord or oddity in the fact that Keats's letter to his brother Tom, 27 June 1818, should bring together the mountains' height and his sense of his own height. But one needs to see the scale of Keats's response in order to see how it can accommodate this self-consciousness freed from embarrassment's self-consciousness:

We arose this morning at six, because we call it a day of rest, having to call on Wordsworth who lives only two miles hence—before breakfast we went to see the Ambleside water fall. The morning beautiful—the walk easy among the hills. We, I may say, fortunately, missed the direct path, and after wandering a little, found it out by the noise—for, mark you, it is buried in trees, in the bottom of the valley—the stream itself is interesting throughout with "mazy error over pendant shades." Milton meant a smooth river—this is buffetting all the way on a rocky bed ever various—but the waterfall itself, which I came suddenly upon, gave me a pleasant twinge. First we stood a little below the head about half way down the first fall, buried deep in trees, and saw it streaming down two more descents to the depth of near fifty feet—then we went on a jut of rock nearly level with the second fall-head, where the first fall was above us, and the third below our feet still—at the same time we saw that the water was divided by a sort of cataract island on whose other side burst out a glorious stream—then the thunder and the freshness. At the same time the different falls have as different characters; the first darting down the slate-rock like an arrow; the second spreading out like a fan—the third dashed into a mist—and the one on the other side of the rock a sort of mixture of all these. We afterwards moved away a space, and saw nearly the whole more mild, streaming silverly through the trees. What astonishes me more than any thing is the tone, the coloring, the slate, the stone, the moss, the rock-weed; or, if I may so say, the intellect, the countenance of such places. The space, the magnitude of mountains and waterfalls are well imagined before one sees them; but this countenance or intellectual tone must surpass every imagination and defy any remembrance. I shall learn poetry here and shall henceforth write more than ever, for the abstract endeavor of being able to add a mite to that mass of beauty which is harvested from these grand materials, by the finest spirits, and put into etherial existence for the relish of one's fellows. I cannot think with Hazlitt that these scenes make man appear little. I never forgot my stature so completely—I live in the eye; and my imagination, surpassed, is at rest—[1]

The strength of Keats's imagination is its peaceful accommodation; the surpassing imagination of Wordsworth, Milton, and Hazlitt can all be intimated here, not only without any quarrelling for ascendancy among themselves but also without any discrepancy between their kind of grandeur, beauty, size, and the landscape's kind. To speak of 'the countenance of such places' is to lead without obtrusion into the watching person and his own height. The touching

[1] i. 300-1.

admission—'I never forgot my stature so completely'—is what authenticates the whole fine self-abnegation which contemplates and renders the landscape so livingly. Keats was alert to something importantly true about the dignity and beauty of nature: that among the sane, fortifying, and consolatory powers it has is the power to free us from embarrassment, to make embarrassment unthinkable ('I never forgot my stature so completely'). For Wordsworth,

> The thought of death sits easy on the man
> Who has been born and dies among the mountains.
> ('The Brothers')

Likewise, the thought of blushing—less grand but not trivial or self-absorbed.

If this is so, we can measure how distant we now are from the Romantics' respectful gratitude to nature by recalling what man has made of waterfalls even mightier than Keats's. I am thinking of Dan Jacobson's saddened acerb observations on the twentieth-century commercial trash that now surrounds the Niagara Falls:

But what about the falls? Oh yes, they're still there, falling away industriously, overwhelmed rather than merely profaned by what Parkman would call the pettiness of man. The smaller, American falls, one learns from the guide, have actually been switched off on more than one occasion in the past, to enable hydro-electric works to be done; and also to try to remove some of the rocks which have tumbled down the face of the falls and piled up messily in front, thus making them so much the less lofty and imposing. From the far bank, the yellow and brown skyscrapers of downtown Niagara NY appear to stand directly above the American falls; and above them again are enormous neon signs advertising the United Hotel and O'Keefe's Ale. The Canadian or Horseshoe Falls are much the more spectacular of the two. The water roars down; the spray rises high; a moving yet stationary line of pale green wavers forever on the all but closed circle of the rim, between the dark green rush of the river and the pure white of torrent. However, among the observation towers and neon signs and car parks, the Horseshoe Falls look from a distance rather like some kind of wildly inspired Pop Art joke: the waters run away incessantly down what is simply the biggest plug-hole in the world.

Standing in the throng of people on the pavement, immediately above the white uproar of the cataract, one can't help wondering, in fact, if there isn't some therapeutic or self-defensive intention in all the rubbish with which the spectacle has been surrounded. What else could one do with it? In making such a stupendous gesture Nature embarrasses us: it seems so excessive, so pointless. We are not explorers, we are not believers like Father Hennepin, we are not 19th-century romantics, we are just tourists.[1]

'Nature embarrasses us': this is a profound insight of Mr. Jacobson's, appallingly remote from Keats's gratitude for having his imagination surpassed. 'I cannot think with Hazlitt that these scenes make man appear little'; but there is a littleness of humiliation which is not humility, and Hazlitt might ask: Why, if modern man does not feel humiliatedly little, does he so belittle and belitter these scenes?

That the cluster of feelings is not a chance collocation is clear from others of Keats's letters. The transitions, which are trains of feeling as much as trains of thought, in his superb letter to Bailey of 18 July 1818, knit a wonderful continuity of self-awareness: from courteous explanation; through apology and embarrassment ('made me blush'); his own work; apology and embarrassment towards women; rejoicing at others' happiness; his height; mountains; poetry—it is like a list of the things he cared most about and was most self-awarely aware of:

My dear Bailey,
    The only day I have had a chance of seeing you when you were last in London I took every advantage of—some devil led you out of the way—Now I have written to Reynolds to tell me where you will be in Cumberland—so that I cannot miss you—and when I see you the first thing I shall do will be to read that about Milton and Ceres and Proserpine—for though I am not going after you to John o' Grotts it will be but poetical to say so. And here Bailey I will say a few words written in a sane and sober Mind, a very scarce thing with me, for they may hereafter save you a great deal of trouble about me, which you do not deserve, and for which I ought to be

[1] *The Listener*, 25 Nov. 1971.

ba[s]tinadoed. I carry all matters to an extreme—so that when I have any little vexation it grows in five Minutes into a theme for Sophocles —then and in that temper if I write to any friend I have so little selfpossession that I give him matter for grieving at the very time perhaps when I am laughing at a Pun. Your last Letter made me blush for the pain I had given you—I know my own disposition so well that I am certain of writing many times hereafter in the same strain to you—now you know how far to believe in them—you must allow for imagination—I know I shall not be able to help it. I am sorry you are grieved at my not continuing my visits to little Britain—yet I think I have as far as a Man can do who has Books to read to [and] subjects to think upon—for that reason I have been no where else except to Wentworth place so nigh at hand—moreover I have been too often in a state of health that made me think it prudent no[t] to hazard the night Air—Yet further I will confess to you that I cannot enjoy Society small or numerous—I am certain that our fair friends are glad I should come for the mere sake of my coming; but I am certain I bring with me a Vexation they are better without—If I can possibly at any time feel my temper coming upon me I refrain even from a promised visit. I am certain I have not a right feeling towards Women—at this moment I am striving to be just to them but I cannot —Is it because they fall so far beneath my Boyish imagination? When I was a Schoolboy I though[t] a fair Woman a pure Goddess, my mind was a soft nest in which some one of them slept though she knew it not—I have no right to expect more than their reality. I thought them etherial above Men—I find then [them] perhaps equal—great by comparison is very small—Insult may be inflicted in more ways than by Word or action—one who is tender of being insulted does not like to think an insult against another—I do not like to think insults in a Lady's Company—I commit a Crime with her which absence would have not known—Is it not extraordinary? When among Men I have no evil thoughts, no malice, no spleen—I feel free to speak or to be silent—I can listen and from every one I can learn—my hands are in my pockets I am free from all suspicion and comfortable. When I am among Women I have evil thoughts, malice spleen—I cannot speak or be silent—I am full of Suspicions and therefore listen to no thing— I am in a hurry to be gone—You must be charitable and put all this perversity to my being disappointed since Boyhood—Yet with such feelings I am happier alone among Crowds of men, by myself or with a friend or two—With all this trust me Bailey I have not the least idea that Men of different feelings and inclinations are more short sighted than myself—I never rejoiced more than at my Brother's Marriage and shall do so at that of any of my friends—. I must absolutely get over this—but how? The only way is to find the root of evil, and so cure it "with backward mutters of dissevering Power" That is a difficult thing; for an obstinate Prejudice can seldom be produced but from a gordian complication of feelings, which must take time to unravell and care to keep unravelled—I could say a good deal about this but I will leave it in hopes of better and more worthy dispositions—and also content that I am wronging no one, for after all I do think better of Womankind than to suppose they care whether Mister John Keats five feet hight likes them or not. You appeared to wish to avoid any words on this subject—don't think it a bore my dear fellow—it shall be my Amen—I should not have consented to myself these four Months tramping in the highlands but that I thought it would give me more experience, rub off more Prejudice, use [me] to more hardship, identify finer scenes load me with grander Mountains, and strengthen more my reach in Poetry, than would stopping at home among Books even though I should reach Homer—By this time I am comparitively a a mountaineer—I have been among wilds and Mountains too much to break out much about the[i]r Grandeur.[1]

It is his sense of the 'gordian complication of feelings' which enlivens the very prose, moving from 'Mister John Keats five feet hight' to 'grander Mountains, and strengthen more my reach in Poetry'.

Similarly, when Keats was momentarily disillusioned with landscape it was natural for him to believe that a landscape needed to be in the vicinity of love if it were to be loved. He wrote to Fanny Brawne: 'I am getting a great dislike of the picturesque; and can only relish it over again by seeing you enjoy it'[2]—the sentiment is a vivid epitome of that vista, of the watcher watched, which is so crucial to Keats's poetry ('seeing you enjoy it', where 'enjoy' is 'enjoy seeing'). Then he needs once more his old figure of 'maidenhead' (it takes up from 'touch'd' and is followed by covert bawdy) in explaining to Dilke why the Isle of Wight made too small an impression upon him, and—one may think—did not abolish his smallness:

I have been so many finer walks, with a back ground of lake and mountain instedd of the sea, that I am not much touch'd with it, though I credit it for all the Surprise I should have felt if it had taken my cockney maidenhead—But I may call myself an old Stager in the picturesque, and unless it be something very large and overpowering I cannot receive any extraordinary relish.[1]

The combination in Keats of intense self-awareness and a richly co-operative creative subconscious was such as to make it natural for him to be liable to and alive to slips and leaps of the mind. These are both bred from and breed embarrassment. The intelligence of Keats's letter to James Rice, 24 November 1818, is manifest in its self-knowledge and in its lucidity; 'it seems downright preintention' is a formulation effortlessly precise and poised.

My dear Rice,
    Your amende honorable, I must call 'un surcroit d'amitié' for I am not at all sensible of any thing but that you were unfortunately engaged and I was unfortunately in a hurry. I completely understand your feeling in this mistake, and find in it that ballance of comfort which remains after regretting your uneasiness—I have long made up my Mind to take for granted the genuine heartedness of my friends notwithstanding any temporery ambiguousness in their behaviour or their tongues; nothing of which how[ev]er I had the least scent of this morning. I say completely understand; for I am everlastingly getting my mind into such like painful trammels—and am even at this moment suffering under them in the case of a friend of ours. I will tell you—Two most unfortunate and paralel slips—it seems downright preintention. A friend says to me 'Keats I shall go and see Severn this Week' 'Ah' says I 'You want him to take your Portrait' and again 'Keats' says a friend 'When will you come to town again' 'I will' says I 'let you have the Mss next week' In both these I appeard to attribute and [an] interested motive to each of my friends' questions—the first made him flush; the second made him look angry—And yet I am innocent—in both cases my Mind leapt over every interval to what I saw was per se a pleasant subject with him—You see I have no allowances to make—you see how far I am from supposing you could show me any neglect. I very much regret the long time I have been obliged to exile from you—for I have had one or two rather pleasant occasions to confer upon with you—What I have

heard from George is favorable—I expect soon a Letter from the Settlement itself—

Your sincere friend

John Keats

I cannot give any good news of Tom—[1]

The humanity and moral intelligence derive partly from its simple decision of friendship: that the way to reassure the needlessly apologetic Rice is for Keats himself to apologize *in absentia*—and needlessly too ('And yet I am innocent')—to 'a friend of ours'. Rice will be released from his embarrassment by Keats's speaking of his own and of that which he innocently inflicted upon their friend— it is a beautiful instance not only of embarrassment as a binding chain-reaction but also of how the whole chain of the embarrassed can be dislinked and released by one imaginative act of sympathy. But I think that it is not only friendship which creates this release in the letter, but also Keats's sense of art. It is not a coincidence that both of Keats's slips concern art (Severn's portrait and Keats's poems), or that the fertility of mind which creates such slips should be spoken of in terms which suggest the fertility of art: 'my Mind leapt over every interval to what I saw was per se a pleasant subject with him.' What Keats sees is that the ordinary daily imagination is the same faculty that leaps to reach the delights of art. We must trust this faculty, as we must trust our friends, 'notwithstanding any temporery ambiguousness in their behaviour or their tongues'. The tact of the whole letter is supreme in its modesty, and it is a tact explicitly devoted to embarrassment; I even think that it was Keats's tact which would not let him risk any slight to Tom, to his own feelings about Tom, or to Rice's, and which therefore saw that the single poignant sentence about his dying brother, 'I cannot give any good news of Tom', could not be accommodated within the letter's tone and its concerns and so must stand as a bleakly separate postscript.

A slip or leap of the tongue or of the mind is the not-consciously intended infliction of embarrassment on others, sometimes because they have just inflicted embarrassment on the speaker. But we do deliberately embarrass people, again sometimes because they have just inflicted embarrassment on us. Keats has a splendidly comic account of the comic therapy (to cure the ingratiations of charm) which one of his friends, Dilke, visited upon another, Brown.

The Place I am speaking of, puts me in mind of a circumsta[n]ce occured lately at Dilkes—I think it very rich and dramatic and quite illustrative of the little quiet fun that he will enjoy sometimes. First I must tell you their house is at the corner of Great Smith Street, so that some of the windows look into one Street, and the back windows into another round the corner—Dilke had some old people to dinner, I know not who—but there were two old ladies among them—Brown was there—they had known him from a Child. Brown is very pleasant with old women, and on that day, it seems, behaved himself so winningly they [that] they became hand and glove together and a little complimentary. Brown was obliged to depart early. He bid them good bye and pass'd into the passage—no sooner was his back turn'd than the old women began lauding him. When Brown had reach'd the Street door and was just going, Dilke threw up the Window and call'd 'Brown! Brown! They say you look younger than ever you did!' Brown went on and had just turn'd the corner into the other street when Dilke appeared at the back window crying "Brown! Brown! By God, they say you're handsome!"[1]

Brown had been embarrassingly 'winning'; Dilke trumps him, and the whole story has a Chaucerian good humour and vitality, like so much else in Keats's letters. What makes it 'very rich and dramatic' is the act of imagination by Dilke, which—as in art seizing a *trouvaille*—seized upon the simple fact of the house's layout in order to plague Brown twice over. The one cry would not have done; alone, it might have seemed shrill or sour; it is the preposterousness of 'the *other* street' and the further cry that makes us feel that Dilke has the right to smile, and that even Brown, though he may have blushed, is unlikely to have scowled.

It has to be a finely judged thing, inflicting embarrassment (the *fabliau* must not get cruel). One feels in this case that both Dilke and now Keats have judged it perfectly. Although it is a pity to

---

[1] To George and Georgiana Keats, 18 Sept. 1819; ii. 190.

risk blurring the anecdote, one of the best and most delicate evocations of embarrassment that I know, I want to quote what introduces and succeeds the anecdote in Keats's letter to his brother George. For Keats comes to this 'dramatic' creation of Dilke's imagination from having spoken of drama and farce, and then of that other farce which was Dilke's upbringing of his son; it is 'farce'— 'Dilke'—and then 'window' which stirs the anecdote into life:

Reynolds has turn'd to the law. Bye the bye, he brought out a little piece at the Lyceum call'd *one, two, th[r]ee, four, by advertisement.* It met with complete success. The meaning of this odd title is explained when I tell you the principal actor is a mimic who takes off four of our best performers in the course of the farce—Our stage is loaded with mimics. I did not see the Piece being out of Town the whole time it was in progress. Dilke is entirely swallowed up in his boy: 't is really lamentable to what a pitch he carries a sort of parental mania—I had a Letter from him at Shanklin—He went on a word or two about the isle of Wight which is a bit of hobby horse of his; but he soon deviated to his boy. 'I am sitting' says he "at the window expecting my Boy from School." I suppose I told you some where that he lives in Westminster, and his boy goes to the School there. where he gets beaten, and every bruise he has and I dare say deserves is very bitter to Dilke. The Place I am speaking of, puts me in mind of a circumsta[n]ce occured lately at Dilkes—

As for what succeeds the anecdote, this thinks further about imagination, first in terms of its own attempt at description, then in praise of Robert Burton—and what Burton is imagining with such fertility is the fertile credulity of the lover:

"Brown! Brown! By God, they say you're handsome!" You see what a many words it requires to give any identity to a thing I could have told you in half a minute. I have been reading lately Burton's Anatomy of Melancholy; and I think you will be very much amused with a page I here coppy for you. I call it a Feu de joie round the batteries of Fort St Hyphen-de-Phrase on the birthday of the Digamma. The whole alphabet was drawn up in a Phalanx on the cover of an old Dictionary. Band playing "Amo, Amas &c" "Every Lover admires his Mistress, though she be very deformed of herself, ill-favored, wrinkled, pimpled, pale, red, yellow, tann'd, tallow-fac'd, have a

swoln juglers platter face, or a thin, lean, chitty face, have clouds in
her face, be crooked, dry, bald . . .

Or, 'Brown! Brown! By God, they say you're handsome!'

The relationship of sexual attraction to embarrassment and to
imagination is clearly rich in potentiality. I want now to quote
Keats's extraordinary evocation of how a woman's sexual self-
possession and freedom from embarrassment created in him a corresponding self-possession and freedom. He comes to this gradually.
He has been declaring to George and to Georgiana his confidence
that he will outdo the reviewers ('I think I shall be among the
English Poets after my death'): 'It does me not the least harm in
Society to make me appear little and rediculous: I know when a
Man is superior to me and give him all due respect—he will be the
last to laugh at me and as for the rest I feel that I make an impression
upon them which insures me personal respect while I am in sight
whatever they may say when my back is turned—'[1] He is still
thinking of such belittling and of respect a few lines later when he
comes to the envy of the Reynolds sisters in the face of the sexual
magnetism of their visiting cousin Jane Cox.

The Miss Reynoldses are very kind to me—but they have lately dis-
pleased me much and in this way—Now I am coming the Richardson.
On my return, the first day I called they were in a sort of taking or
bustle about a Cousin of theirs who having fallen out with her
Grandpapa in a serious manner, was invited by Mrs R—to take
Asylum in her house—She is an east indian and ought to be her
Grandfather's Heir. At the time I called Mrs R. was in conference
with her up stairs and the young Ladies were warm in her praises
down stairs calling her genteel, interresting and a thousand other
pretty things to which I gave no heed, not being partial to 9 days
wonders—Now all is completely changed—they hate her; and from
what I hear she is not without faults—of a real kind: but she has
othe[r]s which are more apt to make women of inferior charms hate
her. She is not a Cleopatra; but she is at least a Charmian. She has a
rich eastern look; she has fine eyes and fine manners. When she comes
into a room she makes an impression the same as the Beauty of a
Leopardess. She is too fine and too conscious of her Self to repulse any

Man who may address her—from habit she thinks that nothing *particular*. I always find myself more at ease with such a woman; the picture before me always gives me a life and animation which I cannot possibly feel with any thing inferiour—I am at such times too much occupied in admiring to be awkward or on a tremble. I forget myself entirely because I live in her. You will by this time think I am in love with her; so before I go any further I will tell you I am not—she kept me awake one Night as a tune of Mozart's might do—I speak of the thing as a passtime and an amuzement than which I can feel none deeper than a conversation with an imperial woman the very 'yes' and 'no' of whose Lips is to me a Banquet. I dont cry to take the moon home with me in my Pocket not [nor] do I fret to leave her behind me. I like her and her like because one has no *sensations*—what we both are is taken for granted—You will suppose I have by this had much talk with her—no such thing—there are the Miss Reynoldses on the look out—They think I dont admire her because I did not stare at her—They call her a flirt to me—What a want of knowledge? she walks across a room in such a manner that a Man is drawn towards her with a magnetic Power. This they call flirting! they do not know things. They do not know what a Woman is. I believe tho' she has faults—the same as Charmian and Cleopatra might have had—Yet she is a fine thing speaking in a worldly way: for there are two distinct tempers of mind in which we judge of things—the worldly, theatrical and pantomimical; and the unearthly, spiritual and etherial—in the former Buonaparte, Lord Byron and this Charmian hold the first place in our Minds; in the latter John Howard, Bishop Hooker rocking his child's cradle and you my dear Sister are the conquering feelings. As a Man in the world I love the rich talk of a Charmian; as an eternal Being I love the thought of you. I should like her to ruin me, and I should like you to save me.

I have quoted this at length because I wished to show the generous feeling both in Keats's disapproval of the envious and in the final humour with which it is made clear that he does not fret: the humour which says with childlike and unhurtful dexterity to his sister-in-law, 'I should like her to ruin me, and I should like you to save me'. But the centre of the passage is its release from embarrassment. 'The Beauty of a Leopardess' is that of an animal unembarrassable and therefore unembarrassing; 'too fine and too conscious of her Self' catches the paradox of a proper self-consciousness.

The wrong self-consciousness is that which manifests itself as an unawareness of other people's susceptibilities; far from dissolving embarrassment this precipitates it. Keats deplored this in Leigh Hunt, in a passage which shows that the *congeries* of embarrassment, taste, Mozart, and 'fine things' ('Yet she is a fine thing'), was not limited to the vicinity of Jane Cox:

He understands many a beautiful thing; but then, instead of giving other minds credit for the same degree of perception as he himself possesses—he begins an explanation in such a curious manner that our taste and self-love is offended continually. Hunt does one harm by making fine things petty and beautiful things hateful—Through him I am indifferent to Mozart, I care not for white Busts—and many a glorious thing when associated with him becames a nothing—[1]

Jane Cox is too conscious of herself to feel at all self-conscious, and because of this she offers as it were the benign contagion of unembarrassment. Keats forgets his self-consciousness in her company: 'I always find myself more at ease with such a woman . . . I am at such times too much occupied in admiring to be awkward or on a tremble. I forget myself entirely because I live in her.' Once more, 'awkward' and 'on a tremble' are Keats's special indication of embarrassment. Then there is the firm, humorously spelled-out disclaimer that he is in love with her; the comparison, which had earlier been with a 'picture' is now with 'a tune of Mozart's', beautiful, delighted-in personally but not one's own, an art that frees from embarrassment. Art is suggested too by the delicate paradox of Keats's feelings for her: 'I speak of the thing as a passtime and an amuzement than which I can feel none deeper'—it wonderfully catches the paradox of art's deep amusement. Clinching the whole thing, and embodying the self-possession for which the ordinarily embarrassed are rightly grateful to the unembarrassable, is this: 'I like her and her like because one has no *sensations*—what we both are is taken for granted.' That Jane Cox and he are moved to the right kind of taking for granted is validated by the extraordinary turn of wording: 'I like her and her like because . . .' For a moment one blinks and then sees it straight. For Keats has said that he is not in love with her; he has spoken of 'such a woman', and

[1] To George and Georgiana Keats, 17 Dec. 1818; ii. 11.

he explicitly is not moved by her uniqueness. So he needs to insist that it is part of why he likes her that she so clearly is one of—what? several? a type? a kind? We have only to substitute 'I like her and her sort', or 'and her kind', 'and her type', 'and such women'—each of them too aloofly classificatory and unaffectionate—to see how much the delicacy, humour, and humanity of Keats's feelings depend upon his not using a word which could in any way slight her while nevertheless making the point which he needs to make. 'I like her and her like . . .': the perfect ease and grace of the transference from the one sense to the other are tenderly unembarrassed by the difficulty of getting the whole feeling exactly right. Keats's self-possession when it comes to animating the language is an exhilarating counterpart to her self-possession as 'she walks across a room'; Keats's too is 'a magnetic Power'. When we experience his wonderfully perceptive account of these difficult and delicate feelings (a hair's-breadth from infatuation or worldliness or beauty-worship), we are ourselves too much occupied in admiring to be awkward or on a tremble.

III

DARWIN, BLUSHING, AND LOVE

THE only man of genius to write at length about blushing, Charles Darwin, made it the climactic and concluding chapter of his book on *The Expression of the Emotions in Man and Animals* (1872). For Darwin, it was the quintessential human expression, far more so than smiling or laughing: 'Blushing is the most peculiar and the most human of all expressions. Monkeys redden from passion, but it would require an overwhelming amount of evidence to make us believe that any animal could blush.'[1]

That Keats's Lamia blushes is more mysterious than that she speaks (and the use of 'lisping', with its snake-like sibilant, is part of this suggestion):

> Ravish'd, she lifted her Circean head,
> Blush'd a live damask, and swift-lisping said . . .
> *(Lamia, I. 115–16)*[2]

That an animal does not blush—and so cannot embarrass with its embarrassment—is what makes other than a superficiality of praise Keats's saying of Jane Cox, 'When she comes into a room she makes an impression the same as the Beauty of a Leopardess'. It is this calm and calmative unembarrassability in animals that makes them so frequent and delightful a feature within paintings of nudes, where they gaze goodhumouredly upon the lovely nude or have their eyes elsewhere, in either case without the faintest tingle of embarrassment, and so make it easy and right for us to look upon the nude and upon them with the same equanimity.

In finding blushing to be irreducibly human, Darwin was co-operating with more than one of Romanticism's insistences: not

[1] p. 310.
[2] Contrast the unthinking verse of *Otho the Great*: 'Otho calls me his Lion, — should I blush / To be so tam'd?' (IV. ii. 43–4).

only upon this question of what the irreducibly human was (a question that spurs Byron as much as Wordsworth) but also the related stress upon what humanity has in common—in Wordsworth, say, the ordinary sorrows of man's life; in Byron, by a kind of tautology or pun, a 'generous common humanity' (the phrase is Dr. Leavis's). It was in the name of a common humanity that Romanticism so often spoke—a humanity shared by all the races of man, including those who might not seem to blush. Dr. Burgess in his book on blushing (1839) had quoted from Humboldt: 'And how can those be trusted who know not how to blush? says the European, in his inveterate hatred to the Negro and the Indian';[1] and Burgess's chapter was entitled 'Different Varieties of the Human Race'. Establishing that the dark-skinned races do indeed blush was not just a foolishness or a pedantry since it was involved in a sense of their full humanity.

Again, a relationship with Romanticism is clear from Darwin's admirably chosen word 'self-attention' for the phenomenon of blushing; for the first time, self-attention had become the supreme subject and animus for the artist, and likewise for the first time blushing had become a phenomenon that asked serious, wide, and deep scrutiny: Dr. Burgess's rich and humane book on blushing was published in 1839. When Darwin considers 'The Nature of the Mental States which induce Blushing', he says: 'These consist of shyness, shame, and modesty; the essential element in all being self-attention. . . . It is not the simple act of reflecting on our own appearance, but the thinking what others think of us, which excites a blush' (pp. 326–7). Self-attention and the vistas of thinking what others think of us: these are among the many vistas and reflections which so preoccupied the Romantics; one recalls Clough's saying of Wordsworth that 'he is apt to wind up his short pieces with reflections upon the way in which, hereafter, he expects to reflect upon his present reflections'.[2] Just as there is a Chinese-boxes regression or a rippling chain-reaction about these vistas in Romanticism, so there is if embarrassment itself goes in for self-attention. There is both an introspective sequence of ripplings

---

[1] p. 30; Darwin, p. 319, took this up from Burgess.
[2] *Prose Remains* (1888), p. 315.

within oneself, and a sequence of ripplings outward through other people; like certain Romantic poets, or like Romantic poets in certain moods, the embarrassed person may feel that his self is both the pool which imagination disturbs into widening ripples, and the stone which disturbs into widening ripples the pools that are others' selves. Goffman tells of the ripples or chain-reactions of embarrassment:

In addition to his other troubles, he has discredited his implicit claim to poise. He will feel he has cause, then, to become embarrassed over his embarrassment, even though no one present may have perceived the earlier stages of his discomfiture. But a qualification must be made. When an individual, receiving a compliment, blushes from modesty, he may lose his reputation for poise but confirm a more important one, that of being modest. Feeling that his chagrin is nothing to be ashamed of, his embarrassment will not lead him to be embarrassed. On the other hand, when embarrassment is clearly expected as a reasonable response, he who fails to become embarrassed may appear insensitive and thereupon become embarrassed because of this appearance.[1]

Not only was it natural for Darwin to invoke the poets (Coleridge and Shakespeare), it was natural too for his formulations to recall, and even perhaps draw upon, the ideas about poetry that sustained Romanticism. There is the crucial question of sincerity and role-playing, and that of the contradictory impulses which create embarrassment but also create art: 'As there generally exists at the same time a strong wish to avoid the appearance of shame, a vain attempt is made to look direct at the person who causes this feeling; and the antagonism between these opposite tendencies leads to various restless movements in the eyes' (p. 322). Not just of the eyes; of the mind, and of the pen. When Goffman says 'In the forestalling of conflict between these [incompatible] principles, embarrassment has its social function',[2] he might be speaking too of

---

[1] *Interaction Ritual*, p. 108. Sandor Feldman has another such chain-reaction: 'they will blush when they observe a person who does not blush in situations in which they would blush' ('Blushing, Fear of Blushing and Shame', *Journal of the American Psychoanalytic Association*, x (1962)).

[2] Goffman's abstract of his article (*American Journal of Sociology*, lxii (1956)), this omitted from *Interaction Ritual*.

a function of literature, especially as it has thrived since the Romantics.

The sense too that the blush was necessarily deeply ambiguous (and one remembers Keats's speaking of 'any temporery ambiguousness in their behaviour or their tongues') is at home with the belief that language itself is so. When George Eliot remarks that 'A blush is no language: only a dubious flag-signal which may mean either of two contradictories',[1] she is in danger of forgetting the extent to which this shows that a blush is like, not unlike, language.

Romanticism, with its preoccupation with the subjective and the objective, was naturally fascinated by the blush, so intensely both. The blush too could sum up so much of what was rightly felt about spontaneity and the extent to which the deepest feelings are somehow involuntary and yet are our responsibility; some of the essential paradoxes about spontaneity, will, and freedom could come together in the blush:

We can cause laughter by tickling the skin, weeping or frowning by a blow, trembling from the fear of pain, and so forth; but we cannot cause a blush, as Dr. Burgess remarks, by any physical means,—that is, by any action on the body. It is the mind which must be affected. Blushing is not only involuntary; but the wish to restrain it, by leading to self-attention, actually increases the tendency.[2]

Burgess's prose thrills with a sense of this humanizing challenge to will, for all his proper high respect for human will:

the irrepressible blush . . . clearly demonstrates the impossibility of the *will* ever being able to overcome or control the *genuine* emotions of the Soul.

No one who has arrived at the years of maturity but must be, more or less, familiar with that peculiar and indescribable *sensation* which immediately precedes the appearance of the blush on the cheek. After the impression is made on the sensorium which is to excite this phenomenon, we become immediately conscious of what is about to take place—we feel that the will is overpowered—and, for the time being, is rendered subordinate to the mental powers, and the emotions of sympathy. Now, from the feeling of our own helplessness,

---

[1] *Daniel Deronda*, Chapter 35. [2] Darwin, pp. 310–11.

like a bad swimmer when out of his depth, we become flurried, and in our eager attempts to avert the threatened result, by endeavouring to expel from the mind or imagination that association of ideas which is about to bring it forth, we only fix it the more firmly, and ensure its full development, to the deep mortification and prostration of our will.[1]

A blush for Burgess, and rightly, is a very important spiritual experience.

So it is not only the obvious association of blushing with sexual attraction or the physicality of the sensation, but also its strange relationship to the involuntary which makes blushing so important to erotic art (which so invigorated Romanticism); for both love and desire have a strange relationship to the involuntary. 'They blush incomparably more in the presence of the opposite sex than in that of their own. . . . No happy pair of young lovers, valuing each other's admiration and love more than anything else in the world, probably ever courted each other without many a blush.'[2]

Yet the fascination of blushing was—and is—that so much about it remains mysterious. Its biological origin, for one thing, as Darwin observed:

The belief that blushing was *specially* designed by the Creator [as a check and a sign] is opposed to the general theory of evolution, which is now so largely accepted. . . . Those who believe in design, will find it difficult to account for shyness being the most frequent and efficient of all the causes of blushing, as it makes the blusher to suffer and the beholder uncomfortable, without being of the least service to either of them. They will also find it difficult to account for negroes and other dark-coloured races blushing, in whom a change of colour in the skin is scarcely or not at all visible.

No doubt a slight blush adds to the beauty of a maiden's face; and the Circassian women who are capable of blushing, invariably fetch a higher price in the seraglio of the Sultan than less susceptible women.[3] But the firmest believer in the efficacy of sexual selec-

---

[1] pp. 53, 133–4.   Darwin, p. 328.

[3] Darwin here, as elsewhere, acknowledges a debt to Burgess:

'The Circassian women, who are so celebrated for their beauty, and so sought after by the keepers of the seraglios of Persia and Turkey, although not perfectly civilized, are occasionally seen to blush deeply, according to Lady M. Wortley Montague's account.

'It is even considered an acquisition by the Sultan, as giving proof of their not

tion will hardly suppose that blushing was acquired as a sexual ornament (p. 338).

Then again, and likewise no further forward apparently than it was in Darwin's day, there is the question of whether and why it is the face alone which blushes: 'In most cases the face, ears and neck are the sole parts which redden; but many persons, whilst blushing intensely, feel that their whole bodies grow hot and tingle; and this shows that the entire surface must be in some manner affected.'[1] Few Victorians other than the doctor had the opportunity to attest: 'He unfastened the collar of her chemise in order to examine the state of her lungs; and then a brilliant blush rushed over her chest, in an arched line over the upper third of each breast, and extended downwards between the breasts. . . .'[2] (A very vivid instance, incidentally, of the doctor's relation to embarrassment.) It is, I think, not only the scholar's caution but a faint embarrassment which lends a momentary pompous stiffness to Darwin's prose when he remarks that 'The foregoing facts show that, as a general rule, with English women, blushing does not extend beneath the neck and upper part of the chest'.[3] An attempted physiological explanation has long been the face's habitual exposure to the air, but as Darwin says 'the hands are well supplied with nerves and small vessels, and have been as much exposed to the air as the face or neck, and yet the hands rarely blush'.[4] To Dylan Thomas's sense of the hand's pitilessness, 'Hands have no tears to flow', we might add a sense of their imperviousness—hands have not the face to blush. James Russell Lowell said of Keats in 1854 that in him 'the moral seems to have so perfectly interfused the physical man, that you might almost say he could feel sorrow with his hands'.[5]

Further, the mysteries of blushing are not limited to the biological and the physiological. There is the whole complex of feelings

being ultra barbarous, and those females who are thus capable of exhibiting their internal emotions, invariably bring a higher price than their less susceptible sisterhood' (p. 43).

[1] p. 312. Also Burgess, pp. 114 ff.
[2] Darwin, p. 314.
[3] p. 314. Feldman: 'I have no information about the blushing of nudists, nor about the extent of redness on them if they blush.'
[4] p. 316.
[5] *Keats: The Critical Heritage*, p. 360.

which we have about our faces. Empson has said, 'I remember a fellow lodger who was very cross because he found his razor had been used—a man's face, he said, is the most private part of his body';[1] and yet though preposterous in a way, the fellow lodger seems to me to be right. Dr. Burgess called the cheek 'that external arena of the emotions of the soul—that focus of every involuntary exhibition of internal feeling and sympathy' (p. 115); and more truly a focus, of course, when on fire.

Then there are the questions which begin in physiology—do you blush when alone, or in the dark, or when alone reading a book? do you blush in your sleep?[2] do the blind, or the blind from birth, blush? (Darwin tackles these matters.) Such questions end in philosophy: is the idea of private embarrassment absurd or meaningless? If in philosophy, then in theology; Darwin takes with proper seriousness the position of Christian believers who must think themselves never alone or unobserved:

On the other hand, a man may be convinced that God witnesses all his actions, and he may feel deeply conscious of some fault and pray for forgiveness; but this will not, as a lady who is a great blusher believes, ever excite a blush. The explanation of this difference between the knowledge by God and man of our actions lies, I presume, in man's disapprobation of immoral conduct being somewhat akin in nature to his depreciation of our personal appearance, so that through association both lead to similar results; whereas the disapprobation of God brings up no such association (pp. 333–4).

If it is true that the believer is not embarrassed into a blush before his God, this seems to me a very important index of different systems of values. But then different systems of values are very much involved in blushing. Much as God may move men to shame but not, apparently, to embarrassment, so the French tradition, or certainly the existentialist one, always seeks to assimilate all embarrassment to shame, guilt, and unworthiness, and not to shy-

---

[1] *Kenyon Review*, xix (1957), 392.
[2] Pope, *The Rape of the Lock*, I. 23–4:

> A Youth more glitt'ring than a *Birth-night Beau*,
> (That ev'n in Slumber caus'd her Cheek to glow)

Pope's parentheses mimic the parenthesis of sleep.

ness, modesty, and innocence. In 'The Phenomenological Approach to the Problem of Feelings and Emotions', F. J. J. Buytendijk asserts that 'Blushing is an outburst of oppression which finds its source inside us, in an unacceptable unworthiness, and which finds its outlet in our face, because that is where our self-being is really in the world.'[1] But I believe that the Romantics were truer to blushing in seeing that it was precisely because it could be an index of modest innocence and not of unworthiness that blushing was of such human interest and was so apt to art. Dr. Burgess remarks of 'the blush of modesty or bashfulness':

> It may, indeed, be very interesting to see a young lady in a drawing room blushing for some trivial cause, as the blush invariably heightens the charms of beauty; and as it is, in this instance, considered to be a test of purity and innocence, many fond parents will, perhaps, co-incide with the Sultan's ideas respecting the fair Circassians, and think it rather an acquisition than otherwise in their daughters; but I am of opinion that a blush is no test whatever of either purity or inno-cence, for many libertines and prostitutes may be seen to blush as deeply as individuals of the most exalted purity and virtue (p. 55).

Keats knows the blush of guilt (though even there the recognition of guilt is itself from one point of view a matter for approbation or at any rate hope—'unblushing' is always a penetrating accusation, and enough to make some people blush). But Keats knows too the blush of innocence:

> How she would start, and blush, thus to be caught
> Playing in all her innocence of thought.
> ('I stood tip-toe', 99–100)

He knows, indeed, the blush which is made up of both:

> 'Why pierce high-fronted honour to the quick
> For nothing but a dream?' Hereat the youth
> Look'd up: a conflicting of shame and ruth
> Was in his plaited brow: yet, his eyelids
> Widened a little, as when Zephyr bids
> A little breeze to creep between the fans

---

[1] *Feelings and Emotions*, ed. M. L. Reymert (1950), p. 138.

Of careless butterflies: amid his pains
He seem'd to taste a drop of manna-dew,
Full palatable; and a colour grew
Upon his cheek, while thus he lifeful spake.
(*Endymion*, I. 759–68)

So when Darwin speaks of self-attention and of thinking what others think of us, we should recall Coventry Patmore's insistence in 1848 that there is in Keats 'this habitual self-contemplation': 'With the peculiar order of poets to which Keats must be said to have belonged, at least up to the time of the composition of *Hyperion*, such self-consciousness becomes an integral portion of the effect.'[1]

'No happy pair of young lovers', said Darwin, 'probably ever courted each other without many a blush.' Yet love stands oddly to embarrassment, in that the blush of exploratory mutuality (could you love someone whom you could not possibly imagine blushing?) is so different from the blush that fears ridicule from outside. The intensity of embarrassment which Jerome Sattler sums up as 'being penetrated, uncovered, or exposed to the other' clearly has much in common with, as well as strong connections with, erotic intensity. D. H. Lawrence said: 'It's such a pity preachers have always dinned in: Go thou and do likewise! That's not the point. The point is: It is so, let it be so, with a generous heart.'[2] This achieves its own generosity through a recognition of the very difficulty of generosity and through a sense that the glory of love, its impassioned physicality, is precisely what makes it vulnerable to a sense of the distasteful. It is natural to Keats's robustness that he should think love inherently open to mockery; the openness of love must be this. By the same token, his objection to the enfeebling Werther-ish romanticism of love as a moping and will-less affectation is an objection to the thin tiny struggling, as of a fly in a milk-pot, to which such lovers are reduced by a solemnity which is ridiculous in its fatigued self-congratulation on being transcendently superior to ridicule. Since I believe that a good many of Keats's mis-spellings are Joycean or Carrollean acts of imagination, their portmanteaux

---

[1] *Keats: The Critical Heritage*, p. 334.
[2] Letter to Lady Ottoline Morrell, 28 Dec. 1928.

hastily packed, I think it a small bonus that he spells ridiculous 'rediculous' (like a blush) and irresistible 'irrisistable' (unable to resist risibility):

I saw Haslam he is very much occupied with love and business being one of Mr Saunders executors and Lover to a young woman He show'd me her Picture by Severn—I think she is, though not very cunning, too cunning for him. Nothing strikes me so forcibly with a sense of the rediculous as love—A Man in love I do think cuts the sorryest figure in the world—Even when I know a poor fool to be really in pain about it, I could burst out laughing in his face—His pathetic visage becomes irrisistable. Not that I take Haslam as a pattern for Lovers—he is a very worthy man and a good friend. His love is very amusing. Somewhere in the Spectator is related an account of a Man inviting a party of stutter[e]rs and squinters to his table. 't would please me more to scrape together a party of Lovers, not to dinner—no to tea. The [There] would be no fighting as among Knights of old—

> Pensive they sit, and roll their languid eyes
> Nibble their tosts, and cool their tea with sighs,
> Or else forget the purpose of the night
> Forget their tea—forget their appetite.
> See with cross'd arms they sit—ah hapless crew
> The fire is going out, and no one rings
> For coals, and therefore no coals betty brings.
> A Fly is in the milk pot—must he die
> Circled by a humane society?
> No no there mr Werter takes his spoon
> Inverts it—dips the handle and lo, soon
> The little struggler sav'd from perils dark
> Across the teaboard draws a long wet mark.
> Romeo! Arise! take Snuffers by the handle
> There's a large Cauliflower in each candle.
> A winding-sheet—Ah me! I must away
> To no 7 just beyond the Circus gay.
> 'Alas' my friend! your Coat sits very well:
> Where may your Taylor live'?' 'I may not tell—
> 'O pardon me—I'm absent now and then'
> Where *might* my Taylor live?—I say again

I cannot tell. let me no more be teas'd—
He lives in wapping *might* live where he pleas'd[1]

Keats's goodness is never saintly; the acerbity of his lack of
sympathy with factitious feelings, with self-deluding pangs and
the heightened sensibility, is the proper counterpart to his
gentle sympathy with the true. Thus the imaginary lovers in
the verses are treated with a lavish scorn and mimicry such
as Keats would have thought it quite wrong to treat his friend
Haslam with; and even with Haslam, Keats is obliged to
distinguish Haslam, the man and the friend, from Haslam the
lover. It is the amplitude of the humour which makes Keats's
awareness feel so completely different even from a contemporary
exposition of much the same notions, such as Shelley: 'In the human
world, one of the commonest expressions of love is sexual intercourse, & in describing the deepest effects of abstract love the
author could not avoid the danger of exciting some ideas connected
with this mode of expression, & he has exposed himself to the
danger of awakening ludicrous or unauthorized images.' Keats
would never have been betrayed into the total defensiveness of
this (as if the possibility of the ludicrous were simply an unfortunate
side-effect rather than a true concomitant of the true), or into its
stiff pomposity (sexual intercourse as 'this mode of expression'), or
into the genuinely unfortunate ludicrousness, risky at that date as
now, by which Shelley says in such a context that 'he has exposed
himself'.

Shelley was chary; Keats's greatness was that though subtly
considerate and alert he was unchary. His muse was, in his own
words, 'the unchariest muse'—the least chary of muses. It is itself
a wonderfully unchary phrase, juxtaposing that humdrum but
strange superlative (a coinage?[2] even 'chariest' is rare enough) with
the traditional dignity of the word *muse*. But it is part of the phrase's
energy that Keats should have created it in order to enforce the
sense of a reticence demanded even of his unmisgiving genius.

---

[1] To George and Georgiana Keats, 17 Sept. 1819; ii. 187–8.

[2] *O.E.D.* has under 'unchary' only Shakespeare's 'I have said too much unto
a heart of stone / And laid mine honour too unchary on't' (*Twelfth Night*, III. iv
187–8), before Keats's 'unchariest'.

The embrace of Venus and Adonis should make any would-be describer feel ridiculous:

> Who, who can write
> Of these first minutes? The unchariest muse
> To embracements warm as theirs makes coy excuse.
>
> (*Endymion*, II. 531–3)

'Hence with denial vain, and coy excuse, / So may som gentle Muse . . .': how good-humoured is the tension between the words of Milton's 'Lycidas' and Keats's right to rule them with the word 'unchariest'. Mrs. Allott in her edition of Keats cites not only 'Lycidas' but *Hamlet*, I. iii. 36, 'The chariest maid'. One can see that *maid* is apt to the passage from *Endymion*, a poem moreover whose story of love and the moon might lead one to complete the *Hamlet* quotation:

> The chariest maid is prodigal enough
> If she unmask her beauty to the moon.

Yet though Keats's muse was unchary, it was not unthinking; the taut conclusive reticence of that line and a half had replaced what was in the manuscript an endless going on and on about the fact that he should not say a word. I give the lines which lead into this because I think that Keats found the intense blush of Venus contagious; he was to remove both the blushing and the pother at the same time.

> Queen Venus bending downward, so o'ertaken,
> So suffering sweet, so blushing mad, so shaken
> That the wild warmth prob'd the young sleeper's heart
> Enchantingly; and with a sudden start
> His trembling arms were out in instant time
> To catch his fainting love.—O foolish rhyme
> What mighty power is in thee that so often
> Thou strivest rugged syllables to soften
> Even to the telling of a sweet like this.
> Away! let them embrace alone! that kiss
> Was far too rich for thee to talk upon.
> Poor wretch! mind not these sobs and sighs! begone!
> Speak not one atom of thy paltry stuff,
> That they are met is poetry enough.

Anybody who would write of love's embraces must be in some
way chary, must deal intelligently and sensitively with the possibilities of embarrassment, since embarrassment may make us mean-
minded about the embraces of others. Some sense of the particular
tone and temper of Keats's intelligence here may be gained by
recollecting the timbre of some other non-dramatic writers. The
greatness of Chaucer in *Troilus and Criseyde* (perhaps the best erotic
poem in the language) is the cool translucency of his verse, the way
in which any sense of embarrassment within our contemplation,
any voyeurism, is precluded: first by Pandarus's having espoused
voyeurism and having left, and second by the generality, the
ordinariness, the height given by a poetic diction at once simple and
traditional, as much so as the parts of the body themselves:

> Hire armes smale, hire streghte bak and softe,
> Hire sydes longe, flesshly, smothe, and white
> He gan to stroke, and good thrift bad full ofte
> Hire snowisshe throte, hire brestes rounde and lite:
> Thus in this hevene he gan hym to delite,
> And therwithal a thousand tyme hire kiste,
> That what to don, for joie unnethe he wiste.
>
> (III. 1247–53)

'Thus in this hevene': it is indeed as if the crystalline buoyancy of
the verse has gained an Olympian height[1] or gained that final
station in the spheres from which Troilus will look down upon love.
But the lines here do not look down upon love, do not disdain it;
they look not with contemptuous laughter but with humour. 'And
good thrift bad full ofte . . .': how small and demeaning would any
modern equivalent be— '. . . not going to waste'? This, like the
humour of Troilus's being carried away ('That what to don, for
joie unnethe he wiste'), succeeds as humour and as insight because
it cools embarrassment while it sees the well-nigh flustered lover
at risk.

---

[1] Twenty lines later, Troilus thanks Love for having

> me bistowed in so heigh a place

and the words 'in this hevene' recur fifty lines on:

> And lat hem in this hevene blisse dwelle,
> That is so heigh that al ne kan I telle!

At another extreme is the very different coolness of Marlowe's
Hero and Leander. He makes something like the same joke as
Chaucer; he too sets himself to concede a possible embarrassment
for all concerned and to preclude it by humour; but the humour and
the remoteness are not what they were in Chaucer, those of an
archangel, but those of an experienced man of the world affectionately bantering the tiro:

> Albeit Leander, rude in love, and raw,
> Long dallying with Hero, nothing saw
> That might delight him more, yet he suspected
> Some amorous rites or other were neglected.
> Therefore unto his body hers he clung;
> She, fearing on the rushes to be flung,
> Strived with redoubled strength; the more she strivèd,
> The more a gentle pleasing heat revivèd,
> Which taught him all that elder lovers know.
> And now the same 'gan so to scorch and glow,
> As in plain terms (yet cunningly) he craved it;
> Love always makes those eloquent that have it.
>
> (II. 61–72)

The cool clarity of Marlowe's manner is not intended to cool the
erotic heat but the heat of embarrassment. The feminine rhymes
(suspected/neglected), the wary largesse ('Some amorous rites or
other'), these are the reassurance of badinage addressed to us
though at play upon the lovers.

There is another kind of cool remoteness that gives the bracing
tingle to Dryden's contemplation of love's embraces, in his translation from Book IV of Lucretius:

> So Love with fantomes cheats our longing eyes,
> Which hourly seeing never satisfies;
> Our hands pull nothing from the parts they strain,
> But wander o're the lovely limbs in vain:
> Nor when the Youthful pair more clossely joyn,
> When hands in hands they lock, and thighs in thighs they
>   twine
> Just in the raging foam of full desire,
> When both press on, both murmur, both expire,

They gripe, they squeeze, their humid tongues they dart,
As each wou'd force their way to t'others heart:
In vain; they only cruze about the coast,
For bodies cannot pierce, nor be in bodies lost:
As sure they strive to be, when both engage,
In that tumultuous momentany rage,
So 'tangled in the Nets of Love they lie,
Till Man dissolves in that excess of joy.
Then, when the gather'd bag has burst its way,
And ebbing tydes the slacken'd nerves betray,
A pause ensues; and Nature nods a while,
Till with recruited rage new Spirits boil;
And then the same vain violence returns,
With flames renew'd th' erected furnace burns.
Agen they in each other wou'd be lost,
But still by adamantine bars are crost;
All wayes they try, successeless all they prove,
To cure the secret sore of lingring love.

W. B. Yeats said that 'the finest description of sexual intercourse ever written was in Dryden's translation of Lucretius, and it was justified; it was introduced to illustrate the difficulty of two becoming a unity: "The tragedy of sexual intercourse is the perpetual virginity of the soul." '[1] For if Dryden's accents are those of experience, it is not the experience of a man of the world but of mankind and of the world. His remoteness, free from embarrassment, is not that of Chaucer's archangel or of Marlowe's man of the world, but of a philosopher who can look back through time and see how 'successeless' is human aspiration in love. The very word 'successeless', like 'adamantine', has a cooled and chastened quality; the dignity of Dryden's style is compounded of the heroic and the mock-heroic, so that 'their humid tongues' reminds us of the warm salivation, and words it grandly but not euphemistically; similarly with 'the gather'd bag', an extraordinary melting of the mock-heroic and the heroic. There is certainly the play of humour —'and Nature nods a while', 'th' erected furnace'—which again cools the embarrassments of our proximity to the lovers' proximity.

[1] Yeats in conversation with John Sparrow; A. Norman Jeffares, *W. B. Yeats: Man and Poet* (1949; 1962 edn., p. 267).

The pathos is a recognition of the ridiculous; the vistas of language (so many kinds of diction) and of experience offer something quite other—in their philosophical detachment and sorrowing concern— than the sharp intuition of the ridiculous which vexed Connie Chatterley.

Or—a glacial coolness, an unembarrassability which aims to leave us in doubt as to whether we should be shocked into embarrassment —there is the Swiftian observation of Samuel Beckett. Its distance and height are not those of archangel, man of the world, or chastened philosopher, but the hauteur of the meticulous fearful pedant.

Mr Hackett decided, after some moments, that if they were waiting for a tram they had been doing so for some time. For the lady held the gentleman by the ears, and the gentleman's hand was on the lady's thigh, and the lady's tongue was in the gentleman's mouth. Tired of waiting for the tram, said[1] Mr Hackett, they strike up an acquaintance. The lady now removing her tongue from the gentleman's mouth, he put his into hers. Fair do, said Mr Hackett. Taking a pace forward, to satisfy himself that the gentleman's other hand was not going to waste, Mr Hackett was shocked to find it limply dangling over the back of the seat, with between its fingers the spent three quarters of a cigarette.

I see no indecency, said the policeman.

We arrive too late, said Mr Hackett. What a shame.

Do you take me for a fool? said the policeman.

Mr Hackett recoiled a step, forced back his head until he thought his throatskin would burst, and saw at last, afar, bent angrily upon him, the red violent face.

Officer, he cried, as God is my witness, he had his hand upon it.

God is a witness that cannot be sworn. (*Watt*)

The precision, unexpectedness, and variety of Beckett's distaste make it something quite other than squeamishness; whatever else the attitude is, it is not shallow, easy, or gratifyingly malcontent. The weird footnote; the finicking stiffness of gait by which the very words move like a malign inventive ungenerous old man; the cool

---

[1] Much valuable space has been saved, in this work, that would otherwise have been lost, by avoidance of the plethoric reflexive pronoun after *say*. [Beckett's note.]

mock-dignity conferred by cliché ('Tired of waiting for the tram, said Mr Hackett, they strike up an acquaintance'); the travesty of love's bounty ('to satisfy himself that the gentleman's other hand was not going to waste'—or, 'and good thrift bad full ofte'): all these combine in the intense embarrassment of Mr. Hackett before the policeman whom he has officiously, pruriently, summoned. The policeman's face is a 'red violent face'. Yet what indeed is seen? 'I see no indecency, said the policeman'—and what have we seen? God knows what God witnessed. It is as if the rich sense of a lover lovingly watched, and all watched by us, which is so expansive a feeling in Keats's poetry, is here desiccated into travesty. Yet the travesty is linguistically vital (see how 'throatskin' stretches the prose to bursting-point) and comically so; it is determined to temper the embarrassments of physicality, prurience, voyeurism, and officialdom's contretemps, by plunging them into cold clarity.

Last of these writers (last because he asks a continuing consideration in relation to Keats) is Byron. *Don Juan* is full of warm evocations of erotic life; what Swinburne called the 'especial and exquisite balance and sustenance of alternate tones' is nowhere truer to Byron's genius—and his genius truer to it—than in the tremorous humane vacillations which genially encompass his feelings and thoughts about love's oddity, its ludicrousness, and the way we should be embarrassed in its presence but need not be in imagining its presence.

> They look upon each other, and their eyes
>   Gleam in the moonlight, and her white arm clasps
> Round Juan's head, and his around hers lies
>   Half buried in the tresses which it grasps.
> She sits upon his knee and drinks his sighs,
>   He hers, until they end in broken gasps;
> And thus they form a group that's quite antique,
> Half naked, loving, natural, and Greek.
>
>   (II. 194)

The romantic feeling is at once conventional and genuine, and it tautens with the neo-classical turn of the syntax, 'Half buried in the tresses which it grasps'—a lovely emblem of love's mutuality, of the differences between the sexes, and of their different kinds of strength. With the next line, the balance is deliberately being shown to be precarious. 'She sits upon his knee' (not a posture favourable to dignity, especially not to false dignity), 'and drinks his sighs': the verse drinks in its cliché, but then it finds the abrupt reciprocity—'He hers'—disconcerting even though it is the right thing ('The lady now removing her tongue from the gentleman's mouth, he put his into hers. Fair do, said Mr Hackett'). The final comic rhyme of antique/Greek is by no means denigratory though tauntingly crisp; 'antique' and 'Greek' do after all belong together. And the effect of 'Half naked' is to endow the following epithets with ungrudging wholeness and fullness: 'loving, natural, and Greek'.

It is beautifully supple, and Byron can achieve this same intimacy (informal and inward) when he might have seemed to be dealing only in abstractions. He fleshes them.

> And that's enough, for love is vanity,
> Selfish in its beginning as its end,
> Except where 'tis a mere insanity,
> A maddening spirit which would strive to blend
> Itself with beauty's frail inanity,
> On which the passion's self seems to depend.
> And hence some heathenish philosophers
> Make love the mainspring of the universe.

> Besides Platonic love, besides the love
> Of God, the love of sentiment, the loving
> Of faithful pairs (I needs must rhyme with dove,
> That good old steamboat which keeps verses moving
> 'Gainst reason. Reason ne'er was hand and glove
> With rhyme, but always leant less to improving
> The sound than sense.)—besides all these pretences
> To love, there are those things which words name senses,

> Those movements, those improvements in our bodies
> Which make all bodies anxious to get out
> Of their own sand-pits to mix with a goddess,
> For such all women are at first no doubt.
> How beautiful that moment, and how odd is
> That fever which precedes the languid rout

Of our sensations! What a curious way
The whole thing is of clothing souls in clay!

(IX. 73-5)

'Those movements, those improvements in our bodies': it is a
triumph of the understated and of the definitive; it moves—after
having talked about rhymes, sound and sense—from 'movements'
to 'improvements', 'improvements' being an improvement on
'movements'. How odd, languid, and curious the whole movement
of the lines is; what a curious way the whole thing is of clothing it
in words. Yet how free it is from 'all these pretences to love', and
how cool in its aplomb, its fineness being, as so often in Byron, not
a refinement or superiority but a thoroughgoing decency. But note
that the second stanza incorporates its sense of the embarrassment
endemic in talking about love, let alone rhyming about it; the long
parenthesis about rhyming staves off the embarrassment to which
the pretensions of art make it liable, and comes to a temporary rest
when it reaches (eight lines after 'Besides Platonic love . . .') the
fundamental candour: '. . . there are those things which words name
senses'; and only then can it vault into the untrammelled un-
anxious zest of 'Those movements, those improvements in our
bodies . . .'. 'How beautiful that moment . . .'

The beauty of Byron's erotic poetry, as—despite all the differences—of Chaucer's, Marlowe's, and Dryden's (and of Beckett's
prose), derives from the coolness, from not raising the possibly
torrid or hotly embarrassing any more than is necessary for a tacit
recognition of its being elsewhere possible. Keats is one of the very
few erotic poets who come at embarrassment from a different angle
of necessity: from the wish to pass directly through—not to bypass
(however principled and perceptive the bypassing)—the hotly
disconcerting, the potentially ludicrous, distasteful, or blush-
inducing.

IV

KEATS, BYRON, AND 'SLIPPERY BLISSES'

'IT seems downright preintention', said Keats of the embarrassing way in which 'my Mind leapt over every interval to what I saw was per se a pleasant subject with him'.[1] Keats's mind, so alertly prefigurative, was especially liable to puns and to portmanteaux, often of course quite premeditatedly; his letters are full of conscious effects of which Lewis Carroll or James Joyce would have been proud. There is the punning letter about the room's furnishings, which ends 'N.B. I beg leaf to withdraw all my Puns—they are all wash, an base uns—'.[2] There is the characteristic vista'd quality of punning on the word pun itself, with 'a Pun mote'[3] finding room too for pound note and *bon mot*. Or the Joycean homage to suggestive place-names:

Here's Brown going on so that I cannot bring to Mind how the two last days have vanished—for example he says 'The Lady of the Lake went to Rock herself to sleep on Arthur's seat and the Lord of the Isles coming to Press a Piece and seeing her Assleap remembered their last meeting at Corry stone Water so touching her with one hand on the Vallis Luces while [t]he other un-Derwent her White-haven, Ireby stifled her clack man on, that he might her Anglesea and give her a Buchanan and said.'[4]

Keats was aware, too, of the way in which a downright pre-intention could create portmanteaux; there is his famous 'purplue': 'I have lick'd it but it remains very purplue [*corrected to* purple]— I did not know whether to say purple or blue, so in the mixture of the thought wrote purplue which may be an excellent name for a colour made up of those two.'[5]

---

[1] See p. 42.   [2] To Dilke, 24 Jan. 1819; ii. 36.
[3] To George and Georgiana Keats, 24 Sept. 1819; ii. 214.
[4] To Tom Keats, 17 July 1818; i. 333–4.
[5] To Fanny Brawne, Feb. (?) 1820; ii. 262.

The letters are full of mis-spellings which have this further dimension. There is the wish to spell ridiculous 'rediculous' (blushingly so) and irresistible 'irrisistable' (laughably so);[1] and there is Keats's sense of an intimate relation between the enchanting and the enhancing, so that he can run through the expected epithets: 'With beautiful enchanting, gothic picturesque fine, delightful, enchancting, Grand, sublime—';[2] and where the acrostic to his sister-in-law has in one version, as the E of KEATS, 'Enhanced has it been . . .', and in another 'Enchanted has it been . . .'.[3]

Again, a relation between deceiving people and demeaning them is involved in slight/sleight, as when Keats writes to Fanny Brawne: 'If you think me cruel—if you think I have sleighted you— do muse it over again and see into my heart—My Love to you is "true as truth's simplicity and simpler than the infancy of truth" as I think I once said before How could I slight you?'[4] Nor is this limited to the letters; the manuscripts of the poems are full of richly suggestive mis-spellings. A famous instance is this:

> A Casement high and tripple archd there was
>   All gardneded with carven imageries
> Of fruits and flowers and bunches of knot grass . . .

Walter Jackson Bate has remarked that at this point Keats 'writes so rapidly that his word "garlanded" [which is there in the previous draft] is momentarily lost in this garden of flowers and fruits, and he puts down "gardneded" '.[5] As a reconstruction of Keats's process this is admirable and itself imaginatively moved ('lost in this garden'), but it ignores the question of whether the word 'garden' should for the reader too be a shadowy presence within or behind 'garland'. Is this part of the tacit richness of the line, or only part of that imaginative scaffolding which is taken down once the poem stands? Such a question recurs so often in reading Keats as to suggest an ever-diminishing likelihood of coincidence.

---

[1] See p. 59.
[2] To Reynolds, 11 July 1818; i. 322.
[3] i. 304; ii. 195.
[4] June (?) 1820; ii. 294. Compare 'The Cap and Bells', I: 'To pamper his slight wooing', where a manuscript has 'sleight'; a cancelled stanza elsewhere speaks of a 'cuning sleight'.
[5] *John Keats*, p. 450.

First there are those possible suggestivenesses which do not depend upon mis-spelling but which involve spelling. Thus I think that the line 'Spenserian vowels that elope with ease' gains some of its convincing rightness from the association of vowels and ease with e's: 'Your sisters by this time must have got the Devonshire ees—short ees—you know 'em—they are the prettiest ees in the Language.'[1] Or there is the feeling of rightness that 'champaign' owes to 'athirst':

> Some were athirst in soul to see again
> Their fellow huntsmen o'er the wide champaign . . .
>
> (*Endymion*, I. 385–6)

Diana (queen and huntress, chaste and fair) is known to be a hunter when she is praised as a haunter:

> 'O Haunter chaste
> Of river sides, and woods, and heathy waste,
> Where with thy silver bow and arrows keen
> Art thou now forested?'
>
> (*Endymion*, II. 302–5)

We are implicitly asked to ponder the relation of haunting to hunting. Similarly, editors are right not to accept the Aldine edition's emendation of 'arbour' to 'harbour', but critics would be wrong to preclude all sense of harbour in the lines:

> It was a sounding grotto, vaulted vast,
> O'er studded with a thousand, thousand pearls,
> And crimson mouthed shells with stubborn curls,
> Of every shape and size, even to the bulk
> In which whales arbour close, to brood and sulk
> Against an endless storm.
>
> (*Endymion*, II. 878–83)

Or there is the blending of paining and plaining, with 'that grief of hers/Sweet-paining on his ear' (*Endymion*, II. 855–6) followed half a dozen lines later by 'Moanings' which had in manuscript been 'Plainings'.

---

[1] To Reynolds, 21 Sept. 1819; ii. 168.

It is these and many other such instances which make me believe that Keats's mis-spellings are often indications of how his imagination was working, and are sometimes indications of an achieved suggestiveness which works within the poem itself. Thus his propensity to mis-spell 'exalt' as 'exhalt' intimates a relation between the grandeur and the breathing:

> Ere long I will exalt [exhalt *MS.*] thee to the shine
> Of heaven ambrosial; and we will shade
> Ourselves whole summers by a river glade;
> And I will tell thee stories of the sky,
> And breathe thee whispers of its minstrelsy.
> (*Endymion*, II. 809–13)[1]

The spelling of 'jeopardy' as 'jeapardy' intimates a relation with jealousy:

> till it flush'd
> High with excessive love. 'And now,' thought he,
> 'How long must I remain in jeopardy [jeapardy *MS.*] . . .
> (*Endymion*, II. 900–2)

More straightforwardly, there is 'deligh[t]cious' (*Hyperion*, II. 266) or 'cheery-brandy' (in 'He is to weet'); or

> every sense
> With spiritual honey fills to plentitude

—a variant upon the scarcely less Keatsian

> every sense
> Filling with spiritual sweets to plenitude,
> As bees gorge full their cells.
> (*Endymion*, II. 38–40)

This last example naturally calls up 'To Autumn', and there I believe that the mis-spellings are especially felicitous, and some of them indeed living within our sense of the poem's richness.

> Thy hair soft-lifted by the winmowing wind
> . . .
> And sometimes like a gleaner thou dost keep
> Stready thy laden head across a brook.[2]

---

[1] Compare 'exaltation/exhaltation' into 'breath of life' in *Endymion*, II. 680–7; and 'swoons' into 'exalt/exhalt' in III. 861–3.

[2] To Woodhouse, 21 Sept. 1819; ii. 170.

Perhaps the potentialities within 'winmowing' and 'Stready' (straight and steady) form no part of the achieved poem. Yet the various spellings for 'Drows'd with the fume of poppies'—Dos'd, Dosed, Dazed, Dased—seem to me part of the rich opiate, its drowsing at one with its dosing, dozing, and dazing.

Does 'adicted to every word'[1] have its subterranean pun? Keats would not have objected on principle to such an idea. He knew that the imagination has its pre-intention: 'for things which [I] do half at Random are afterwards confirmed by my judgment in a dozen features of Propriety.'[2] 'He has said, that he has often not been aware of the beauty of some thought or expr^n until after he has composed & written it down—It has then struck him with astonishm^t—& seemed rather the prod^n of another person than his own—He has wondered how he came to hit upon it.'[3]

One word to which he was addicted was 'sooth'. Once more I find John Jones richly incomplete:

Did he spell the verb ['soothe'] that way ['sooth'] in order to bring it visually—and thus magically-truly—closer to 'smooth'? Or perhaps its private rationale is to be found in the private Keatsian adjective 'sooth' which exists in his poetry alongside the public 'sooth' (meaning of course 'true') and appears to conflate 'smooth' and 'soothing'—at any rate in St Agnes Eve's 'jellies soother than the creamy curd'. The superlative form 'soothest'—again unexampled outside Keats—in the invocation 'O soothest Sleep!' of the sonnet to Sleep might well mean no more than 'most soothing'.[4]

This is beautifully apt on the relation of sooth as soothing to sooth as smooth, and certainly this compacts a great deal of Keats's sense of the truly human needs. It is because of this relation that it would be both right and wrong to emend (as Garrod and Jones both half-suggest) 'sooth' to 'smooth' in:

> nor had any other care
> Than to sing out and sooth their wavy hair.
> ('Sleep and Poetry', 179–80)

---

[1] Draft preface to Endymion.
[2] To Haydon, 11 May 1817; i. 142.
[3] Woodhouse; The Keats Circle, i. 129.
[4] John Keats's Dream of Truth, p. 61.

But Jones is apparently indifferent to 'sooth' as 'true'; he mentions it, but as 'alongside' the other senses (does he mean it occurs at other places?), and it is not clear whether he thinks that Keats's imagination was truly exercised, within this very word, by the conjunction of the true, the smooth, and the soothing. Yet 'O soothest Sleep!' ('To Sleep', 5) is acutely moving because it so compacts the three; Adam, awakening from that dream of soothing and of smoothness which became truth, might cry 'O soothest Sleep!'. The word, if what it intimates is itself true (and Keats believed it was), puts heart in us, encourages us, even in the moment when the truth that we are confronting is a painful one:

> 'None can usurp this height,' returned that shade,
> 'But those to whom the miseries of the world
> Are misery, and will not let them rest.
> All else who find a haven in the world,
> Where they may thoughtless sleep away their days,
> If by a chance into this fane they come,
> Rot on the pavement where thou rotted'st half.—'
> 'Are there not thousands in the world,' said I,
> Encourag'd by the sooth voice of the shade. . .
> (*The Fall of Hyperion*, I. 147–55)

It is an odd little indication of the unity of Keats's imagination that the consolatory dignity of that last line should have been fed by some of the same sources of imaginative truth as Keats's amiable joke about the Emperor Elfinan, 'He lov'd girls smooth as shades, but hated a mere shade'.

Elfinan was Byron. Keats's hostility to Byron went deep. His only attempt at Byronic verse, the satirical fantasy 'The Cap and Bells', gets most of such energy as it has from a drawling contempt for Byron. Walter Jackson Bate says of it:

The poem would be written under the pseudonym of one of Byron's feminine admirers——'Lucy Vaughan Lloyd', residing at Chin-a-Walk, Lambeth. Certainly the satiric hero of the poem, the Emperor Elfinan, is as much like Byron as the Prince Regent. In one place Keats (as Byron himself did with other poets) uses direct quotations for burlesque. He takes Byron's sentimental poem to Lady Byron, written two months after she left him ('Fare thee well! and if for ever, / Still for ever, fare thee well'). Elfinan, hopping in his insect way about the room, looks at his scorned fiancée, Bellanaine: 'Poor Bell!' he says (using Byron's pet name for his wife, Annabel): ' "Farewell! and if for ever! Still / For ever fare thee well!"—and then he fell / A laughing!—snapp'd his fingers . . .'[1]

It was Byron's snapping his fingers, his flippant lordliness, which so repelled Keats. On one occasion he was moved to high praise of Byron:

Do not think my dear Brother from this that my Passions are head long or likely to be ever of any pain to you—no
"I am free from Men of Pleasure's cares
By dint of feelings far more deep than theirs"
This is Lord Byron, and is one of the finest things he has said—[2]

In fact, one of the finest things Byron had not said, since (as Maurice Buxton Forman pointed out) the lines are from Leigh Hunt's *Rimini* (III. 121–2).

And had been kept from men of pleasure's cares
By dint of feelings still more warm than theirs.

Even more than deep feelings, warm feelings are what Byron's sang-froid feels it right to call in question.

Keats was not, I think, right in supposing that all Byron did was laugh and gloat; but he was right that such an accusation was integral to the effect which Byron intended to make; 'why is this not just gloating?' is still the question for the admirer of Byron. We need Byron's salutary scepticism (when alive, it is as alive to the sentimentalities of cynicism as to any others) as much as we need Keats's scorn for scorn. The antagonism was a true one, a clash of whole systems of thinking and feeling, and not just a personal dislike or a mere rivalry. On his desperate racked journey to Italy when he was dying, Keats was moved to a fierce urgency and a wild injustice in directly assimilating Byron's principled preference

---

[1] *John Keats*, p. 624.
[2] To George and Georgiana Keats, 14 Oct. 1818; i. 396.

of 'extreme obduracy of heart' to the coarse insolence of the sailors. The account is Joseph Severn's:

—When we had passed the bay of Biscay, where we had been in danger & great fright from a storm of three days—Keats took up Ld Byrons Don Juan accidentally as one of the books he had brought from England & singular enough he opened on the description of the Storm, which is evidently taken from the Medusa frigate & which the taste of Byron tryes to make a jest of—Keats threw down the book & exclaimed, "this gives me the most horrid idea of human nature, that a man like Byron should have exhausted all the pleasures of the world so compleatly that there was nothing left for him but to laugh & gloat over the most solemn & heart rending since [scenes] of human misery this storm of his is one of the most diabolical attempts ever made upon our sympathies, and I have no doubt it will fascenate thousands into extreem obduracy of heart—the tendency of Byrons poetry is based on a paltry originality, that of being new by making solemn things gay & gay things solemn—On another occasion when we were in the dull Quarantine with the other passengers (who were two English Ladies) the captain requested the sailors on deck to continue singing just to amuse us—I confess I did not understand or listen sufficiently to be aware of the kind of thing they were singing, but my surprise was great when on a sudden Keats rose with rather a frantic look & exclaimed that nothing could teach him the extent of mans depravity, that it must be part of a demon existance, that it would be difficult for these sailors in any way to rise up to the level of brutes beasts." I soon found that Keats had painfully understood they were sin[g]ing abominable songs when they knew the Ladies below in the cabin were listening—this he added is only another tho more sincere spec[i]men of the unmanly depravity which Byron so publicly assumes to feel or tries to make others feel—'tis all the same system of a crampd & wilfull nature the one by a preverted education —the other by no education at all.[1]

It was a related antagonism which made Keats so dislike the hauteur of Lord Chesterfield. Complaining about Dilke's handwriting, Keats wrote to him:

I would endeavour to give you a facsimile of your word Thistlewood if I were not minded on the instant that Lord Chesterfield has done

[1] *The Keats Circle*, ii. 134–5.

some such thing to his Son. Now I would not bathe in the same River with lord C. though I had the upper hand of the stream. I am grieved that in writing and speaking it is necessary to make use of the same particles that he did.[1]

It is a fine comic inversion of the social situation (the class gulf) which makes Keats speak of Lord Chesterfield as vulgar, dirtying ('the same River . . . the same particles . . .'); Chesterfield—and it is a piercing insight—is seen as deeply common. But I believe that, as with Byron, Keats's objection is to an affected coolness, a manner or code which would think it a betrayal and a weakness to be awkward or to blush. It is probably just a trivial coincidence that this same paragraph of Keats's letter to Dilke should say, still of handwriting, 'Look at Queen Elizabeth's Latin exercises and blush'. It is not, I think, a coincidence that a social psychologist like Goffman should find it natural to quote Chesterfield:

The fixed smile, the nervous hollow laugh, the busy hands, the downward glance that conceals the expression of the eyes, have become famous as signs of attempting to conceal embarrassment. As Lord Chesterfield puts it:

They are ashamed in company, and so disconcerted that they do not know what they do, and try a thousand tricks to keep themselves in countenance; which tricks afterwards grow habitual to them. Some put their fingers to their nose, others scratch their head, others twirl their hats; in short, every awkward, ill-bred body has his tricks.[2]

'Awkward' is the word which Keats again and again redeemed, both in admitting it and in turning it to a human victory (a victory too for those whose awkwardness he redeemed at the same time); and the issue between him and Chesterfield is indeed about the true sense we should give to 'ill-bred'.

Yet it is Byron's hostility to Keats, rather than Keats's to Byron, which is especially revealing. G. M. Matthews has pointed out the 'sexual resentment' which so often animated contemporary criticism of Keats, and he penetratingly insists upon the way in which this

[1] 4 Mar. 1820; ii. 272. [2] *Interaction Ritual*, p. 102.

was a class matter (and, like all class matters, involving large questions of judgement and sympathy):

This sort of socio-sexual revulsion is an oddly persistent feature of
Keats criticism. . . . Its origin seems to lie in the disturbance created
by a deep response to Keats's poetic sensuality in conflict with a
strong urge towards sexual apartheid. At any rate, Byron's astonishing
outbursts must have had some such components. That is, it was more
or less accepted—since Crabbe and Wordsworth had insisted on it—
that the domestic emotions of the lower classes were a fit subject for
poetry; but that a poet of the lower classes should play with *erotic*
emotions was insufferable, unless these were expressed in a straight-
forward peasant dialect, as with Burns or Clare.[1]

But though Byron's outbursts—'Johnny Keats's *p-ss a bed* poetry'
—are indeed astonishing, they are not surprising. First, because an
important element in Keats's writing is that it should permit of the
possibility of such a reaction; to react so is wrong (in underrating
Keats's sense of responsibility and delicacy), but not as wrong as it
would be to experience the poetry as altogether precluding any
such response. In a similar way, it would be wrong to laugh at the
scene in *King Lear* when Gloucester imagines himself to be jumping
from the cliff, but less wrong than a denial that the possibility of
laughter (the comedy of the grotesque) is importantly active
within our response. Second, there is the fact that Byron's own
remarkable achievements, as a man and as a poet, owe their strength
and their insights to quite opposite impulses from Keats's. In his
company there is only as much recognition of the possibility of
embarrassment as will give savour, release, and width to the feeling
that embarrassment is unthinkable. The experience is tonic and
humane, and in Byron it represented a life-long struggle against 'a
shyness naturally inherent in my Disposition'.[2] Those were the
words he wrote to his half-sister Augusta when he was sixteen. He
was highly embarrassed, and his nonchalance or his panache is
continually an act of courage. As with all courage, therefore, it renders particularly difficult the status of play-acting; if you can pretend to be brave on the scaffold, are you not brave? The distinction

[1] *Keats: The Critical Heritage*, p. 35.
[2] *Byron: A Self-Portrait*, ed. Peter Quennell (1950), i. 6.

is elided to the point at which only the mean-minded will be pre-occupied with it. It is not a simple accusation, or simply an accusa-tion, against Byron that he affected nonchalance; certain true and benign ways of seeing and of behaving are available to those who succeed in doing so with flexibility and integrity.

Of Keats's early life, the pains, the embarrassments, and the insecurities are patent enough: the death of his father when he was eight, the remarriage of his mother two months after (and her leaving her husband soon after), the crusty aloofness of his guar-dian, the false start in medicine, and the unjust vulnerability to the cheaply snobbish jeers of the reviewers. But Byron's early life, though very different, was no less harsh. There was the death of his father when Byron was three and a half : 'I was not so young when my father died, but that I perfectly remember him; and had very early a horror of matrimony, from the sight of domestic broils. . . . He seemed born for his own ruin, and that of the other sex.'[1] There were the family degradations and debts which reduced Byron's mother from an heiress to a penurious widow; and then there was the death of Byron's great-uncle, of which at ten Byron was the beneficiary but also the victim, in becoming the sixth Baron Byron. The anomalies and insecurities of Byron's social standing were later to be compounded by his very talents. Lord Holland remarked to Thomas Moore: 'It was *not* from his birth that Lord Byron had taken the station he held in society, for till his talents became known, he was, in spite of his birth, in any thing but good society, and *but* for his talents would never, perhaps, have been in any better.'[2] Then there was his club-foot, which was anguish and embarrassment to him. When he added, in the second edition of *English Bards and Scotch Reviewers*, the couplet about 'the paralytic puling of Carlisle', he was mortified to hear that men sup-posed him to be alluding to a nervous disorder of Lord Carlisle's: 'I thank Heaven I did not know it—and would not, could not, if I had. I must naturally be the last person to be pointed on defects or maladies.'[3] What made the club-foot even worse to him was the way in which his mother ridiculed it; she did so, apparently, from

---

[1] Leslie A. Marchand, *Byron: A Biography* (1957), i. 32.
[2] Ibid. i. 330 n.   [3] Ibid. i. 168 n.

his earliest days, and did so indeed on the very last occasion on which he saw her. His mother was desperate, possessive, loving, and impossible; when Byron was at Cambridge he feared the vacations because of his 'Horror of entering Mrs. Byron's House'.[1] Part of the horror was that, from his youngest days, he had been bitterly embarrassed by her.

He was embarrassed by others, too. In two succeeding paragraphs of an early letter he admits it:

> Met with another "*accidency*"—upset a butter-boat in the lap of a lady—look'd very *blue*—spectators grinned—"curse 'em!" . . .
> Saw a girl at St. Mary's the image of Anne★★★, thought it was her—all in the wrong—the lady stared, so did I—I *blushed*, so did *not* the lady, —sad thing—wish women had *more modesty*.[2]

What makes this rueful, not self-pitying, is the buoyancy of the depiction; it is an invigorating stroke that chooses 'blue' (glum) as the epithet for red-faced embarrassment. But then Byron's letters are full of rich evocations of his own embarrassment. Sometimes they are as plain and straight as could be wished:

> I had not so much scope for risibility the other day as I could have wished, for I was seated near a woman, to whom, when a boy, I was as much attached as boys generally are, and more than a man should be. I knew this before I went, and was determined to be valiant, and converse with *sang froid*; but instead I forgot my valour and my nonchalance, and never opened my lips even to laugh, far less to speak, and the lady was almost as absurd as myself, which made both the object of more observation than if we had conducted ourselves with easy indifference.[3]

Or there are the farcical heightenings of an imbroglio of embarrassment: 'After about an hour, in comes—who? why, Signor Segati, her lord and husband, and finds me with his wife fainting upon the sofa, and all the apparatus of confusion, dishevelled hair, hats, handkerchiefs, salts, smelling-bottles—and the lady as pale as ashes, without sense or motion. . . .'[4] There is too the sense of the bitterest embarrassment, that which becomes humiliation and

[1] Marchand, i. 106.   [2] *Byron: A Self-Portrait*, i. 30–1.
[3] Ibid., i. 43.   [4] Ibid., ii. 394.

so can become tragedy, in the sad impossible relation with Lady
Caroline Lamb:

To Lady Melbourne

My dear Lady M.,—God knows what has happened, but at four
in the morning L^y Ossulstone looking angry (and at that moment,
ugly), delivered to me a confused kind of message from you of some
scene—this is all I know, except that with laudable logic she drew
the usual feminine deduction that I "*must* have behaved very ill". If
L^y C. is offended, it really must be anger at my *not* affronting her—
for one of the few things I said, was a request to know her will and
pleasure, if there was anything I could say, do, or not do to give her
the least gratification. She walked away without answering, and after
leaving me in this not very dignified situation, and showing her
independence to twenty people near, I only saw her dancing and in
the doorway for a moment, where she said something so very violent
that I was in distress lest Ld Y. or L^y Rancliffe overheard her. I went
to supper, and saw and heard no more till L^y Ossulstone told me your
words and her own opinion, and here I am in stupid innocence and
ignorance of my offence or her proceedings. If I am to be haunted
with hysterics wherever I go, and whatever I do, I think she is not the
only person to be pitied. I should have returned to her after her
doorway whisper, but I could not with any kind of politeness leave L^y
Rancliffe to drown herself in wine and water, or be suffocated in a
jelly dish, without a spoon, or a hand to help her; besides if there
was, and I foresaw there would be something ridiculous, surely I was
better absent than present.[1]

I have quoted from Byron's letters at such length because they make
clear that his notable nonchalance, even when it could be cruel, was
not shallow or trivial. As a poet his greatest achievements all seem
to me to be saddened scrutinies of different kinds of misguided
superiority to the possibility of embarrassment and to the simplest
human feelings; saddened, not caustic, because it is the flicker of
another possibility which moves us even in those who 'moving
others are themselves as stone'. I think of the astonishing lines
about General Suwarrow, a kind of poetry quite unlike anything
else that I know, where the scrutiny which Suwarrow gives to the

---

[1] *Byron: A Self-Portrait*, i. 164–5.

suffering is expanded into the scrutiny devoted to him, and where an admiration of Suwarrow's strength coincides with a dismay at his habitual narrowness to produce a full judgement, not at all a disparagement:

> Suwarrow, who had small regard for tears
>   And not much sympathy for blood, surveyed
> The women with their hair about their ears,
>   And natural agonies, with a slight shade
> Of feeling;
>
> (*Don Juan*, VII. 69)

There is an analogous admiration yet dismay in Byron's large response to the large, yet not monolithic, Catherine the Great:

> And Catherine, who loved all things (save her lord,
>   Who was gone to his place) and passed for much,
> Admiring those (by dainty dames abhorred)
>   Gigantic gentlemen, yet had a touch
> Of sentiment; and he she most adored
>   Was the lamented Lanskoi, who was such
> A lover as had cost her many a tear
> And yet but made a middling grenadier.
>
> (IX. 54)

It is this, the momentary relapse into simple feeling of those not much amenable to feeling, which Byron can catch with drily admiring perplexity:

> And thus Gulbeyaz, though she knew not why,
> Felt an odd glistening moisture in her eye.
>
> (V. 120)

There is nonchalance as heroism, as when Pedrillo dies in the cannibalism of the shipwreck with a calm at once admirable and sheeplike; Byron's lines vacillate yet never lurch here, since they are truly perplexed by such simplicity and faith:

> He but requested to be bled to death.
>   The surgeon had his instruments and bled
> Pedrillo, and so gently ebbed his breath
>   You hardly could perceive when he was dead.

He died as born, a Catholic in faith,
    Like most in the belief in which they're bred,
And first a little crucifix he kissed,
    And then held out his jugular and wrist.

(II. 76)

For it is one of the many paradoxes of Byron that his own non-chalance is so often devoted to scrutinizing the varieties of non-chalance; he is moved to pity by the blank superiority which can condescend even to the universe:

In the great world—which being interpreted
    Meaneth the West or worst end of a city
And about twice two thousand people bred
    By no means to be very wise or witty,
But to sit up while others lie in bed
    And look down on the universe with pity—
Juan, as an inveterate patrician,
Was well received by persons of condition.

(XI. 45)

Blushes and embarrassment are frequent in *Don Juan*. But they never work upon us, as Keats's do, by implicating us in the hot tinglings of sensation; they are always seen from outside, and the feeling that is induced in us as we read is not of sharing others' embarrassment but of being for once permitted to feel no such thing. The limpidity and lucidity of Byron's style act as a *cordon sanitaire* against contagious embarrassment; the style is therefore best fitted to notice important things when the kind of embarrass-ment it contemplates is one which it may be good for us not exactly to share. The altogether generalizable, for instance, where it would be inordinate to share in tremblings which are so markedly *un*individual:

Then there were sighs, the deeper for suppression,
    And stolen glances, sweeter for the theft,
And burning blushes, though for no transgression,
    Tremblings when met and restlessness when left.
All these are little preludes to possession,
    Of which young passion cannot be bereft,

And merely tend to show how greatly love is
Embarrassed at first starting with a novice.

(I. 74)

Or there is the embarrassment of a particular predicament which is
a consequence of a professional hazard, and where we should not
too much sympathize with the awkward plight of the Sultana's
eunuch:

Baba with some embarrassment replied
    To this long catechism of questions, asked
More easily than answered, that he had tried
    His best to obey in what he had been tasked.
But there seemed something that he wished to hide,
    Which hesitation more betrayed than masked.
He scratched his ear, the infallible resource
To which embarrassed people have recourse.

(VI. 100)

Once Don Juan is in England, the importance of embarrassment
necessarily increases. 'Though modest, on his unembarrassed brow/
Nature had written "gentleman" ' (IX. 83). But that Juan is
approaching at last a woman whom he may find himself having to
be true to after a different fashion from his usual one, that he may
be meeting his match, is clear from the blush which Aurora mildly
inflicts upon him. His brow ceases to be unembarrassed. Aurora
smiles.

'Twas a mere quiet smile of contemplation,
    Indicative of some surprise and pity.
And Juan grew carnation with vexation,
    Which was not very wise and still less witty,
Since he had gained at least her observation,
    A most important outwork of the city,
As Juan should have known, had not his senses
By last night's ghost been driven from their defences.

But what was bad, she did not blush in turn
    Nor seem embarrassed. Quite the contrary;
Her aspect was as usual, still, not stern,
    And she withdrew, but cast not down her eye,

Yet grew a little pale. With what? Concern?
  I know not, but her colour ne'er was high,
Though sometimes faintly flushed and always clear,
  As deep seas in a sunny atmosphere.
                                                    (XVI. 93–4)

The feelings that we share are altogether Aurora's, not Juan's; the mock-heroic but genuine courtesy which allows the hero of the poem not to blush but to grow 'carnation with vexation' (the further internal rhyme is teasing) ensures that we retain the cool unembarrassability of Aurora and of Byron. It is greatly to Juan's credit, and to his peril, that he blushes; it would only blur and intrude if we were to do likewise. We do not blush in turn or seem embarrassed. Quite the contrary.

It is* to Byron's credit that he conceived of the crucial moment which is to mature Juan's love as a moment of embarrassment. Since Byron, like any good and sensitive man ,was not unembarrass-able (though he effected fine things through the gentlemanly pretence that he was), it will not quite do, unfortunately, to claim that Byron was unembarrassable except by Keats. What is true, nevertheless, is that he was moved by Keats to an intensity and violence of embarrassment quite unlike anything else he ever expressed. 'Mr Keats, whose poetry you enquire after, appears to me what I have already said: such writing is sort of mental masturbation—he is always f—gg—g his *Imagination*. I don't mean he is *indecent*, but viciously soliciting his own ideas into a state.'[1] Yet Byron did mean that Keats was indecent; the metaphors return with an indecent insistence:

The *Edinburgh* praises Jack Keats or Ketch, or whatever his names are: why, his is the Onanism of Poetry—something like the pleasure an Italian fiddler extracted out of being suspended daily by a Street Walker in Drury Lane. This went on for some weeks: at last the Girl went to get a pint of Gin—met another, chatted too long, and Cornelli was *hanged outright before she returned*. Such like is the trash they praise, and such will be the end of the *outstretched* poesy of this miserable Self-polluter of the human mind.[2]

[1] Marchand, *Byron*, ii. 886.
[2] *Byron: A Self-Portrait*, ii. 533; 'Onanism' is supplied from Marchand, *Byron*, ii. 886.

The 'trash' was of a kind that made Byron hot at being seen with it: 'Johnny Keats's *p-ss a bed* poetry. . . . There is such a trash of Keats and the like upon my tables, that I am ashamed to look at them.'[1]

One may think that these outbursts tell us more about Byron's imagination than about Keats's, but I think that Byron's violence of embarrassed disgust is a false reaction to something truly in Keats. For one thing, Byron is not alone in having spoken in such terms; for another, many of Keats's readers have felt that there is some obscure relation between Keats's delight (and their delight in Keats) and sexual gratifications such as at least lend themselves to being misconstrued as masturbation. The depth and ubiquitousness of Keats's preoccupation with blushing may legitimately remind us that many psycho-analysts have stressed the link between masturbation and blushing. The coarse jibe at '*p-ss a bed* poetry' was a shrewd shot in the dark. Sandor Feldman writes in 'Blushing, Fear of Blushing, and Shame':

> Freud thought that there is a connection between shame and involuntary urination in sleep. Many observers, including myself, have found excessive blushing in enuretics. . . . There is a connection between enuresis and masturbation. I had had in analysis adult male and female enuretics all of whom masturbated in their sleep while dreaming. . . . Blushers often connect shame with masturbation and seek signs of detection on the faces of those who observe them. In the course of the analysis of blushers I have found that it is not so much the masturbation itself as the masturbatory fantasy which is the essential stimulus for shame and blushing.[2]

Hitschmann, moreover, makes a contribution to a different puzzle (Darwin: 'and yet the hands rarely blush'): 'Blushing hands of patients with self-reproach of masturbation are recorded.'

The focus for a great deal of this sense that Keats is sexually perturbing is the accusation that there is something voyeuristic about his art. It has from the start been an accusation that could easily rebound, like the other deplorings of prurience. *The British*

---

[1] *Letters and Journals*, v. 93–4.

[2] *Journal of the American Psychoanalytic Association*, x (1962). Similarly, Benedek, *International Journal of Psycho-Analysis*, vi (1925); and Hitschmann, *Psychoanalytic Review*, xxx (1943).

Critic in June 1818 reproved Keats for his 'Pan, whom he represents, rather indecorously, we must acknowledge, as a god "who loves to see the Hamadryads *dress*" ';[1] but *The British Critic* should have been watching its own voyeuristic imagination before making this accusation and intensifying it with italics, since Keats's lines go like this:

> Who lov'st to see the hamadryads dress
> Their ruffled locks . . .
> *(Endymion,* I. 236–7)

Yet even there it will not do to think that *The British Critic* was altogether wrong; with cunning humour and decorum, Keats did intimate a glimpse of nakedness before rounding the corner into the perfectly proper thing. In any case, the general sense of watching the naked is very strong in Keats: in the daisy's joke in the 'Daisy's Song', so that the day's-eye is lucky to be an eye; in the Oread that 'peep'd' in *Endymion,* I. 671; or in the imaginative transference of the power to peer when Keats learns from Milton's 'opening eyelids of the morn':

> until the rosy veils
> Mantling the east, by Aurora's peering hand
> Were lifted from the water's breast . . .
> *(Endymion,* III. 112–14)

'Rosy' and 'mantling' ('let it mantle rosy-warm') are the blush of morning, and may serve to remind us that the link between blushing and seeing is preserved in a wrinkle of the language. To blush is 'to cast a glance' *(O.E.D.* vb. 2), and a blush is a glance *(O.E.D.* sb. 2 and 3); Byron made charming play with this little linguistic survival in praising British beauties:

> But this has nought to do with their outsides.
> I said that Juan did not think them pretty
> At the first blush, for a fair Briton hides
> Half her attractions, probably from pity . . .
> *(XII. 74)*

---

[1] *Keats: The Critical Heritage,* p. 92.

The psychologists need not rely upon the linguistic coinciding since the connection between blushing and voyeurism or scopophilia is one of their commonplaces. In 'A New Approach to the Therapy of Erythrophobia', Edmund Bergler speaks in terms which are clearly apt to art though necessarily perilous for art.

The exhibitionistic tendency that was warded off is smuggled into the symptom: by blushing the erythrophobe makes himself really conspicuous, i.e., exhibits himself. It is also noteworthy that traces of the original voyeur wishes themselves are included in the final symptom. In the first place, according to Freud, every exhibitionist identifies himself with the voyeur, and by this detour enjoys voyeur pleasure. In the second place, the erythrophobe projects his own wishes to peep upon his surroundings. As virtually all analytic observers stress, these patients have pseudoparanoid ideas of being watched and observed. Thus peeping pleasure finds surreptitious satisfaction along the projective by-path of identification with an onlooker, buttressed by the moral alibi, 'Others, not I, are looking'. The erythrophobe makes use of others as a mirror in order to look at himself with a clear conscience.[1]

Art, with its discipline and respect, can convert such impulses to true ends; the writer and the reader, like the ereutophobe but unsuccumbing, make use of imagined others as a mirror in order to look at themselves with a clear conscience—genuinely clear, not self-flattering. Again, the vistas of voyeuristic embarrassment resemble those of art, especially of Keats's art: 'Another adult male patient once noticed that an old man was looking at a scene in which a young man was heavily courting a girl in public. The patient blushed.' Yet all such blushing asserts decorum, and like all decorum it is an equivocal blend of innocence and experience. Feldman's point about social expectation is also a point about the double purpose of blushing which can be duplicity but can be largeness of mind: 'At that time women were *expected* to blush whenever an embarrassing situation arose. . . . Women had to blush in order to "prove" their "innocence" and they did so to advantage. Thus they gave evidence of their chastity and at the same time revealed their interest in sexual matters.'[2]

---

[1] *Psychoanalytic Quarterly*, xiii (1944).
[2] *Journal of the American Psychoanalytic Association*, x (1962).

The critic of Keats cannot afford in this matter to be defensive—
not unless he really believes Keats to be indefensible. For the case
for some of Keats's most impassioned poetry is essentially the case
for a purified and liberated scopophilia: for a contemplating which is
more than permissible since it is so enabling and free of anxiety, and
yet is still felt to be surprising because it includes a sense of possible
guilt, shabbiness, or prurience held off by an unmisgiving largeness
of mind.

> Full on this casement shone the wintry moon,
> And threw warm gules on Madeline's fair breast,
> As down she knelt for heaven's grace and boon;
> Rose-bloom fell on her hands, together prest,
> And on her silver cross soft amethyst,
> And on her hair a glory, like a saint:
> She seem'd a splendid angel, newly drest,
> Save wings, for heaven:—Porphyro grew faint:
> She knelt, so pure a thing, so free from mortal taint.
> ('The Eve of St. Agnes', XXV)

The best criticism of these lines was written while Keats was still
alive, by John Scott in the *London Magazine*, September 1820:

Let us take also a passage of another sort altogether—the description
of a young beauty preparing for her nightly rest, overlooked by a
concealed lover, in which we know not whether most to admire the
magical delicacy of the hazardous picture, or its consummate,
irresistible attraction. 'How sweet the moonlight sleeps upon this
bank', says Shakspeare; and sweetly indeed does it fall on the half
undressed form of Madeline:—it has an exquisite moral influence,
corresponding with the picturesque effect.[1]

'The magical delicacy of the hazardous picture': it is itself a
beautifully delicate evocation, and the sense of the hazardous is not
simply absent but is alive as relief. Nevertheless, the purifying
moonlight is at once succeeded, complemented, by a different kind
of erotic imagining, one that raises more directly the question of
potential improprieties absorbed yet not (rightly not) abolished:

> Anon his heart revives: her vespers done,
> Of all its wreathed pearls her hair she frees;

[1] *Keats: The Critical Heritage*, p. 224.

> Unclasps her warmed jewels one by one;
> Loosens her fragrant boddice; by degrees
> Her rich attire creeps rustling to her knees:
> Half-hidden, like a mermaid in sea-weed,
> Pensive awhile she dreams awake, and sees,
> In fancy, fair St. Agnes in her bed,
> But dares not look behind, or all the charm is fled.
> (XXVI)

'Of all its wreathed pearls her hair she frees': the whole impulse and movement of the stanza are devoted to an act of freeing (Keats's first thought, 'strips', suggests diminution not unconstrained liberty), and as we hidden watch this hidden man watching this woman undress, the freeing is from all the ordinary concomitants of being engaged in such a thing; the whole enterprise is 'hazardous' because it is committed to the belief that engaging in fantasy, when it is responsible and self-respecting, can help us to live in the world of fact; the essential tact and precariousness are that the fantasy must incorporate a recognition of fact such as will make it clear that we are neither to feel a disabling guilt at imagining such innocent contemplation nor think that out in real life we could retain innocence in acting so. For the lines contain a strong respect for rules and self-discipline as the condition of achievement, even of magical achievement. 'But dares not look behind, or all the charm is fled': this is the proper fear incorporated within these else unfearing lines, since it is a fear of throwing it all away by unthinkingness or inattention; Madeline holds before herself the adjuration that the young virgins who wish for visions of delight must 'Nor look behind, nor sideways'. The same sense of constraints, of rules to be observed, affects even Porphyro, for the observing of Madeline's undressing has a decisive moment. He sees, and so we see, her freeing her hair and unclasping her jewels and loosening her fragrant bodice (while 'fragrant' beautifully ventures upon a different appeal to the senses): but then at this point, seeing is complemented by hearing:

> by degrees
> Her rich attire creeps rustling to her knees:

How rich the effect and the pleasure are; the gratifications of the
enkindled ear (the least sensual of the senses)—

> by degrees
> Her rich attire creeps rustling to her knees:—

outdo those of the gazing eye, for a reader (imagining within the
imaginative world of the poem) as for Porphyro. It is characteristic
of Keats's honourable hedonism that this elicits, not a consciousness
of sacrificial worthiness, but a keener pleasure. It was to be the
special pain of his relationship with Fanny Brawne, racked as it was
by his ill health, that it entailed for him the wrong kind of secrecy
(including the secret, apparently, of his engagement, which he
felt obliged to hug to himself and to try to keep from his friends—
he, the most open of men), and that it gave him neither the dis-
interested contemplation that is imagination nor the urgently
personal acts of love that are its actuality.

There is still another dimension to the stanza's triumph. Who
but Keats would have ventured upon the hazards of sea-weed?
'Half-hidden, like a mermaid in sea-weed'. Yet the sea-weed to me
epitomizes the central strength and sanity of Keats's erotic poetry:
its creation of a double sense, both within and without the eroti-
cism, so that we both are and are not one of the lovers themselves.
The point about a word like sea-weed, and about the thing itself,
is that it arouses strong mixed feelings; it is both fascinating in its
tactile pungent oddity and yet faintly repellent. It would need a
Gaston Bachelard to do justice to the psycho-analysis of sea-weed,
which is a really suggestive and strange thing to contemplate; children can unmisgivingly delight in sea-weed, but adults would be
reluctant to admit the compound of sensations it can elicit. Why this
matters is that in Keats's line it is 'sea-weed' which precipitates the
double sense, fascinatingly attractive to the lover (and so to us in
so far as we are he) and at the same time odd, faintly repellent, and
faintly ludicrous. It is the incorporation, within the large apprehension, of this faintly embarrassing possibility of response that
makes Keats's poetry at once truthful and generous. Truthful,
because we cannot, even in imagination, become the lovers whom
we see and sympathize with; generous, because it becomes neither

aloof nor embittered by its recognition of the possibility of embarrassment or distaste in a full imagination of the physicality of others' love. It is not hard to be undisconcerted, unenvious, unprurient in the face of others' physicality in love, if your sympathetic imagination simply lets no full sense of physicality in; and on the other hand it is not hard to have a full sense of such physicality while letting its embarrassment dominate your response and turn it to distaste or monkishness. But what is hard, and what gives the sense of warm spaciousness to Keats's imagination, is to let the inevitable sense of a possibility of the distasteful or the ludicrous be accommodated within a full magnanimity. It is not only the damaged men in Zola who feel pain when they contemplate the loving happiness of lovers embracing; the freedom from envy and prurience is not simply and easily available provided that we refuse to be 'anti-life' or warped, and the saying 'It is so, let it be so, with a generous heart' is a hard saying. Until quite recently, the young were discouraged from holding hands in public because it gave the middle-aged such pains in the stomach; this was not good, but nor would it be good to make out that only those who are in a bad way would ever feel any such thing. Keats's poetry is animated by a very real sense of the threats to calm and to benignity which can spring from any active imagining of and noticing of other people's intimacies and pleasures; his respect for fantasy is a concomitant of his being so simply realistic in his hopes and expectations about human goodness.

'Half hidden like a Syren of the Sea': that had been Keats's earlier version. Walter Jackson Bate has said: 'Recalling that the association with "sirens" has an unpleasant side, he finally replaces it with ". . . Half hidden, like a mermaid in sea-weed".'[1] But this ignores the fact that sea-weed too has an unpleasant side; what was wrong with 'Syren' was that it included an unpleasant side of the wrong sort; it is important that this replacement was not simply pleasant but has its own ambivalence of feeling, located differently from that in 'Syren' where the ambivalence was a moral not a physical response; it is the morality of physical response that interests Keats, not that of untrustworthiness. More faintly, a

---

[1] *John Keats*, p. 449.

physical ambivalence comparable to that in 'sea-weed' is at work in 'warmed': 'her warmed jewels'. For the body-heat of those we love is intensely lovable, but the possibility of a faint physical repellence is nevertheless there, and it is again part of Keats's doubleness of sympathy—we are and are not Porphyro—that 'warmed' should be so different a word in its physical weight (a weight of ambivalence) from the epithet which is its counterpart in the previous line: 'wreathed pearls', 'warmed jewels'. Beckett's Mr. Hackett retorts to the policeman: 'If you imagine that I have not your number, said Mr Hackett, you are mistaken. I may be infirm, but my sight is excellent. Mr Hackett sat down on the seat, still warm, from the loving. Good evening, and thank you, said Mr Hackett.' (*Watt*) Such comic distaste is indeed absent from Keats, but it is not merely omitted. 'Full nakedness', cries Donne. The fullness of the nakedness in Keats's best poetry comes from the fact that though it is not open to Henry James's words as accusation, it is open to their disconcerted sense of paradox, especially in the watching that goes on within the scene we watch: 'A young woman, also naked—more than naked, as one somehow feels Gérôme's figures to be—reclines beside him and looks lazily on.'[1]

I have said that it is hard, when contemplating the loving physicality of others, to let the inevitable sense of a possibility of the distasteful be accommodated within a full magnanimity. The ambivalence of such physicality (ambivalent within oneself, and ambivalent because others are not oneself) involves a recognition of the need for such generosity. But, it might be retorted, though such magnanimity is indeed hard in life, it is easy enough in imagination; Keats, after all, is not contemplating the actual otherness of other people but only the imagined otherness of those whom he is making up—people not truly other at all, and all too accommodating as beneficiaries of this merely imaginary magnanimity.

Such an objection might argue that Keats's generosity is not hard won but easily won; and that by the same token it is easy for us too to feel a warm glow which could not withstand the chill jealous winds of actuality; and that in any case there is never any simple carry-over of emotions, sympathies, or attitudes which we experience in literature into our daily emotions, sympathies, or attitudes.

Can we praise and value works of imagination as we should praise and value behaviour? I think that we can, should, and do. It is not just that writing is itself a form of behaviour; nor that the generosity which I find in Keats's poems is to me so strikingly like that which animates his letters—and letters, though they entail imagination, are not airily free from the contingencies of the actual: letters are directly behaviour in the most ordinary sense.

One reason why it is not all too easy for Keats is that the imagination has its own unremitting responsibilities. Rules, constraints, and self-discipline are explicitly invoked as guiding Madeline herself; they are implicitly manifested in the art with which Keats creates Madeline. Art and the imagination are not free to do as they like; they are indeed more free to choose than we often are in daily life, but the choices made are then inseparable from responsibilities. Even so patent and distinct a choice as that of a stanza-form is a consequence of prior responsibilities (Keats's sense of what the story asks, and of his attitudes and responsibilities towards it), and is then the creator of further responsibilities. Granted, the responsibilities of fantasy are often less assured or less palpable than those of fact; 'The Eve of St. Agnes' is a kind of dream, and though it is not true that in dreams anything goes, it is true that it is exceptionally difficult to say why not everything does go. Yet 'in dreams begin responsibilities.'

Moreover, observation suggests that it is by no means easy for a writer to be fully generous towards his imagined creations. There are a great many writers of talent, and even some of genius, whose work is vitiated by the ungenerosity with which it contemplates those whom it has called into being—the ungenerosity that is mean-minded or spiteful or condescending or censorious. So that even if one acknowledges that it was a different thing for Keats to manifest generosity towards Niobe in a poem and towards Fanny Brawne in a letter, one may still urge not only that the Keats of the letters is markedly the same man as the Keats of the poems, but also that the virtue of generosity is the same wherever we find it. The contingencies and coercions within life which threaten generosity are distinguishable from, but not distinct from, such contingencies and coercions within art.

Envy and jealousy and prurience, which are perversions of imagination and not merely absences of it, can imperil the humanity of art as they can imperil the humanity of daily behaviour. Certainly art has its freedom which life does not, but such freedoms are the purposeful suspension of responsibility, not the ignoring or abolishing of it. As to the question of whether there can be a carry-over of sympathies from literature into daily life, here one is necessarily proffering a trust and a hope rather than an assurance or a substantiation. When Keats not only lets us see so vividly the undressing of Madeline and Porphyro's watching it, but lets us share his richly intimate equanimity, he gives us an example of how we should—in the largest sense—behave. His art, though not didactic, is concerned to educate our thoughts, feelings, and sympathies, and it does so by being exemplary. Of course such an example can be resisted, ignored, or crushed by all the things in life which can make it gratifying to behave ill and to feel ill will rather than to behave well and to feel good will. But to say this is simply to say what is true of anything that might hope to help by example: personal conduct, for instance, which we know perfectly well to be no guarantee of anything whatever in those who are given the opportunity to observe it—no guarantee but a hope at least.

Imagination can be abused (the sadist does not simply lack imagination); among the uses of it is that it can be exemplary. I grant that when in daily life one subsequently comes up against those usual embarrassments which are an invitation to ungenerosity one might not be in the least assisted by having entered into an imagined meeting—in art—with such an embarrassment. But that one might not be assisted is not to say that one could not be and is not to say anything about the (undiscoverable) odds; the trust in art's power to enlarge our sympathies and to make us more alive to things (and not just when ensconced within art) is not different from the trust in bringing children up with love and with respect.

The trust that something can be carried over does, I admit, lead to a suspiciously simple sense of the workings of the imagination. That the imagination works in other ways than Keats's, which is exemplary and celebratory, may be conceded. But though there are risks in this assimilation of the artistic imagination to the daily imagination, they seem to me to be less impoverishing or distorting than any theorizing which would disjoin the two. The right antithesis, as T. S. Eliot said, is not that of literature to life: 'It is the function of a literary review to maintain the autonomy and disinterestedness of literature, and at the same time to exhibit the relations of literature—not to "life", as something contrasted to literature, but to all the other activities, which, together with literature, are the components of life.'[1] So it is an essential strength of Dr. Leavis's criticism, disturbing though it may seem at first, that it can so unmisgivingly locate within the same world of human sympathies and human judgement an imagined adultery and an actual one, that of Anna Karenina and that of Frieda Lawrence:

Anna was not an amoral German aristocrat—that seems to me an obvious opening comment. Frieda didn't give up *her* children without some suffering (*Look! We Have Come Through*), but she got over that, and attained a floating indolence of well-being as, placidly undomesticated, she accompanied Lawrence about the world (we always see *him* doing the chores). There are delicacies in the way of offering to push further our divinations from such evidence concerning Frieda as we have, but we can see that what Tolstoy makes present to us in Anna is certainly something finer.[2]

I should therefore wish to qualify Lionel Trilling's pages on Keats in his excellent essay on 'The Fate of Pleasure'. No one has better stated the root-antinomy of Keats:

Keats's intellect was brought into fullest play when the intensity of his affirmation of pleasure was met by the intensity of his skepticism about pleasure. The principle of pleasure is for Keats, as it is for Wordsworth, the principle of reality—by it, as Wordsworth said, we *know*. But for Keats it is also the principle of illusion. In *The Eve of St. Agnes*, to take the most obvious example, the moment of pleasure at the centre of the poem, erotic pleasure expressed in the fullest possible imagination of the luxurious, is the very essence of reality: it is all we know on earth and all we need to know. And it is the more real as

---

[1] *The Criterion*, i (1923), 421.　　[2] '*Anna Karenina*' and Other Essays (1967), p. 22.

reality and it is the more comprehensive as knowledge exactly because in the poem it exists surrounded by what on earth denies it, by darkness, cold, and death, which make it transitory, which make the felt and proclaimed reality mere illusion.

But we must be aware that in Keats's dialectic of pleasure it is not only external circumstances that condition pleasure and bring it into question as the principle of reality, but also the very nature of pleasure itself. If for Keats erotic enjoyment is the peak and crown of all pleasures, it is also his prime instance of the way in which the desire for pleasure denies itself and produces the very opposite of itself. . . .

Keats, then, may be thought of as the poet who made the boldest affirmation of the principle of pleasure and also as the poet who brought the principle of pleasure into the greatest and *sincerest* doubt.[1]

This is clear and rich in its evocation of the way in which Keats contains—both includes and restrains—two of the external challenges to pleasure: that from harsh necessities, and that from pleasure's rounding on itself in that it palls. But for me it is not these considerations alone which are sufficient to re-create a sense of what Keats's poetry fully feels like, or sufficient to justify what I do indeed think to be justified: Trilling's assured emphasis upon bringing 'the principle of pleasure into the greatest and *sincerest* doubt'. For the challenge which Keats's poetry most triumphantly contains is not a challenge *to*, but the challenge *of*, pleasure: the demanding challenge that a full and livingly imaginative apprehension of the pleasures of others cannot but make upon us.

It is therefore not an objection to Keats's erotic writing that it can cause a twinge of distaste, since the accommodation of distaste can be a humanly and artistically valuable thing, especially when it coexists with a frank delight. *The British Critic*[2] deplored 'the following exquisite nonsense to describe a kiss' (the fifth and sixth lines of the stanza):

> 'Love! thou art leading me from wintry cold,
>   'Lady! thou leadest me to summer clime,
> 'And I must taste the blossoms that unfold
>   'In its ripe warmth this gracious morning time.'

---

[1] *Beyond Culture*, pp. 65–7.   [2] *Keats: The Critical Heritage*, p. 231.

So said, his erewhile timid lips grew bold,
  And poesied with hers in dewy rhyme:
Great bliss was with them, and great happiness
Grew, like a lusty flower in June's caress.

('Isabella', IX)

M. R. Ridley outdid *The British Critic*: ' "And poesied with hers in
dewy rhyme", which, apart from conveying a sensation of somewhat tasteless lusciousness, seems to convey as little meaning as is
possible for seven English words arranged in a grammatical clause.'[1]
But the line is tastelessly luscious only if one ignores all the meaning, and of course the meaning affects the sensation. The kiss is a
rhyme because it rhymes (pairs) their lips ('And pair their rhymes
as Venus yokes her doves', *Don Juan*, V. 1) and doubly so because
the upper and lower lips already rhyme with each other. It is 'dewy'
because the lips are wetted by saliva, a fact at once romantically
expressed and attractive (as if the reader were either the kisser or
the kissed), and also disconcerting (the reader is neither, and the
saliva on lips is something which cannot but be faintly uneasy to
contemplate unless one is not just contemplating it). The essential
thing was for Keats to apply 'dewy' directly to 'lips', and not to
allow any gap such as might allow the physical immediacy of the
sense (saliva, after all) to slip away through a slackness; you can
see the same complex of feelings, including the pair of lips and the
song ('a glee'), coming to nothing elsewhere:

              a glee
  Circling from three sweet pair of Lips in Mirth;
  And haply you will say the dewy birth
      Of morning Roses—

('To the Ladies . . .', 3–6)

'Dewy', though at the opposite pole as a verbal device, works rather
as the tautology does in Bob Dylan's exultant cry of memory, 'Her
mouth was watery and wet'.[2] And 'poesied'?: because a kiss is a
creative act, like writing a poem; like a poem, it both recognizes
what already exists and brings something new into existence; it
both is bred from, and breeds love. ('Brown has been walking up

---

[1] *Keats' Craftsmanship* (1933; 1964 edn.), p. 28.   [2] 'I Don't Believe You.'

and down the room a breeding—now at this moment he is being delivered of a couplet—and I dare say will be as well as can be expected—Gracious—he has twins!')[1]

A kiss does not use words, but then 'poesied' and 'rhyme' are aware of that; it is a fine stroke of the poetical imagination which sees the simple creativity of a kiss as its honourable equal. The poet does not belittle his art, though he archaizes it with an effect of modesty ('to poesy' has a different effect from 'poesy' the noun). Poetry is a nobleness of life, and so is a kiss. The creativity fulfils itself in the last couplet:

> Great bliss was with them, and great happiness
> Grew, like a lusty flower in June's caress.

—where the tautology (like 'Her mouth was watery and wet') of bliss and happiness is an exultation, a cup running over, while at the same time indicating a difference of sense through the verbs. 'Great bliss was with them': bliss,[2] an accompaniment, ecstatically out of the ordinary; 'and great happiness / Grew', as ordinary, continuing, and expansive. The erotic fervour is unmistakable and burgeoning, as in the choice of 'lusty', so sure to call up lust and so confident of holding it off.

Keats intimates that a full kiss upon the lips is uniquely moving and creative, and that it is so because of its dewiness and because of its reciprocity, the rhyme of lips upon lips. And perhaps because of the impossibility of talking at that moment, the relief from talk, since this poesy, this rhyme, is not a matter of saying anything. Moreover, you cannot kiss your own mouth (except in the mirror, and there—with perfected narcissism—it is the only part of you that you can kiss), and this for a more total reason than that you cannot kiss some parts of yourself; the full sense of self in a kiss upon the lips is supremely dependent upon non-self and its perfect complement. For Keats, a kiss is creative, an act of love which makes love; as is well known, we kiss not only because we love but so that we may love. At such a moment a kiss is a self-fulfilling prophecy. Keats's 'pre-figurative imagination' delighted in, and

---

[1] To George and Georgiana Keats, 19 Feb. 1819; ii. 66.
[2] Byron: ' "Kiss" rhymes to "bliss" in fact as well as verse' (*Don Juan*, VI. 59).

fully trusted, this self-fulfilling power. 'It seems downright pre-intention': the subconscious which created slips of the tongue was, it is true, the same which created nightmare:

> As feels a dreamer what doth most create
> His own particular fright, so these three felt.
> (*Endymion*, IV. 889–90)

But it was the same, too, which created our hopes for those we love; in the words of Keats's letter to George and Georgiana, 'If I had a prayer to make for any great good, next to Tom's recovery, it should be that one of your Children should be the first American Poet. I have a great mind to make a prophecy and they say prophecies work out their own fullfillment.'[1] The prophecy which Keats made was a poem for this as yet unborn child.

'The Genius of Poetry must work out its own salvation in a man: It cannot be matured by law & precept, but by sensation & watch-fulness in itself—That which is creative must create itself.'[2] 'The Imagination may be compared to Adam's dream—he awoke and found it truth.' And Adam's dream was a dream of love, of a woman to love and to be loved by. The dream ushered not just a woman or even the woman into Adam's life, but ushered woman into life. 'I have the same idea of all our Passions as of Love they are all in their sublime, creative of essential Beauty.'[3] 'Things real—such as existences of Sun Moon & Stars and passages of Shakspeare—Things semireal such as Love, the Clouds &c which require a greeting of the Spirit to make them wholly exist.'[4] It is, to say the least, a very beautiful coincidence in a matter of coinciding that Dr. Burgess, writing about blushing in 1839, should have brought together in a quotation from Dr. Muller the four humanizing creativities, of the reproductive organs, of pregnancy, of digestion, and of blushing:

The mutual action or *affinity* between the *blood* and the *tissues* of the body, which is an essential part of the process of nutrition, is, under many circumstances, greatly encreased: and an accumulation of blood into the dilated vessels of this organ is the result. It is seen, for

---

[1] 14 Oct. 1818; i. 398.
[3] To Bailey, 22 Nov. 1817; i. 184–5.
[2] To Hessey, 8 Oct. 1818; i. 374.
[4] To Bailey, 13 Mar. 1818; i. 243.

example, in the reproductive organs when excited; in the uterus during pregnancy, stomach in digestion, &c. The local accumulation of blood with the dilatation of old and the formation of *new vessels*, is, however, seen most frequently in the embryo, in which new organs are developed in succession by a process of this kind (vital turgescence of the blood-vessels). *This condition* may be excited very suddenly, as is seen in the instantaneous injection of the cheeks with blood *in the act of blushing* (pp. 112–13).

Keats knew of the vital turgescence that for his lovers 'Grew, like a lusty flower in June's caress'; he later knew too of the dark dilatation and accumulation, not a vital but a mortal turgescence: before he saw the 'bright blanch'd' face of Moneta,

> I had a terror of her robes,
> And chiefly of the veils, that from her brow
> Hung pale, and curtain'd her in mysteries
> That made my heart too small to hold its blood.
> (*The Fall of Hyperion*, I. 251–4)

'The authenticity of the Imagination', the creative prophecy of the imagination and of love, meet supremely when the imagination takes love as its great example and its theme; grandly, in Adam's dream, *Paradise Lost*, VIII. 452–90; modestly, in the rich felicity, a felicity that does indeed incorporate the possibility of a tastelessness such as is endemic in the full imagining of another's kiss, in

> So said, his erewhile timid lips grew bold,
> And poesied with hers in dewy rhyme.

The nineteenth-century critic Alexander Smith deplored Keats's 'nauseous sweetness':[1]

'He still wrote in a style of babyish effeminacy about
   "Plums/Ready to melt between an infant's gums" '

Yet it is odd that the fact that he needed the word 'babyish' did not at all move the critic to wonder whether at least some distaste could not be valid and enriching. The point about babies' gums is again that they evoke such powerfully mixed feelings, at once sweetly delightful and disconcerting in their pink wet physicality and toothlessness. Once again we are to have a double sense, both

---

[1] *Keats: The Critical Heritage*, p. 365.

within and without the situation; in so far as we imagine ourselves as the infant's parents, we are ready to melt in sympathetic pleasure at its innocent little gums; in so far as we are not any such thing, the possibility of embarrassment and faint repellence is altogether right; it is characteristic of Keats's imagination that it should combine a good-hearted rebuke to any timorousness of sympathetic identification, with the same rebuke to any unrealistic and exorbitant claims to transcend obvious simplicities of feeling—such as not feeling about the gums of other people's babies as you do about the gums of your own baby. The word *gums* itself quite naturally elicits such double feelings; in this, it resembles some of Keats's other attractive yet disconcerting physicalities, like 'spongy'. The tenderness of the young gums is outdone by the utterly accommodating tenderness of the plums:

> and here, undimm'd
> By any touch, a bunch of blooming plums
> Ready to melt between an infant's gums . . .
>   (*Endymion*, II. 449–51)

'Bunch' makes the hyperbolic delight clear enough; and 'blooming' is at once flourishing, and like flowers (so that a bunch of them is a feast for the eyes), and still fresh with the bloom upon the plum. Yet this intricacy of phrasing coexists with the infant's sense of the deepest gratification, that of the mouth; and given Keats's predilection for intelligent synaesthesia, it is worth recalling Empson's comment that 'it throws back the reader upon the undifferentiated affective states which are all that such sensations have in common; perhaps recalls him to an infantile state before they had been distinguished from one another'.[1] It was Aubrey de Vere in 1849 who said:

Shelley admired the beautiful, Keats was absorbed in it; and admired it no more than an infant admires the mother at whose breast he feeds. That deep absorption excluded all consciousness of self. . . . There is a peculiar significance in the expression, 'a child of song', as applied to him. Not only his outward susceptibilities retained throughout the freshness of infancy, but his whole nature possessed that integrity

---

[1] *Seven Types of Ambiguity* (1930; 1947 edn.), p. 13.

which belongs but to childhood, or to the purest and most energetic genius.[1]

What makes Keats's lines something more than a relapse into the infantile or babyish is their combining the full feeling of undifferentiated sensation (for the baby, everything concentring in the mouth) with the adept little differentiations that make 'blooming' a complicated part of the effect. In truncating the phrase, Alexander Smith was making things easy for himself; in finding it 'nauseous', he was over-reacting but reacting to something truly and rightly there. A baby's toothlessness is not nauseous but it is strange and slightly embarrassing to contemplate; to delight in a baby's gums and its toothlessness (the plums melting unbitten) is to intimate but to stave off the nauseous infancy of old toothlessness: 'She favoured voluminous tempestuous shifts and petticoats and other undergarments whose names I forget. They welled up all frothing and swishing and then, congress achieved, broke over us in slow cascades. And all I could see was her taut yellow nape which every now and then I set my teeth in, forgetting I had none, such is the power of instinct.' That extraordinarily dismaying and comical piece of erotic writing from Beckett's *Molloy* may seem to take no cognizance whatever of Keats's world. Yet 'tempestuous shifts and petticoats'? 'The tempestuous petticoat' is after all from the diminutive precursor of Keats, Robert Herrick.

I take these instances precisely because they are the notorious and unforgettable ones; my point is that the critic, in the nineteenth century as now, was too quick to assume that there could not possibly be any point in Keats's inducing (as part of the sensation and response) a hot tingle and discomfort. Granted, there is not an immensely wide range of worthwhile effect and comprehension which lies open to such a use of language, but the effect is neither simple nor trivial, since it compacts a necessary struggle within the sympathetic imagination: its recognition, when confronted by the physicality of others (and especially of those loved by others), of a generosity to be attained without sentimentality (that is, without the pretence that there is no possibility of distaste or embarrassment) and without morbidity (which is fixated upon those

[1] *Keats: The Critical Heritage*, p. 342.

possibilities). In short, to apply Dr. Leavis's words where he might not wish, a 'relation between Keats's sensuousness and his seriousness'.

One can come upon another notorious example in its place:

> Enchantress! tell me by this soft embrace,
> By the most soft completion of thy face,
> Those lips, O slippery blisses, twinkling eyes,
> And by these tenderest, milky sovereignties—
> These tenderest, and by the nectar-wine,
> The passion—
>
> *(Endymion,* II. 756–61)

I cannot see why 'Those lips, O slippery blisses' has been so scorned, except that scorn can be the recourse of embarrassment and of a timorous imagination finding itself unduly, even improperly, moved. The phrase is famous for its exultant patterning of sounds: 'Those' into 'O slippery', and 'lips' into 'slippery'; I think that the effortlessness, naturalness, and yet surprise with which 'lips' slips into 'slippery' is a bliss to experience. True, it insists upon the saliva which we shall meet if we kiss; but I think that a good thing to insist upon, given that Keats does not remain fixated upon it (the list slips flickering on; the pace of the line is quite different from that of the line which precedes and the line which follows it). For the effect of 'slippery' is the morally apt and percipient one: of demanding that we recognize salivation, that we admit to being disconcerted by it, that we be conscious that we are not disconcerted by it when within a moment of ecstatic love such as the lines themselves embody, and that our being disconcerted and embarrassed should not be rested upon but can be incorporated within a large response to others' responses. Again, too, the poetry is not a simple infantilism or sensation; I think of the tenderness by which the unexpected, yet beautifully full and whole, word 'completion' cannot but suggest the word 'complexion': 'By the most soft completion of thy face'. (Keats elsewhere in *Endymion* has 'freckled' exert the pressure which is here exerted by 'soft . . . face': 'Their freckled wings; yea, the fresh budding year / All its completions'; I. 259–60.)[1]

---

[1] Milton calls up 'embroidered' in a comparable way in *Paradise Lost,* IX. 437–8:
> Among thick-wov'n Arborets and Flours
> Imborderd on each Bank, the hand of Eve.

Keats is not fixated upon the fact that the lips are slippery; the effect of buoyancy, of healthy unloitering recognition, is not just a matter of the line's pace, but also of the way in which the lips' slipperiness simply takes its place with the other liquidities; what ends as nectar-wine, and had been the life-giving milkiness of her breasts, had been 'twinkling eyes'—the eyes twinkle with moisture; it is the proper brightness of all these liquidities that allows the verse to incorporate 'slippery blisses' and yet—since it is patently an audacious piece of writing—to give the sense that the imagination (ours now, and ours in daily life, and the poet's imagination) does have to make its benign effort in order to achieve such effortlessness.

Professor G. Wilson Knight was aware of the notoriety of a Keatsian moment which he sought to reinstate: ' "O, he had swoon'd, drunken from pleasure's nipple" (*Endymion*, II. 868) suggests a typical blend of intoxication with health-giving nourishment.'[1] But this needs to be qualified and amplified. Qualified, in that it is an important part of Keats's effect that those words should not constitute a single iambic line. The movement of 'O, he had swoon'd, drunken from pleasure's nipple' would be altogether too swooning, too easily completing, too lapsing into complacency; the movement of what Keats wrote is quite different:[2]

> O he had swoon'd
> Drunken from Pleasure's nipple; and his love
> Henceforth was dove-like . . .

I think, too, that Mr. Wilson Knight's 'typical' needs to be strengthened; the glory of Keats's observation here is, to begin with, its

---

[1] *The Starlit Dome* (1941; 1971 edn.), p. 260.

[2] We do a similar damage (one that creates a tone of self-satisfaction, of a perfect fit) to two great Shakespearean moments when our memory mislineates them: not 'Simply the thing I am shall make me live'; but

> Simply the thing I am
> Shall make me live. Who knows himself a braggart . . .
> (*All's Well*, IV. iii. 310–11)

Not 'I am a man more sinned against than sinning', but:

> 'I am a man
> More sinned against than sinning.' 'Alack, bare-headed?'
> (*King Lear*, III. ii. 59–60)

A wonderful contrariety of the sinning and the bare head, at once touching and styptic.

immediate felicity: a baby *does* swoon from the nipple, its eyelids
waver and then it is received into a full intoxication. The force is,
of course, the contrast between what such a swoon and such a
drunkenness are, when compared to those of adult life; we in our
turn should be invigorated by the simple delight of the baby, a full
gratification free from guilt or anxiety. And what enables us, with
Keats's guiding, to feel a full pleasure comparable to the infant's is
precisely the fact that though infancy is irrecoverably lost, adult love
can re-create its full innocence of gratification. Freud's words are
vivid not only in themselves but as a commentary upon Keats: 'No
one who has seen a baby sinking back satiated from the breast and
falling asleep with flushed cheeks and a blissful smile can escape the
reflection that this picture persists as a prototype of the expression
of sexual satisfaction in later life.'[1] At which point we recollect that
Keats's lines, though they have all the force of an immediate
description, are in fact a metaphor of adult love.

Yet it is not just the two so different drunkennesses which create
the penetrating ambivalence of Keats's words. The single word
'nipple' gathers a great deal to itself (as 'sea-weed' and 'gums' did
elsewhere). Clearly nobody can speak on any of these suggestivenesses and sensations without being aware that he risks manifesting
his own oddity; nevertheless 'nipple' is a word of quite a different
kind from 'breast' or 'bosom'. Clearly a breast or a bosom may
arouse mixed feelings in us, but this is not concentrated into the
very shape and sound of the word, into a disconcerting or embarrassing specificity and physicality, such as is compacted into the
word 'nipple'—a word for which there was significantly no home in
Byron's *Don Juan*, for all Byron's width and indecorousness. It is not
a word of an animality or—differently—a coarseness which make it
inappropriate to a human being, as may be 'dug' or 'udder'. It is a
word different, too, from 'teat', though that has its own strange
effect. Keats: 'The Heart . . . is the teat from which the Mind or
intelligence sucks its identity.'[2] Yet 'nipple' is a peculiarly forceful
and active word. It is true, plainly, that this is not just a matter
of the word, a forcefulness independent of the thing, since female

---

[1] *Three Essays on Sexuality* (1905).
[2] To George and Georgiana Keats, 21 Apr. 1819; ii. 103.

fashions and much else make it clear that the nipple is indeed especially intimate. (There are those who will say that this is culturally determined; indeed, and so is all our life and so is Keats's poetry.) But this is a verbal forcefulness and ambivalence coinciding with those of the thing itself. It sums up a classic pastoral predicament: that only the infant, who cannot speak (*infans*) let alone speak the word 'nipple', can fully, altogether unmisgivingly, appreciate the nipple. I think that the word plays an important part in our feelings, and that the effect of Keats's lines is therefore importantly different from the effect of, say, Bronzino's 'Allegory of Passion'; in the painting, the nipple is important, and it arouses mixed feelings, but it is not (because of the very medium) spoken of as a nipple, it is simply shown; and therefore it cannot arouse the particular mixed feelings, or cannot in the same way arouse them, as those elicited by the word. A nipple, a picture of a nipple, and the word 'nipple' all are different in effect. Having things spoken of is after all an embarrassment of a different kind; the infant who cannot say 'nipple' cannot blush either: infants do not blush.

That the word does have this odd contrariety of effect—at once fascinating, attractive, splendidly unsentimentalizable, and yet embarrassing, sometimes perhaps somewhat repellent—is clear from the memorable literary moments which speak of it. In Swift's description of the Brobdingnagian nurse suckling the baby, 'nipple' does not evoke the same feelings as 'breast' and 'dug':

I must confess no object ever disgusted me so much as the sight of her monstrous breast, which I cannot tell what to compare with, so as to give the curious reader an idea of its bulk, shape and colour. It stood prominent six foot, and could not be less than sixteen in circumference. The nipple was about half the bigness of my head, and the hue both of that and the dug so varified with spots, pimples and freckles, that nothing could appear more nauseous. . . .

('A Voyage to Brobdingnag', Chapter I)

As is usual with Swift, the ferocity and surprise are not a matter of an emotion unknown to us, but of one which we recognize but usually (and mostly rightly) play down. But I think that the strength of Keats, of 'Pleasure's nipple', is a matter of doing something other than avert the eyes from these violent, embarrassed, and disconcerted feelings about nipples; Pleasure's nipple is what no actual nipple could be, except in a moment of deep love: pure pleasure to contemplate.

Since I think that it is the potentiality of embarrassment, recognized and subsumed, which animates the lines, it may be objected that I am imagining this potentiality in order to redeem embarrassingly bad verse. But Keats's sequence of feeling here makes it clear that the recognition is his:

> O he had swoon'd
> Drunken from Pleasure's nipple; and his love
> Henceforth was dove-like.—Loth was he to move
> From the imprinted couch, and when he did,
> 'Twas with slow, languid paces, and face hid
> In muffling hands.
>
> (*Endymion*, II. 868–73)

The evocation of embarrassment becomes the clearer if one recalls that 'hands' had in the manuscript been 'arms'; one thinks of 'Some with their faces muffled to the ear / Between their arms'.[1]

Walter Jackson Bate, who deplores 'Those lips, O slippery blisses' and 'Pleasure's nipple', is consistent in deploring too

> Rise, Cupids! or we'll give the blue-bell pinch
> To your dimpled arms . . .
>
> (*Endymion*, II. 505–6)

But again the assumption is that the physicality could not be intended to hint a potentiality of distaste, and could not be of value if it were, whereas I believe that the memorability of this tiny vignette is a matter of the mixed feelings that we have about a small tender bruise (to be regarded with affection and yet as a powerful reminder of how strange and vulnerable flesh is) and about dimples. Dimples upon our own babies are simply delightful; on other people's, we may feel a qualm (pudgy? overweight? flesh so obviously not within control?), and so we may even have the potentiality for a qualm when it comes to the infant loves, Keats's Cupids. There is a comparable contrariety in the wonderful lines that follow, redeeming 'lazy' through its here being an activity, and pacifying

[1] See p. 25.

'fists' as only infant innocence can do, and seeing 'yawns' as lovable
not as embarrassing or impolite:

> 'Rise, Cupids! or we'll give the blue-bell pinch
> To your dimpled arms. Once more sweet life begin!'
> At this, from every side they hurried in,
> Rubbing their sleepy eyes with lazy wrists,
> And doubling over head their little fists
> In backward yawns.
>
> (*Endymion*, II. 505–10)

Once again I am claiming that what might seem to be literary
usages from quite a different world are nevertheless presences
(potentialities present) in Keats's phrasing, phrasing which even
those who dislike these moments find it impossible to forget. When
Pope wishes to evoke the powerful mixed feelings deserved by
Sporus, with his 'Cherub's face', it is natural for him to make use of
a variant of dimple: 'As shallow streams run dimpling all the way.'
Or there is Robert Frost, in 'Design': 'I found a dimpled spider,
fat and white . . .' For the strange little physicality of 'dimple' is
not just a matter of the thing itself (though again one can see why
as a physical phenomenon it might call up mixed feelings) or of the
shape and sound of the word, but of the fact that it is one of the
words which put strongly before us a disconcerting fact about
attractive physicality: that what can be simply attractive in a baby
(its dimples, its gums) may not be so in a woman or in a man.
Sporus is associated with dimpling, and his toothlessness is the
subject of Pope's most mordant wit:

> Eternal Smiles his Emptiness betray,
> As shallow streams run dimpling all the way.[1]

The disturbance of this delicate balance in the word, a balance which
can simply be disturbed by choosing 'dimpled' instead of 'dimple',
is what makes it a forceful component of a euphemism; in the old
days when the word 'navel' was thought to be somehow rude (and
it still is one of the disconcerting or embarrassing physical pheno-
mena and words), the popular press came up with the rich euphemism 'waist-dimple', perfect in its combination of ghastly delicacy

---

[1] *An Epistle to Dr. Arbuthnot*, 315–16.

with ripe prurience. A diminutiveness which is simply coy when applied to a full-grown woman can be a charming release from timorousness elsewhere; it is this which gives a true clear sensation of its own sweet delight to Keats's lines about the minnows, totally and unwrestlingly at ease with bellies as we cannot quite ordinarily be:

> How they ever wrestle
> With their own sweet delight, and ever nestle
> Their silver bellies on the pebbly sand.
>
> ('I stood tip-toe', 75-7)

The contrasting rhyme 'wrestle' and 'nestle' (with the effect made gentle by their being feminine rhymes) is an epitome of the way in which Keats's poetry can accommodate what are ordinarily incompatible impulses.

Our mixed feelings about freckles create another Keatsian instance, but a more important one is nostrils. Like all the body's orifices it has the potentiality for distaste and awe. When Keats tries to ignore this, he produces mere prettiness: 'Her nostrils, small, fragrant, faery-delicate' (*Otho the Great*, V. v. 68). But when he allows the physicality to realize itself as possibly embarrassing, he produces a poetry of awe:

> These raven horses, though they foster'd are
> Of earth's splenetic fire, dully drop
> Their full-veined ears, nostrils blood wide, and stop.
>
> (*Endymion*, IV. 398-400)

Or a poetry which creates a physicality at once disturbing and magnetic:

> when her lips and eyes
> Were clos'd in sullen moisture, and quick sighs
> Came vex'd and pettish through her nostrils small.
>
> (*Endymion*, II. 468-70)

The response to a word like 'nostrils' may seem remote from anything of size or weight, but since what is involved includes both man's full sense of his physicality and man's notions of dignity, even a great epic moment may turn upon small verbal choices. Cowden

Clarke recalled his introducing Keats to 'some of the "famousest" passages' in Chapman's Homer:

The last was the whole of the shipwreck of Ulysses in the Fifth Book of the *Odyssey*. I think his expression of delight, during the reading of those dozen lines, was never surpassed:—

> Then forth he came, his both knees faltering, both
> His strong hands hanging down, and all with froth
> His cheeks and nostrils flowing, voice and breath
> Spent to all use, and down he sunk to death.
> *The sea had soaked his heart through*; all his veins
> His toils had rack'd t' a laboring woman's pains.
> Dead weary was he.

On an after-occasion I showed him the couplet of Pope's upon the same passage:—

> From mouth and nose the briny torrent ran,
> *And lost in lassitude lay all the man.*[1]

Cowden Clarke was right to think that the lines which he italicized were the heart of the matter: 'The sea had soaked his heart through.' But the richer dignity of Chapman's lines is also a result of their unmisgiving immediacy and particularity in 'nostrils', especially as 'all with froth / His cheeks and nostrils flowing'; Pope, once he wished the sea-water to be 'the briny torrent', had to prefer nose to nostril—and the nemesis which lies in wait for false dignity gratified itself with 'nose . . . ran' as would not have been so with 'nostril'.

No one would deny that Keats was preoccupied with breasts and that sometimes he could not think in their vicinity. But faced with such a mere relapse as 'That warm, white, lucent, million-pleasured breast' ('Sonnet: To Fanny'), we should ask what made this so debilitated; and the answer, I think, is that in imagining the breast only as pleasure (as 'million-pleasured') it loses the truthful tension which Keats elsewhere apprehends.

How highly you estimate the sonnet 'Bright star!' will depend upon whether the marked absence from it of any mixed feelings in contemplating and describing a breast is a triumph of the 'pure

---

[1] *Keats: The Critical Heritage*, pp. 390–1.

ablution' of love or is somewhat staged and thin in its willed non-recognition of the possibility of an unease in those of us who find ourselves in the poem's company but neither as Keats nor as Fanny Brawne.

> Bright star! would I were steadfast as thou art—
>   Not in lone splendour hung aloft the night
> And watching, with eternal lids apart,
>   Like nature's patient, sleepless Eremite,
> The moving waters at their priestlike task
>   Of pure ablution round earth's human shores,
> Or gazing on the new soft fallen mask
>   Of snow upon the mountains and the moors—
> No—yet still steadfast, still unchangeable,
>   Pillow'd upon my fair love's ripening breast,
> To feel for ever its soft fall and swell,
>   Awake for ever in a sweet unrest,
> Still, still to hear her tender-taken breath,
> And so live ever—or else swoon to death.

To me, this watching and gazing, fine though it is, is something less than the full release of Keats's imagination; it is more self-conscious a relief. The manuscript version ran:

> Cheek-pillow'd on my Love's white ripening breast,
>   To touch for ever its warm sink and swell . . .

This had a fuller candour, risking a blush by its audacity and its assimilation of the cheek's physicality to the breasts, and by its sense that one can 'touch' with one's cheek; this creates a more ample and less simply sweet unrest, just as did the relation then of 'snow' to 'white' and to 'warm'. So that the last swoon, 'And so live ever—or else swoon to death', is to me slack and anticlimactic in comparison with

> O he had swoon'd
> Drunken from Pleasure's nipple . . .

It is Keats the man as well as the poet who has these pre-occupations, and I find a truer poignancy than that of the sonnet to Fanny Brawne in two remarks in his letters to her: 'Knowing well that my life must be passed in fatigue and trouble, I have been endeavouring to wean myself from you: for to myself alone what can be much of a misery?' 'I cannot say forget me—but I would mention that there are impossibilities in the world. No more of this—I am not strong enough to be weaned—'[1] The strength with which he here contemplates his own need of strength is a matter of the touching incongruity between 'weaned' and the laconic edge of 'but I would mention that there are impossibilities in the world'.

Like any other true imagination, Keats's is intensely personal and yet not merely so. Geoffrey Grigson has urged a relation between Keats's mother and his nursing of Tom:

'I am certain of nothing but of the holiness of the Heart's affections and the truth of the Imagination': behind that see the unholiness of the lack of affection in a mother who had married another man less than three months after his father had been killed. That fiery particle was not snuffed out by criticism, only by the disease to which his family was prone, and which he caught by the most faithful nursing —in the holiness of the heart's affections—of his brother Tom.[2]

> And very, very deadliness did nip
> Her motherly cheeks . . .
>
> Cheek-pillow'd on my Love's white ripening breast . . .

Such poetry will not dwindle into case-history though we bring it into the vicinity of Dr. Bergler.[3]

She found the upper part of the female body very beautiful, especially the breast. 'The first thing I look at in a woman is the breast'. Then hesitantly, 'After which I compare it with my own'. And the triumphant conclusion: 'So far I have not yet found a woman with a bosom more beautiful than mine'.

An interesting detail relating to the choice of her own cheeks as substitute for the maternal breast must be mentioned. The patient . . . had full cheeks as a child which, people always would tell her, looked like 'milk and blood' ('peaches and cream'). Every visitor would pet them, make friendly remarks on their size, color and firmness. As the patient was brought up with great regard for modesty,

---

[1] 13 Sept. 1819; ii. 160; and Feb. (?) 1820, ii. 257.
[2] *The Listener*, 25 Apr. 1968.
[3] On ereutophobia and breasts, see also Benedek, Feldman, and Hitschmann.

her cheeks were virtually the only part of her body permitted to be exhibited . . . The preoedipal stage is also indicated by the fact that two cheeks made use of psychically in blushing are in obvious correspondence to the two breasts.

The patient was a passionate drinker of milk, which she consumed by the quart. The implied defiance of her mother was: 'I don't need *your* milk.'

In the whole of Keats's letters, there is only one reference to his mother. The sonnet that imagines Fanny Brawne's breast begins 'Bright star!'; the letter that mentions his mother is a letter to Fanny Brawne which ends

Your's ever, fair Star,

John Keats.

—and which then begins its postscript:

> My seal is mark'd like a family table cloth with my Mother's initial F for Fanny: put between my Father's initials. You will soon hear from me again. My respectful Compts to your Mother.[1]

[1] 25 July 1819; ii. 133.

V

TASTE AND DISTASTE

What men or gods are these? What maidens loth?
What mad pursuit? What struggle to escape?
What pipes and timbrels? What wild ecstasy?

THE lines from the 'Ode on a Grecian Urn' are parodied but respected in Aldous Huxley's 'Frascati's',[1] a poem which deliberately has some of the stage-properties but not the properties of a Keats poem.

Bubble-breasted swells the dome
Of this my spiritual home,
From whose nave the chandelier,
Schaffhausen frozen, tumbles sheer.
We in the round balcony sit,
Lean o'er and look into the pit
Where feed the human bears beneath,
Champing with their gilded teeth.
What negroid holiday makes free
With such priapic revelry?
What songs? What gongs? What nameless rites?
What gods like wooden stalagmites?
What steam of blood or kidney pie?
What blasts of Bantu melody?
Ragtime. . . . But when the wearied Band
Swoons to a waltz, I take her hand,
And there we sit in blissful calm,
Quietly sweating palm to palm.

I find the poet's distaste distasteful, though aware that someone can find my distaste for it so too. But what concentrates the poem and the argument is the concluding sweating. Some of its mockery is derived from its allusion to Shakespeare, where Juliet's assurance,

[1] *Leda* (1920).

'And palm to palm is holy palmer's kiss', does indeed have about it a holy innocence, very different from sophistication's self-deceiving self-indulgence at Frascati's. (It is apt that Shakespeare's line should probably have been behind Keats's respectful innocence: 'Lorenzo, a young palmer in Love's eye', 'Isabella', I.)

Sweat can be embarrassed and can embarrass whether it is so or not. Like the wetness of lips, it proffers an immediacy of the physical which can be a true and healthy component of full love or can be active within a distaste which it would be false and unhealthy to brand simply as false and unhealthy. Love poems therefore do well to recognize its existence, and particularly as hand to hand, a lover's reciprocity and complement. In his Shakespeare, Keats marked the lines from *Venus and Adonis*, 143–4:

> My smooth moist hand, were it with thy hand felt,
> Would in thy palm dissolve or seem to melt.

The conditionals ('were it . . . would') have a cooling effect, and even when the poem seizes the moment, it moves swiftly to significance and to the anticipated rather than resting in the immediate physicality:

> With these she seizeth on his sweating palm,
> The precedent of pith and livelihood,
> And trembling in her passion, calls it balm,
> Earth's sovereign salve to do a goddess good.
>
> (25–8)

William Empson has spoken candidly:

C. S. Lewis found the poem disgusting, mainly because Venus sweats. . . . But also the modern conventions about sweat are sharply different from the Elizabethan ones. Many love poems of the time regard the sweat of a lady as somehow a proof of her elegance and refinement; the smell is not recommended as an excitement for our lower nature, the only way it could be praised in a modern novel.[1]

Indeed the conventions change, but this is perhaps more a matter of what is most strongly felt rather than of what is felt at all. The wish in Shakespeare or in Donne (who likewise has recourse to

---

[1] *Shakespeare: Narrative Poems*, Signet Shakespeare (1968), p. xix.

'balm') to set sweat within a context of dignity and abstraction does not necessarily mean that such a context was the easy and obvious one for it; in 'The Ecstasy' Donne seems to me, whether in the interests of spirituality or carnality or of enforcing a sense of their interinanimation, to think of joined sweating hands as we do not effortlessly do, just as we are to be moved newly by the lovers' oeillades:

> Our hands were firmly cimented
> With a fast balm, which thence did spring,
> Our eye-beams twisted, and did thread
> Our eyes, upon one double string.

Aldous Huxley recognized such physicality and its importance to love's largeness of feeling, and insisted upon a distaste at the physical which the poem attributes (or, in my view, purports to attribute) to the narrowness of feeling endemic in love at Frascati's. Shakespeare and Donne recognize the physicality but transmogrify it. Keats's achievement is the one we should expect of the poet who said of *Lamia* that 'there is that sort of fire in it which must take hold of people in some way—give them either pleasant or unpleasant sensation. What they want is a sensation of some sort.'[1] Yet the particular sort of sensation which elicits Keats's powers of description and moral insight is precisely one which will not settle as 'either pleasant or unpleasant sensation', but a blend at once remarkable and ordinary, a blend which can work upon us in the service of a fundamental double truth which literature can prove upon our pulses, easy to know but never easy to recognize, accept, and delight in: that we are not other people and so should never think that we can fully imagine their feelings, and yet that we can imagine others' feelings. (The falsity of presumption beckons to one side, and of indifference to the other.) A deservedly famous passage in *Middlemarch* speaks of one aspect of a true imagination:

> It had been easier to her to imagine how she would devote herself to Mr. Casaubon, and become wise and strong in his strength and wisdom, than to conceive with that distinctness which is no longer reflection but feeling—an idea wrought back to the directness of

[1] To George and Georgiana Keats, 18 Sept. 1819; ii. 189.

sense, like the solidity of objects—that he had an equivalent centre of self, whence the lights and shadows must always fall with a certain difference.   (Chapter 21)

Keats's truth of imagination begins in 'the directness of sense', of physical sensation; but this directness is not such as 'the solidity of objects', which can be conceived of, as say a billiard ball can, from many different angles and still appear the same, but of physical sensations in which an alternativeness of response is inherent. Keats's apprehension of the physical is most drawn to, and most acute in, the conjunction of pleasure and displeasure in physical sensation; and the value of this imagination—'no longer reflection but feeling'—is its necessarily helping to create in us the sense that others have 'an equivalent centre of self', at home within a situation which is not ours, whence pleasure and displeasure must always be felt with a certain difference. The contrariety is not simply located within us, but is a consequence of our knowing—and of our being truly able to imagine, intermittently or partially—that we are located elsewhere than are other people. Erotic experiences could be for Keats the type case, since they can be both intensely alive to our imagination and yet also especially difficult to contemplate without the false perturbation of envy or wincing, as against a true perturbation which recognizes the need to overcome such feelings.

> My river-lily bud! one human kiss!
> One sigh of real breath—one gentle squeeze,
> Warm as a dove's nest among summer trees,
> And warm with dew at ooze from living blood!
> (*Endymion*, IV. 664–7)

I think it not right of Mrs. Allott to annotate the last line with 'An elegant periphrasis for the Indian maid's perspiration'. (I think too, incidentally, that such summary critical judgements are out of place in editorial footnotes.) 'Perspiration' itself has its faintly uneasy elegance; the line is certainly a periphrasis, but is it elegant? On the contrary it seems to me to be (quite properly) at once force-ful and odd. If I wished to be elegantly periphrastical in a lady's company, I do not think that I should speak of anything about her as 'at ooze'. 'Ooze' is one of Keats's strong necessary words precisely because it compacts sensation pleasant and unpleasant. The teasing quality of Keats's periphrasis or euphemism, unlike the decrepit genteelism 'perspiration', is its strange combination of an encompassing indirectness with a directness that is indeflectible; this is an effect not only of diction—'ooze', or 'warm' gathering 'warm' up into itself from the previous line—but also of the advancing prepositions; 'with . . . at . . . from'. Dew from the blood is not merely elegant or romantic (the basis of the metaphor is the salt in both sweat and dew); and the liquidity of dew and blood is, as a matter of physical sensation, counterbalanced by the dry 'nest' of the previous lines, rather as the high 'summer trees' come down to earth with 'dew'. Mrs. Allott dislikes 'one gentle squeeze': 'A phrase illustrating what Colvin calls ". . . the simpering familiar mood which Keats at this time had caught from or naturally shared with Leigh Hunt" '. I cannot see in what way the phrase simpers; it manifests a faint paradox, and a yearning that is simply ordinary, not at all grand, and necessarily an inducer of unease. Then Keats tautens the whole network of feelings with 'melt', Endymion's cry at her departure:

> . . .
> And warm with dew at ooze from living blood!
> Whither didst melt?

John Bayley said of the lines: 'The words are most real—embarrassingly real perhaps—when fantasy is most apparent.' A pity that 'perhaps' flinches from the truth which it needed to be importunate about. But certainly much of the case for Keats is the case for a proper embarrassment and for a proper fantasy, not kept on a tight rein but on a rein nevertheless.

'An indelible sweetness, which remains indefinitely in the mouth even after swallowing, perfectly completes the essence of the slimy.' Sartre's words would lead naturally enough to a reflection by E. H. Gombrich in 'Psycho-Analysis and the History of Art':

The importance of oral gratification as a genetic model for aesthetic pleasure is a subject that would reward closer investigation. After all, food is the first thing on which we train our critical faculties from the moment of birth. The very word taste which we use to describe a person's aesthetic responses suggests this model. But so strong is the Platonic prejudice in favour of the spiritual senses, the eye and the ear, that a blanket of social disapproval seems still to cover such animal gratification as eating and drinking.[1]

Is it disapproval or embarrassment, or perhaps disapproval of embarrassment? Keats announced: 'I have not one opinion upon any thing except in matters of taste';[2] and David Masson acutely was shocked: 'This is one of the most startling and significant sayings ever uttered by a man respecting himself.'[3] A pun flutters there; Keats does not just say it respecting himself: he is a man respecting himself, and our respect for him depends upon seeing how wide, deep, and true was his sense of taste and all that it comprised in relation to art, to others, and to ourselves.

The primacy of eating in Keats is well known and for his adverse critics notorious. Carlyle said that 'Keats is a miserable creature, hungering after sweets which he can't get; going about saying, "I am so hungry; I should so like something pleasant" '.[4] Jane Welsh Carlyle was sure that 'Almost any young gentleman with a sweet tooth might be expected to write such things. "Isabella"[5] might have been written by a seamstress who had eaten something too rich for supper and slept upon her back.' More amiably, though not without condescension, Leigh Hunt dubbed the young John Keats 'Junkets'; and the pseudonym which Hunt appended to 'La Belle Dame sans Merci', as to 'As Hermes once', when it was published in *The Indicator* was 'Caviare'. But Hunt would have appreciated the affinity of this to Keats's belief that 'the Imagination may be compared to Adam's dream—he awoke and found it truth'; for Hunt said of 'Sleep and Poetry' that it was 'a striking specimen of the restlessness of the young poetical appetite, obtaining its food by the very desire of it'.[6]

Not all the eating that fascinated Keats was 'hungering after sweets'; the matter is capacious enough for the staunch and vivid

[1] *Meditations on a Hobby Horse* (1965), p. 39.
[2] To George and Georgiana Keats, 31 Dec. 1818; ii. 19.
[3] *Keats: The Critical Heritage*, p. 374.   [4] Ibid., p. 35.
[5] G. M. Matthews points out that she presumably meant 'The Eve of St. Agnes'.
[6] *Keats: The Critical Heritage*, p. 62.

good sense of anatomical explanation: 'casually illustrating the comment, in his characteristic way, with poetical imagery: the stomach, he said, being like a brood of callow nestlings (opening his capacious mouth) yearning and gaping for sustenance.'[1] The relation in Keats of the acute sense of fact to richly robust fantasy is clear if we juxtapose that with a letter to his friend Rice, itself creating a humorously humdrum juxtaposition in its concluding sentence:

Would you like a true Story "There was a Man and his Wife who being to go a long journey on foot, in the course of their travels came to a River which rolled knee deep over the pebbles—In these cases the Man generally pulls off his shoes and stockings and carries the woman over on his Back. This Man did so; and his Wife being pregnant and troubled, as in such cases is very common, with strange longings, took the strangest that ever was heard of—Seeing her Husband's foot, a hansome on [one] enough, look very clean and tempting in the clear water, on their arrival at the other bank she earnestly demanded a bit of it; he being an affectionate fellow and fearing for the comeliness of his child gave her a bit which he cut off with his Clasp knife—Not satisfied she asked another morsel— supposing there might be twins he gave her a slice more. Not yet contented she craved another Piece. "You Wretch cries the Man, would you wish me to kill myself? take that!" Upon which he stabb'd her with the knife, cut her open and found three Children in her Belly two of them very comfortable with their mouth's shut, the third with its eyes and mouth stark staring open. "Who would have thought it" cried the Widower, and pursued his journey—, Brown has a little rumbling in his Stomach this morning—

> Ever yours sincerely
> John Keats—[2]

Even so, Carlyle and Mrs. Carlyle would be right to retort that in Keats the wish to be given a slice is usually a more sensuous and luxurious matter than this fairy-tale unsentimentality; and that it occurs in the oddest places, as when Keats writes to Haydon: 'I shall expect to see your Picture plumped out like a ripe Peach— you would not be very willing to give me a slice of it.'[3] Yet on

---

[1] Cowden Clarke; quoted by Bate, *John Keats*, p. 117.
[2] Dec. 1819; ii. 236.   [3] 3 Oct. 1819; ii. 221.

reflection it is not odd to assimilate the arts to eating, in the first place for the reasons which Gombrich gives, and in the second for those that Lionel Trilling gives in his penetrating account of Keats:

We are ambivalent in our conception of the moral status of eating and drinking. On the one hand ingestion supplies the imagery of our largest and most intense experiences: we speak of the wine of life and the cup of life; we speak also of its dregs and lees, and sorrow is also something to be drunk from a cup; shame and defeat are wormwood and gall; divine providence is manna or milk and honey; we hunger and thirst for righteousness; we starve for love; lovers devour each other with their eyes; and scarcely a mother has not exclaimed that oh, she could eat her baby up; bread and salt are the symbols of peace and loyalty, bread and wine the stuff of the most solemn acts of religion. On the other hand, however, while we may represent all of significant life by the tropes of eating and drinking, we do so with great circumspection. Our use of the ingestive imagery is rapid and sparse, never developed; we feel it unbecoming to dwell upon what we permit ourselves to refer to.

But with Keats the ingestive imagery is pervasive and extreme. He is possibly unique among poets in the extensiveness of his reference to eating and drinking and to its pleasurable or distasteful sensations. To some readers this is likely to be alienating, and indeed even a staunch admirer might well become restive under, for example, Keats's excessive reliance on the word 'dainties' to suggest all pleasures, even the pleasures of literature. It is surely possible to understand what led Yeats to speak of Keats as a boy with his face pressed to the window of a sweet-shop. The mild and not unsympathetic derogation of Yeats's image suggests something of the reason for the negative part of our ambivalence toward eating and drinking. The ingestive appetite is the most primitive of our appetites, the sole appetite of our infant state, and a preoccupation with it, an excessive emphasis upon it, is felt—and not without some reason—to imply the passivity and self-reference of the infantile condition. . . .

But Keats did not share our culture's fear of the temptation to the passive self-reference of infancy. He did not repress the infantile wish; he confronted it, recognized it, and delighted in it. Food—and what for the infant usually goes with food, a cosy warmth—make for him the form, the elementary idea, of felicity. He did not fear the seduc-

tion of the wish for felicity, because, it would seem, he was assured
that the tendency of his being was not that of regression but that of
growth. The knowledge of felicity was his first experience—he made
it the ground of all experience, the foundation of his quest for truth.
Thus, for Keats, the luxury of food is connected with, and in a sense
gives place to the luxury of sexuality. The best known example of this
is the table spread with 'dainties' beside Madeline's bed in 'The Eve
of St. Agnes'. And in that famous scene the whole paraphernalia of
luxurious felicity, the invoked warmth of the south, the bland and
delicate food, the privacy of the bed, and the voluptuousness of the
sexual encounter, are made to glow into an island of bliss with the
ultimate purpose of making fully apparent the cold surrounding
darkness; it is the moment of life in the infinitude of not-being.[1]

In one respect this valuable criticism is not Keatsian: it is faintly
embarrassed. I deduce this from its strange embarrassment about
using the word embarrassment. 'The moral status of eating and
drinking', 'we feel it unbecoming to dwell upon what we permit
ourselves to refer to', 'likely to be alienating', 'might well become
restive', 'fear of the temptation': all these are true ways to speak,
but they are uncharacteristically timorous. At no point is it clearly
said that the ambivalence of eating and drinking is an ambivalence
of embarrassment. I hear the creaking of embarrassment where it
usually is not, in Trilling's prose: in 'ingestion', in 'tropes' (not a
word from the real world or from Keats's world, or from Trilling's,
I should have thought), in the great circumspection of 'with great
circumspection', in 'the ingestive imagery' in two successive sen-
tences where it has a wooden bloodlessness, and even in the staunch
jocose unembarrassability of 'even a staunch admirer'.

What is at issue becomes clearer if we take the passage from
Keats's letters which leads into Trilling's account; Trilling has been
speaking of the apocryphal anecdote about Keats's putting cayenne
pepper on his tongue the better to appreciate the coolness of claret:

It does not, after all, go beyond Keats's own account of his pleasure
in the nectarine. 'Talking of pleasure,' he writes to Dilke, 'this
moment I was writing with one hand, and with the other holding

[1] *The Opposing Self*, pp. 16–18.

to my mouth a Nectarine—good God how fine. It went down soft, slushy, oozy—all its delicious embonpoint melted down my throat like a beatified Strawberry.'

Perhaps it is some qualm, unbeknown to Trilling, which leads even him to think that Keats is here overdoing it, and so to omit 'pulpy' ('soft pulpy, slushy, oozy') and 'large' ('like a large beatified Strawberry'). Still, Trilling is clearly right to think it a crucial and extraordinary piece of writing. Masson in 1860 delighted in the freshening power of it: 'he goes on to describe the nectarine in language that would reawaken gustativeness in the oldest fruiterer';[1] and Coventry Patmore, with an air of surprise and of doubt as to whether this made the whole thing better or worse, introduced the passage thus: 'To us, Keats seems to have pursued the pleasures and temptations of sense, rather than to have been pursued by them. We often find him feasting coolly over the imagination of sensual enjoyment.'[2] The paradox of the coolness and the heat should be related to the other doubleness; for when Trilling goes on from these lines to speak of Keats's frequent reference to 'eating and drinking and to its pleasurable or distasteful sensations', I wish to take that *or* in a different sense: not to mean that sometimes the sensation is one and sometimes the other, but to mean that any vivid recreation of the pleasurable sensation should involve a recognition of the possibility of distasteful sensation for someone else—for every someone else who is not actually doing the tasting.

The lines about the nectarine involve embarrassment; Keats's delighted hyperbole is a grand overdoing, and if we put the lines back into their context, two things are clear: Keats's relating of the nectarine to reading and writing, and his relating it to another kind of embarrassment. I shall come back later to embarrassment's links with reading and writing; for the moment it will be enough to show that for Keats the sequence of feeling and thinking is manifest, and to suggest that we should trust Keats's intuition about his left hand and his right hand and the simultaneity of their enterprises. I need to quote the whole of this letter to Dilke, because it moves forward through different embarrassments, cleansed for Dilke as for

---

[1] *Keats: The Critical Heritage*, p. 376.   [2] Ibid., p. 333.

Keats by his candour: the embarrassments of having to write an 'interested' and 'requestive' letter; of nerving himself to earning money; of his fixing upon literary journalism; and others. My point is the intimate relation between all these, and reading and writing, and the oozy nectarine:

My dear Dilke,

Whatever I take too for the time I cannot lave [leave] off in a hury; letter writing is the go now; I have consumed a Quire at least. You must give me credit, now, for a free Letter when it is in realty an interested one, on two points, the one requestive, the other verging to the pros and cons—As I expect they will lead me to seeing and conferring with you in a short time, I shall not enter at all upon a letter I have lately received from george of not the most comfortable intelligence: but proceed to these two points, which if you can theme out in sexions and subsexions, for my edification, you will oblige me. The first I shall begin upon, the other will follow like a tail to a Comet. I have written to Brown on the subject, and can but go over the same Ground with you in a very short time, it not being more in length than the ordinary paces between the Wickets. It concerns a resolution I have taken to endeavour to acquire something by temporary writing in periodical works. You must agree with me how unwise it is to keep feeding upon hopes, which depending so much on the state of temper and imagination, appear gloomy or bright, near or afar off just as it happens—Now an act has three parts—to act, to do, and to perform—I mean I should *do* something for my immediate welfare—Even if I am swept away like a Spider from a drawing room I am determined to spin—home spun any thing for sale. Yea I will trafic. Any thing but Mortgage my Brain to Blackwood. I am determined not to lie like a dead lump. If Reynolds had not taken to the law, would he not be earning something? Why cannot I—You may say I want tact—that is easily acqui[r]ed. You may be up to the slang of a cock pit in three battles. It is fortunate I have not before this been tempted to venture on the common. I should a year or two ago have spoken my mind on every subject with the utmost simplicity. I hope I have learnt a little better and am confident I shall be able to cheat as well as any literary Jew of the Market and shine up an article on any thing without much knowlege of the subject, aye like an orange. I would willingly have recourse to other means. I cannot; I am fit for nothing but literature. Wait for the issue of this Tragedy?[1] No—there cannot be greater uncertainties east west, north, and south than concerning dramatic composition. How many months must I wait! Had I not better begin to look about me now? If better events supersede this necessity what harm will be done? I have no trust whatever on Poetry—I dont wonder at it—the mavel it [marvel is] to me how people read so much of it. I think you will see the reasonableness of my plan. To forward it I purpose living in cheap Lodg[i]ng in Town, that I may be in the reach of books and information, of which there is here a plentiful lack. If I can [find] any place tolerably comfitable I will settle myself and fag till I can afford to buy Pleasure—which if [I] never can afford I must go Without— Talking of Pleasure, this moment I was writing with one hand, and with the other holding to my Mouth a Nectarine—good god how fine —It went down soft pulpy, slushy, oozy—all its delicious embonpoint melted down my throat like a large beatified Strawberry. I shall certainly breed. Now I come to my request. Should you like me for a neighbour again? Come, plump it out, I wont blush. I should also be in the neighbourhood of Mᵣˢ Wylie, which I should be glad of, though that of course does not influence me. Therefore will you look about Marsham, or rodney street for a couple of rooms for me. Rooms like the gallants legs in massingers time "as good as the times allow, Sir." I have written to day to Reynolds, and to Woodhouse. Do you know him? He is a Friend of Taylors at whom Brown has taken one of his funny odd dislikes. I'm sure he's wrong, because Woodhouse likes my Poetry—conclusive. I ask your opinion and yet I must say to you as to him, Brown that if you have anything to say against it I shall be as obstinate & heady as a Radical. By the Examiner coming in your hand writing you must be in Town. They have put [me] into spirits: Notwithstand my aristocratic temper I cannot help being verry much pleas'd with the present public proceedings. I hope sincerely I shall be able to put a Mite of help to the Liberal side of the Question before I die. If you should have left Town again (for your Holidays cannot be up yet) let me know—when this is forwarded to you—A most extraordinary mischance has befallen two Letters I wrote Brown— one from London whither I was obliged to go on business for George; the other from this place since my return. I cant make it out. I am excessively sorry for it. I shall hear from Brown and from you almost together for I have sent him a Letter to day: you must positively agree with me or by the delicate toe nails of the virgin I will not open your

---

[1] *Otho the Great.*

Letters. If they are as David says 'suspicious looking letters" I wont open them—If St John had been half as cunning he might have seen the revelations comfortably in his own room, without giving Angels the trouble of breaking open Seals. Remember me to Mrs D. —and the Westmonisteranian and believe me

Ever your sincere friend
John Keats—[1]

The interrelationships (and they are not a matter of Keats's psychology alone, but of his important intuitions about our physical and our moral feelings) cluster around the nectarine: 'writing with one hand, and with the other . . .'; 'embonpoint'; 'I shall certainly breed' (which for Keats means bring poetry to birth);[2] and then at once the 'request': 'Should you like me for a neighbour again? Come, plump it out, I wont blush.' The pun on 'plump' (following 'embonpoint'); the promise not to blush (Keats himself not about to become 'a large beatified Strawberry'): what holds it all together is on one side the simple tricky embarrassment of a social request ('Should you like me for a neighbour again?') and on the other the double tricky embarrassment of good-hearted sensual gratification, aware both that it can and that it cannot share its pleasure, and using words to evoke both the intense pleasure and the simultaneous sense that since it is not being literally experienced by another it cannot but have the possibility of distastefully embarrassing. The creativity of heart and mind here is astonishing; Keats certainly breeds. Yet as with so many of the magnificent things in the letters, there is both nothing like it anywhere else and also a good deal that is at one with it. 'Soft pulpy' (no comma, so perhaps it is a compound epithet) clearly belongs in the world of Keats's erotic imaginings; pulp and pulpy are excellent words for the ambivalence of sensation, dependent upon whether you are experiencing, or imagining experiencing:

> And for each briar-berry he might eat,
> A kiss should bud upon the tree of love,
> And pulp and ripen richer every hour,
> To melt away upon the traveller's lips.
> ('Extracts from an Opera')

[1] 22 Sept. 1819; ii. 178–80.   [2] See p. 99.

Or there is the strange mingling of physical and emotional feeling in the manuscript line from 'The Eve of St. Agnes': 'Her anxious lips full pulp'd with rosy thoughts'. That un-Keatsian figure, Henry James, found the word *pulpy* useful to gesture with when he came near Keats's world: 'The consummate expressiveness of the eyes, the magnificent rendering of flush and bloom, warmth and relief, pulpy, blood-tinted, carnal substance in the cheeks and brow, are something of which a more famous master than Mr. Duveneck might be proud.'[1] As always with Keats the dark use is clear enough elsewhere, as in Ted Hughes's sense of the physical price paid, not for self-abandonment but for plethoric restraint, by 'The Retired Colonel' who

> Came, face pulped scarlet with kept rage,
> For air past our gate.

The letter to Dilke is magnificent—and then Keats did a braver thing, which was to keep that hid: he never sent it.[2] This usually does not get mentioned, yet surely it matters that Keats should have decided not to send it, penning instead the simple request that Dilke try to find him some rooms. Keats must have decided that his letter was not just fraught with embarrassing possibilities beautifully freed by friendship and humour but was embarrassing. Perhaps the nub was this sentence, which Keats may rightly have thought that he could neither unsay nor say in any way that could render it an unhurtful thing to say: 'I ask your opinion and yet I must say to you as to him, Brown that if you have any thing to say against it I shall be as obstinate & heady as a Radical.' We all do some such thing to our friends; I think it good of Keats to have seen that we should not, and that not even affectionate exaggeration could make this the right thing to have to say.

---

[1] *The Painter's Eye*, p. 106.

[2] H. B. Forman deduced so, from the lack of postmark, and from Keats's words ('I scarcely know whether I shall send my letter now') in his letter to Brown, 23 Sept. 1819: 'It seems likely that the short letter of the 1st of October to Dilke was sent instead of this longer one.' Hyder Rollins speaks with varying degrees of firmness: 'This letter was not mailed to Dilke' (ii. 178); 'it was probably not sent' (ii. 181); 'Presumably Keats held [it] back' (ii. 218).

And still she slept an azure-lidded sleep,
In blanched linen, smooth, and lavender'd,
While he from forth the closet brought a heap
Of candied apple, quince, and plum, and gourd
With jellies soother than the creamy curd,
And lucent syrops, tinct with cinnamon;
Manna and dates, in argosy transferr'd
From Fez; and spiced dainties, every one,
From silken Samarcand to cedar'd Lebanon.
                    ('The Eve of St. Agnes', XXX)

The Keatsian effect is of a rich description of a meal when you are not necessarily hungry; it is at once a very ambitious thing to try to pull off, and a modest one in that it eschews the presumption of those writers who think that all their readers can, whatever the moment, be made to feel fully hungry, so to speak.[1] For the appetite is large and yet fine;[2] as Leigh Hunt said, 'Here is delicate modulation and super-refined epicurean nicety!

          Lucent syrops, tinct with cinnamon,

make us read the line delicately, and at the tip-end, as it were, of one's tongue.'[3] A critic such as J. M. Newton, who finds Keats's sensuousness shallow and unrelated to anything much that is important, will inevitably be perturbed by the fact that the food never gets eaten: 'The feast is never mentioned again: either the poet forgets it or the lovers never think of eating (and perhaps never *have* thought of eating?).'[4] But Keats's moral sense cannot be accommodated within—though it can accommodate—'waste not, want not'; the nature of the power of that stanza is its rich evocation not of eating but of edibility. There is Madeline asleep, and

---

[1] The art of a letter therefore has to be differently (oppositely) sensitive to some of the same considerations, just because knowing what your audience feels like is much more precisely a possibility: 'Ha! my dear Sister George, I wish I knew what humour you were in that I might accomodate myself to any one of your Amiabilities' (27 June 1818; i. 303); and to Reynolds, 'I wish I knew always the humour my friends would be in at opening a letter of mine, to suit it to them nearly as possible' (13 July 1818; i. 324).

[2] Keats hated the narrowly fine: 'These men say things which make one start, without making one feel, they are all alike; their manners are alike; they all know fashionables; they have a mannerism in their very eating & drinking . . .' (to George and Tom Keats, 21 Dec. 1817; i. 193).

[3] *Keats: The Critical Heritage*, p. 280.   [4] *Cambridge Quarterly*, iv (1969), 277.

Porphyro bringing forth delicately what is nevertheless 'a heap'. Of course this suspended edibility could later in the poem have been succeeded by the actual eating; yet if we try to imagine that, we find it somehow inappropriate (as Mr. Newton rightly implies). Clearly it is not that Keats cannot manage a description of eating, and even one to outdo these astonishing edibilities; the abstention is deliberate, and it is, I think, required by the crucial act of sympathy within the poem. By limiting the feast to edibility, we remain at one with the lovers; like them, we feast our eyes. To watch them (one might say hear them, too) eat such a feast with the energetic delight appropriate to the largesse would inevitably be to intensify the ambivalence of feasting (they feast, and we do not, except in our momentary and necessarily partial identification) to the point at which it would inevitably blur and then eclipse the climax of the poem, their act of love, an intense physicality the ambivalence of which for us is to be neither shirked nor paralleled.

That the feasting and the act of love are related in this way for Keats (and perfectly naturally for us too) is clear from the stanza earlier in the poem which Keats dropped; wilfully dropped, some have thought, in that it made helpfully clear what the feast was doing there at all.

> 'Twas said her future lord would there appear
> Offering as sacrifice—all in the dream—
> Delicious food even to her lips brought near:
> Viands and wine and fruit and sugar'd cream,
> To touch her palate with the fine extreme
> Of relish: then soft music heard; and then
> More pleasure followed in a dizzy stream
> Palpable almost: then to wake again
> Warm in the virgin morn, no weeping Magdalen.

But to have kept this in would have demanded that Madeline should indeed eat; the relish is presented as a condition of the progress to the 'dizzy stream / Palpable almost', and much of the beauty and suppleness of the poem comes from the courtesy extended to the legend; the poem has the legend freely there without either bending it or bending to it. The 'dizzy stream' is permitted to appear in the poem when it should:

Beyond a mortal man impassion'd far
  At these voluptuous accents, he arose,
Ethereal, flush'd, and like a throbbing star
  Seen mid the sapphire heaven's deep repose
  Into her dream he melted, as the rose
Blendeth its odour with the violet,—
  Solution sweet: meantime the frost-wind blows
Like Love's alarum pattering the sharp sleet
Against the window-panes; St. Agnes' moon hath set.

(XXXVI)

The syntax through to the colon ('solution sweet:') melts beautifully: thus 'and like a throbbing star' at first is governed by 'he arose' and then blends in to be governed by 'Into her dream he melted'; it is this that gives the deep feeling of suspension at the line-ending of

    Seen mid the sapphire heaven's deep repose

Then the movement sharpens into the quite different syntax (pointed by the very different way in which this second 'Like . . .' acts) of the concluding lines.

    I do not think that I am making up an orbit within which these things fall; or, though that would deserve our interest, that Keats was merely doing so. The orbit brings into relationship the primitive and the refined, and the emotions which the anthropologist postulates are ones which the poet shapes and releases into health. I am thinking of Havelock Ellis on 'The Evolution of Modesty':

A special form of modesty very strongly marked among savages in some parts of the world. I refer to the feeling of immodesty in eating. . . . Thus among these peoples the act of eating in public produces the same feelings as among ourselves the indecent exposure of the body in public.

It is quite easy to understand how this arises. Whenever there is any pressure on the means of subsistence, as among savages at some time or another there nearly always is, it must necessarily arouse a profound and mixed emotion of desire and disgust to see another person putting into his stomach what one might just as well have put into one's own.[1]

<hr>

[1] *Studies in the Psychology of Sex.*

Keats's poetry comprehends, in both senses of the word, some such deep relation of eating to immodesty and to the possibility of anger and of disgust. Of danger too; it must be remembered that Porphyro is risking his life (because of the feud), and that the risks intensify while eating or in the act of love. The considerations raised by MacCurdy in 'The Biological Significance of Blushing and Shame' are remote in tone but not in substance from this poem which is so warm with blushing, and with danger, eating, and sleep.

In general the indulgence of any appetite tends to raise the threshold for stimuli irrelevant to the satisfaction of the appetite involved. The more powerful the appetite the greater the potential danger, and hence the greater the need for isolation. The sexual and nutritional lusts claim first place. Many animals will not eat while under observation, and it is difficult to witness coitus between the male and female of almost any wild species. Savages, who are immodest in many ways according to our prejudices, never perform the sexual act where they can be seen, except, rarely, as a religious rite. Prof. Malinowski writes me: 'Eating very definitely tends to be secretive. I find from the scanty notices of commensalism among primitive peoples, that eating in company is extremely rare, that eating among strangers is regarded as definitely indecent.' Incapacity to deal with potential dangers is still more obvious during illness and sleep. Consequently both animals and men evince a desire for isolation when ill or sleepy that extends from a pure mandatory instinct to a mere tendency. Malinowski generalizes thus: 'It is characteristic that sexual activities, sleep and excretion are surrounded by protective taboos and mechanisms of concealment and isolation in every society.' . . .

A third factor importing danger into the indulgence of appetites has been suggested to me by Prof. Malinowski. It excites jealousy. Hence to make love or to eat in public is to invite rivals to seize that which is being enjoyed. Our table customs, he thinks, may have as their *raison d'être* the suppression of too expressive delight.[1]

Among the things for which we should value literature, and in particular should value Keats, is the power to do something with such feelings, especially in giving us a sense of what is true and false,

[1] *British Journal of Psychology*, xxi (1930).

what can be both realistic and healthy, about our attitude to our own 'expressive delight', our attitude to that of others which we imagine, and to that of others whom we imagine.

Keats's publisher John Taylor deplored Keats's making the sexual consummation patent in his revision of 'The Eve of St. Agnes' (stanzas XXXV–XXXVI): 'the flying in the Face of all Decency & Discretion is doubly offensive from its being accompanied with so preposterous a Conceit on his part of being able to overcome the best founded Habits of our Nature.'[1] But the depth and passion of Keats's poetry and letters arise from the combination of his true scepticism as to what those habits indeed are, with his true respect for 'the best founded Habits of our Nature'.

When a poet writes an acrostic which, since it is for his sister-in-law, has to include his own surname, and he makes play with this, we should be especially interested to see the acrostic's components. Keats's acrostic to Georgiana reaches 'Keats':

> Kind Sister! aye this third name says you are [;]
> Enhanced has it been the Lord knows where.
> Ah! may it taste to you like good old wine—
> Take you to real happiness and give
> Sons daughters and a Home like honied hive.[2]

This insists upon the importance of tasting and of wine, and upon the climactic importance of the 'honied hive', in its associations with the fecundity of future sons and daughters.

Keats's concern with honey and the honey-like has always disconcerted his critics; my argument is that what should disconcert them, and partly does, is the properties of honey and not just of Keats's poetry. Carlyle cried that 'Keats wanted a world of treacle!',[3] but what Keats wanted was a recognition of the world of feelings active for us within treacle. David Masson said that 'the language in many parts was juvenile, not to say untasteful; such phrases as "honey-feel of bliss" were too frequent.'[4] Yet it was a handsomely co-operative subconscious which led Masson to complain that

---

[1] To Woodhouse, 25 Sept. 1819; *The Keats Circle*, i. 96.
[2] To George and Georgiana Keats, 27 June 1818; i. 304. With variants at ii. 195.
[3] *Keats: The Critical Heritage*, p. 35.   [4] **Ibid.**, p. 371.

'honey-feel' is 'untasteful'; indeed, and it is only because of Keats's ability to retain a sense of the truths accessible to the 'juvenile' and not to the self-consciously adult, that he is able to create the astonishing candour of the line, 'Aye, such a breathless honey-feel of bliss' (*Endymion*, I. 903). What we really want to do with honey is feel it, and not necessarily in our mouths and throats where it can indeed be perilous in its clinging ('breathless'). Geoffrey Grigson deplores in Keats 'a style of, yes, *oozy* neo-classicism whose entablatures are upheld by columns of butterscotch';[1] again, here is criticism in thrall to the metaphors which it claims to find inherently fraudulent or clogging, and again inviting the question: granted that there are many things which an oozy style cannot do, are there no things it can especially do, no truths about life of which honey's ooze, and not stone's stolidity, can speak?

The Friar in *Romeo and Juliet* knew that

> The sweetest honey
> Is loathsome in his own deliciousness
> And in the taste confounds the appetite.
> (II. vi. 11–13)

Honey is therefore well suited to two systems of belief which Keats is not alone in repudiating: a gross hedonism which coarsens its own appreciation of physical sensation, such that not even an excess of honey can bring it to a sense of the loathsome; and a sour puritanism which repudiates the delights of physical sensation on the grounds that after all even honey palls and satiates, such that not even the richly nutritious peaceful simplicity of honey can reconcile it to a pleasure in physical pleasure. Keats's evocations of honey recognize both the inherent precariousness of such delight and in any case the inherent uncertainty of our response to it, since the possibility must always exist that we cannot at a particular moment share the desire for any of the physical sensations which might on other occasions delight us.

Denise Levertov, who has an affectionate respectful poem 'Memories of John Keats' (in *Footprints*, 1972), has another which knows honey in its oddly benign manifestations, these the more

---

[1] *The Listener*, 25 Apr. 1968.

common ones in Keats ('Second Didactic Poem', in *The Sorrow Dance*, 1967):

> The honey of man is
> the task we're set to: to be
> 'more ourselves'
> in the making:
>   'bees of the invisible' working
> in cells of flesh and psyche,
> filling
>   'la grande ruche d'or.'
>
> Nectar,
>   the makings of the
> incorruptible,
>   is carried upon the
> corrupt tongues of
> mortal insects,
> fanned with their wisps of wing
>   'to evaporate
> excess water,'
>   enclosed and capped
> with wax, the excretion
> of bees' abdominal glands.
> Beespittle, droppings, hairs
> of beefur: all become honey.
> Virulent micro-organisms cannot
> survive in honey.
>   The taste,
> the odor of honey:
> each has no analogue but itself.
>
> In our gathering, in our containing, in our
> working, active within ourselves,
> slowly the pale
> dew-beads of light
> lapped up from flowers
> can thicken,
> darken to gold:
>
> honey of the human.

Honey and related words come again and again in Keats; a sense of the great attraction and of the great potentiality for distaste animates the poetry into truthful contrariety, not simple abandonment.

> Her throat was serpent, but the words she spake
> Came, as through bubbling honey, for Love's sake,
> > (*Lamia*, I. 64–5)

There 'serpent', with its own mingling of attraction and possible repellence, assists the double response with which we imagine words bubbling up through honey.[1]

> Another city doth he set about,
> Free from the smallest pebble-bead of doubt
> That he will seize on trickling honey-combs:
> > (*Endymion*, II. 148–50)

The cool clarity of definition which delights in 'the smallest pebble-bead of doubt' is properly in fusion with the sticky 'trickling honey-combs'; and the idea of seizing on honey-combs is not Keats's maladroitness but his dual candour. That a loved one should have a 'honied tongue' (*Endymion*, II. 820); that the net of love should be what it is:

> With tears, and smiles, and honey-words she wove
> A net whose thraldom was more bliss than all
> The range of flower'd Elysium.
> > (*Endymion*, III. 426–8)

—these are Keats's true surprises.

Keats marked in his Shakespeare the middle line of these by Isabella in *Measure for Measure*:

> There have I made my promise,
> Upon the heavy middle of the night,
> To call upon him.
> > (IV. i. 33–5)

[1] Tennyson achieved one of his vivid rhythmical feats because he acknowledged to himself the fascinated delight natural hereabouts along with repulsion:

> and Gareth loosed the stone
> From off his neck, then in the mere beside
> Tumbled it; oilily bubbled up the mere.
> > ('Gareth and Lynette')

There is a feeling of personification here, in 'Upon the heavy middle of the night'; 'heavy' is held by the Arden editor to include 'pregnant', along with 'responsible ' and 'sombre'. Keats's adaptation of the line converted its sombre pregnant physicality into a delighted physicality: 'Upon the honey'd middle of the night' (a living waist, as against Shakespeare's 'the dead waste and middle of the night'). But the grandeur and robustness of Keats's stanza derive from all which complements and curbs this rich line:

> They told her how, upon St. Agnes' Eve,
> Young virgins might have visions of delight,
> And soft adorings from their loves receive
> Upon the honey'd middle of the night,
> If ceremonies due they did aright;
> As, supperless to bed they must retire,
> And couch supine their beauties, lily white;
> Nor look behind, nor sideways, but require
> Of Heaven with upward eyes for all that they desire.
>   ('The Eve of St. Agnes', VI)

The unmisgiving (though ambivalent) largesse of the third and fourth lines is incorporated within strictness and restraint; it is virgins who may receive these adorings, and then only 'If ceremonies due they did aright'—a double insistence; 'must'—'nor . . . nor . . . but . . .': the crisp amplitude of Keats is the accommodation of yearning's overflowing fulfilments—'Upon the honey'd middle of the night'—to the disciplined clarity of what would elsewhere be a 'young' girl's punishment: 'supperless to bed.'

So strong, though, was the erotic undulation in the line which Keats fashioned from Shakespeare, so much did it need its bracing complements, that when Tennyson came to write 'Mariana' he realized that for his purposes 'the middle of the night' must be austerely free of any epithet, and that a safeguard against any suggestions of physicality in 'upon' was to let no word precede it at the start of the stanza:

> Upon the middle of the night,
>   Waking she heard the night-fowl crow . . .

A world of treacle would be a world of ooze, the world of *Antony and Cleopatra*, a play which persistently preoccupied Keats. 'The feel I have of Anthony and Cleopatra':[1] the phrase may call up a passage which Keats marked in his Shakespeare:

> The higher Nilus swells,
> The more it promises; as it ebbs, the seedsman
> Upon the slime and ooze scatters his grain,
> And shortly comes to harvest.[2]
>
> (II. vii. 20–3)

What Keats cannot do is write convincingly of slime and ooze when he means them to be simply odious:

> wipe away all slime
> Left by men-slugs and human serpentry
> (*Endymion*, I. 820–1)

is factitious and unimpinging because it is false to Keats's deepest and most interesting feelings about slime, slugs, and serpents. Likewise there is 'His Druid locks to shake and ooze with sweat' (*Hyperion*, I. 137), which enfeebles a perturbed physicality by excluding the other sensations which Keats usually and rightly sees as intimate with perturbation, for instance attraction. How different, how penetrating, is the mixed feeling of the ooze and the serpent here:

> sweet with the dews
> Of precious flowers pluck'd in Araby,
> And divine liquids, come with odorous ooze
> Through the cold serpent-pipe, refreshfully,—
>
> ('Isabella', LII)

There 'divine' suggests that the calling-up of the distant liquids is as magical and yet rural as water-divining.

> My grotto-sands
> Tawny and gold, ooz'd slowly from far lands
> (*Endymion*, II. 113–14)

---

[1] To Haydon, 8 Apr. 1818; i. 265. I owe the point to Mr. Harry Ricketts.
[2] Compare I. iii. 68–9: 'By the fire / That quickens Nilus' slime'.

Again, it is commonplace to speak of Venus as 'sea-born' (*Endymion*, I. 626); but it is profoundly disconcerting and truthful, a possibility of distaste not at all permitted to overcome awe and sensual pleasure, to call her 'the ooze-born Goddess' (*Endymion*, III. 893). The rich felicity and candour of that one epithet (all life and love must recognize its gratitude to the Nile) seem to me Shakespearean in width and fineness.

It is such physical duality—challenging our imagination and not our mere frisson—which draws Keats to a word like 'sluicy':

> and where her tender hands
> She dabbles, on the cool and sluicy sands:
> (*Endymion*, I. 945–6)

Likewise with the sponge and the oils in *Lamia*, II. 191–4; and with what succeeds 'spongy' in the libation in *Endymion*:

> Now while the earth was drinking it, and while
> Bay leaves were crackling in the fragrant pile,
> And gummy frankincense was sparkling bright . . .
> (I. 227–9)

'Gummy' is so attractive and yet tacky; its meltingness is both checked and accentuated by the very different physicalities with which Keats surrounds it: the porous earth drinking the sheer liquidity of the wine, the crisp crackling of the bay leaves, and the intangible fragrance and fire of the pile; and yet the frankincense is sparkling bright no less than it is gummy. The gummy, with its extraordinary power to attract us into self-indulgence, or to repel us into puritanism: this is the subject of what I consider to be the best writing of Jean-Paul Sartre's that I have read: his prose-poem, if I may call it that, in *Being and Nothingness* on *le visqueux*; that the translation upsets the balance of the ambivalence by rendering this as *slime* and *the slimy* is indicative of how fine the balance of attraction and possible repellence has to be. Sartre's pages are to me the best criticism of Keats ever written not about him.

What mode of being is symbolized by the slimy? I see first that it is the homogeneity and the imitation of liquidity. A slimy substance like pitch is an aberrant fluid. At first, with the appearance of a fluid it manifests to us a being which is everywhere fleeing and yet everywhere similar to itself, which on all sides escapes yet on which one can float, a being without danger and without memory, which eternally is changed into itself, on which one leaves no mark and which could not leave a mark on us, a being which slides and on which one can slide, which can be possessed by something sliding (by a rowboat, a motor boat, or water ski), and which never possesses because it rolls over us, a being which is eternity and infinite temporality because it is a perpetual change without anything which changes, a being which best symbolizes in this synthesis of eternity and temporality, a possible fusion of the for-itself as pure temporality and the in-itself as pure eternity. But immediately the slimy reveals itself as essentially ambiguous because its fluidity exists in slow motion; there is a sticky thickness in its liquidity; it represents in itself a dawning triumph of the solid over the liquid—that is, a tendency of the indifferent in-itself, which is represented by the pure solid, to fix the liquidity, to absorb the for-itself which ought to dissolve it.

Slime is the agony of water. It presents itself as a phenomenon in process of becoming; it does not have the permanence within change that water has but on the contrary represents an accomplished break in a change of state. This fixed instability in the slimy discourages possession. Water is more fleeting, but it can be possessed in its very flight as something fleeing. The slimy flees with a heavy flight which has the same relation to water as the unwieldy earthbound flight of the chicken has to that of the hawk. Even this flight can not be possessed because it denies itself as flight. It is already almost a solid permanence. Nothing testifies more clearly to its ambiguous character as a 'substance in between two states' than the slowness with which the slimy melts into itself. A drop of water touching the surface of a large body of water is instantly transformed into the body of water; we do not see the operation as buccal absorption, so to speak, of the drop of water by the body of water but rather as a spiritualizing and breaking down of the individuality of a single being which is dissolved in the great All from which it had issued. The symbol of the body of water seems to play a very important role in the construction of pantheistic systems; it reveals a particular type of relation of being to being. But if we consider the slimy, we note that it presents a constant hysteresis in the phenomenon of being transmuted into itself. The honey which slides off my spoon on to the honey contained in the

jar first sculptures the surface by fastening itself on it in relief, and its
fusion with the whole is presented as a gradual sinking, a collapse
which appears at once as a *deflation* (think for example of children's
pleasure in playing with a toy which whistles when inflated and
groans mournfully when deflating) and as *display*—like the flattening
out of the full breasts of a woman who is lying on her back.

In the slimy substance which dissolves into itself there is a visible
resistance, like the refusal of an individual who does not want to be
annihilated in the whole of being, and at the same time a softness
pushed to its ultimate limit. For the *soft* is only an annihilation which
is stopped half way; the soft is what furnishes us with the best image
of our own destructive power and its limitations. The slowness of the
disappearance of the slimy drop in the bosom of the whole is grasped
first in *softness*, which is like a retarded annihilation and seems to be
playing for time, but this softness lasts up to the end; the drop is
sucked into the body of the slimy substance. This phenomenon gives
rise to several characteristics of the slimy. First it is *soft* to touch.
Throw water on the ground; it *runs*. Throw a slimy substance; it
draws itself out, it displays itself, it flattens itself out, it is *soft*; touch
the slimy; it does not flee, it yields. There is in the very fact that we
cannot grasp water a pitiless hardness which gives to it a secret sense
of being *metal*; finally it is incompressible like steel. The slimy is com-
pressible. It gives us at first the impression that it is a being which
can be *possessed*. Doubly so: its sliminess, its adherence to itself prevent
it from escaping; I can take it in my hands, separate a certain quantity
of honey or of pitch from the rest in the jar, and thereby *create* an
individual object by a continuous creation; but at the same time the
softness of this substance which is squashed in my hands gives me
the impression that I am perpetually *destroying* it.

Actually we have here the image of destruction-creation. The
slimy is *docile*. Only at the very moment when I believe that I possess
it, behold by a curious reversal, *it* possesses me. Here appears its
essential character: its softness is leech-like. If an object which I hold
in my hands is solid, I can let go when I please; its inertia symbolizes
for me my total power; I give it its foundation, but it does not furnish
any foundation for me. . . . I open my hands, I want to let go of the
slimy and it sticks to me, it draws me, it sucks at me. Its mode of
being is neither the reassuring inertia of the solid nor a dynamism
like that in water which is exhausted in fleeing from me. It is a soft,
yielding action, a moist and feminine sucking, it lives obscurely

under my fingers, and I sense it like a dizziness; it draws me to it as the bottom of a precipice might draw me. There is something like a tactile fascination in the slimy. I am no longer the master in *arresting* the process of appropriation. It continues. In one sense it is like the supreme docility of the possessed, the fidelity of a dog who *gives himself* even when one does not want him any longer, and in another sense there is underneath this docility a surreptitious appropriation of the possessor by the possessed. . . .

At this instant I suddenly understand the snare of the slimy: it is a fluidity which holds me and which compromises me; I can not *slide* on this slime, all its suction cups hold me back; it can not slide over me, it clings to me like a leech. The sliding however is not simply denied as in the case of the solid; it is *degraded*. The slimy seems to lend itself to me, it invites me; for a body of slime at rest is not noticeably distinct from a body of very dense liquid. But it is a trap. The sliding is *sucked* in by the sliding substance, and it leaves its traces upon me. The slime is like a liquid seen in a nightmare, where all its properties are animated by a sort of life and turn back against me. Slime is the revenge of the In-itself. A sickly-sweet, feminine revenge which will be symbolized on another level by the quality 'sugary.' This is why the sugar-like sweetness to the taste—an indelible sweetness, which remains indefinitely in the mouth even after swallowing—perfectly completes the essence of the slimy. A sugary sliminess is the ideal of the slimy; it symbolizes the sugar death of the For-itself (like that of the wasp which sinks into the jam and drowns in it).

But at the same time the slimy is *myself*, by the very fact that I outline an appropriation of the slimy substance. That sucking of the slimy which I feel on my hands outlines a kind of continuity of the slimy substance in myself.

VI

SENSUOUSNESS AND SERIOUSNESS

WHEN Byron uses a word like 'succulent', he does not permit it to flesh itself enough to give you either pleasurable or distasteful sensation; and since it is a word with 'ripe' potentialities for both, he pinions it with 'truculent' and 'look you lent':

> Though somewhat large, exuberant, and truculent
>   When wroth; while pleased, she was as fine a figure
> As those who like things rosy, ripe, and succulent
>   Would wish to look on, while they are in vigour.
> She could repay each amatory look you lent
>   With interest, and in turn was wont with rigour
> To exact of Cupid's bills the full amount
> At sight, nor would permit you to discount.
>
> (Don Juan, IX. 62)

This says some of the things that need to be said about succulence; the other things could not come from a poet whose attitude to distaste and disgust is that which Byron expressed in his candid puzzlement about Burns:

What an antithetical mind!—tenderness, roughness—delicacy, coarseness—sentiment, sensuality—soaring and grovelling, dirt and deity—all mixed up in that one compound of inspired clay!

It seems strange; a true voluptuary will never abandon his mind to the grossness of reality. It is by exalting the earthly, the material, the *physique* of our pleasures, by veiling these ideas, by forgetting them altogether, or, at least, never naming them hardly to one's self, that we alone can prevent them from disgusting.[1]

It is a perfect opposition to Keats.[2] For Keats a true voluptuary

---

[1] *Byron: A Self-Portrait*, i. 240.

[2] Keats on Burns (to Tom Keats, 9 July 1818; i. 320):

'How sad it is when a luxurious imagination is obliged in self defence to deaden its delicacy in vulgarity, and riot in thing[s] attainable that it may not have leisure

would be one who acknowledged the truth; one who did not exalt
into immateriality the *physique*, the physicality, of our pleasures; one
who neither forgot these physicalities, nor never named them hardly
to himself; one who believed that it was only by a recognition of the
possibility of disgust that one could escape the corrosive disgust
which lay in wait for, say, Byron.

There is a double simultaneity in Keats's ambivalence of sensation; the rich pleasure can in the moment of its achievement become
a poisoned satiation, and one man's pleasure can be another man's
poison—this, a matter of the angle of vision or of an experience
which we can in a way enter into with perilous facility.

> And Joy, whose hand is ever at his lips
> Bidding adieu; and aching Pleasure nigh,
> Turning to poison while the bee-mouth sips:
> ('Ode on Melancholy')

I think it unlikely prima facie that the poet who so often calls upon
the word 'cloy' should have been as naïve and unaware about the
possibility of his own verse's cloying as his austere critics assume.
How wide the suggestiveness is, and yet how controlled, when we
are required to ask ourselves just what it would be for a hand to
cloy:

> Echo hence shall stir
> No sighs but sigh-warm kisses, or light noise
> Of thy combing hand, the while it travelling cloys
> And trembles through my labyrinthine hair.
> (*Endymion*, I. 966–9)

Keats is at least theoretically aware (and I see no reason to limit his
awareness to the theoretical) of the perils of pleasure, and of self-
indulgence, satiation, distaste, the clear lines gone.

> The soul is lost in pleasant smotherings:
> ('I stood tip-toe', 132)

to go mad after thing[s] which are not. No Man in such matters will be content
with the experience of others—It is true that out of suffrance there is no greatness,
no dignity; that in the most abstracted Pleasure there is no lasting happiness: yet
who would not like to discover over again that Cleopatra was a Gipsey, Helen a
Rogue and Ruth a deep one?'

> refreshment drowns
> Itself, and strives its own delights to hide—
> > (*Endymion*, II. 343–4)

> We might embrace and die: voluptuous thought!
> Enlarge not to my hunger, or I'm caught
> In trammels of perverse deliciousness.
> > (*Endymion*, IV. 759–61)

It is the contrariety of pleasure which most moves his imagination.
'My strange love came—Felicity's abyss!' (*Endymion*, III. 176). The
poetry does not succumb to what it speaks of, 'Forgetfulness of
everything but bliss' (*The Fall of Hyperion*, I. 104), and this is a
matter not solely of Keats's recognition of those things in life which
are not bliss, but also of those things about bliss itself which are not
simply blissful—especially in contemplating or imagining the bliss
of others.[1] The poetry therefore has something less than its true
amplitude when it chooses ways of speaking which do not involve
this ambivalence:

> And can I ever bid these joys farewell?
> Yes, I must pass them for a nobler life,
> Where I may find the agonies, the strife
> Of human hearts:
> > ('Sleep and Poetry', 122–5)

That this remains merely hortatory is a consequence of the unvexed
antithesis, joys as against agonies and strife. But it is precisely the
particular strife and even agonies which are implicated in human
joys, and especially those of the intense physicality such as both
invites us with its vivid sympathy and cannot but to some degree
rebuff us because of our otherness, which Keats most deeply cares
about and knows about. His evocations of distaste *per se*, even when
they have a bitter pungency, have the narrowness of one decisive

---

[1] There is to me something willed and strained in the famous cry to Fanny
Brawne: 'I have two luxuries to brood over in my walks, your Loveliness and the
hour of my death. O that I could have possession of them both in the same minute'
(25 July 1819; ii. 133). If so, this may be in part because such a conception of
'luxuries' has retained one of its many ambivalences but has jettisoned the corporeal
ambivalence of physical sensation.

alternative ('Instead of . . .') rather than a radiating richness of apprehension:

> Instead of sweets, his ample palate took
> Savour of poisonous brass and metal sick.
> (*Hyperion*, I. 188–9)

'I think Poetry should surprise by a fine excess and not by Singularity.'[1] Yet a fine excess is a paradoxical thing, and one of the objections to singularity is its singleness. Unfortunately the openness of Keats was not something he could always maintain, and the word 'mawkish'[2] is usually the sign both that he is near to things that are urgent for him because his truest imaginings are involved and also that he knows how necessarily open to ridicule is his refusal to ridicule. 'I hate a Mawkish Popularity';[3] there is no immediate cause for our being uneasy at that. But we should be uneasy about Keats's uneasiness in the preface to *Endymion*, 'Thence proceeds mawkishness', since it is for Byron, not for Keats, to have no truck with mawkishness. By September 1819 he had been battered and mocked to the point at which he wrote coolly about how he had perhaps better flinch; but what he was putting at risk was precisely this doubleness of angle, this power to incorporate a sense of another angle from which it would all feel different, which was his most personal and least eccentric experience of life:

I will give you a few reasons why I shall persist in not publishing The Pot of Basil—It is too smokeable—I can get it smoak'd at the Carpenters shaving chimney much more cheaply—There is too much inexperience of live, and simplicity of knowlege in it—which might do very well after one's death—but not while one is alive. There are very few would look to the reality. I intend to use more finesse with the Public. It is possible to write fine things which cannot be laugh'd at in any way. Isabella is what I should call were I a reviewer 'A weak-sided Poem' with an amusing sober-sadness about it. Not that I do not think Reynolds and you are quite right about it—it is enough for me. But this will not do to be public—If I may so say, in my dramatic

---

[1] To Taylor, 27 Feb. 1818; i. 238.

[2] Dr. Burgess in his book on blushing (1839) found it natural to use the word ('mawkish sentiments') to distinguish a false from a true sensibility (p. 21).

[3] To Reynolds, 9 Apr. 1818; i. 267.

capacity I enter fully into the feeling: but in Propria Persona I should be apt to quiz it myself—There is no objection of this kind to Lamia— A good deal to St Agnes Eve—only not so glaring—[1]

Woodhouse resisted such self-criticism of Keats's, but even Woodhouse is, I think, too defensive, too quick to assume that there cannot be any 'sort of revulsion, or resiliency' which a poem might indeed be the worse for advocating or gratifying but the better for accommodating, especially since a poem should not think that it can predict its every reader's frame of mind:

He said he could not bear the former ['Isabella'] now. It appeared to him mawkish. . . . The feeling of mawkishness seems to me to be that which comes upon us where any thing of great tenderness & excessive simplicity is met with when we are not in a sufficiently tender & simple frame of mind to bear it: when we experience a sort of revulsion, or resiliency (if there be such a word) from the sentiment or expression. Now I believe there is nothing in any of the most passionate parts of Isabella to excite this feeling. It may, as may Lear, leave the reader far behind: but there is none of that sugar & butter sentiment, that cloys & disgusts.[2]

'The Genius of Poetry must work out its own salvation in a man: It cannot be matured by law & precept, but by sensation & watchfulness in itself.'[3] The relation between sensuousness and seriousness is also a relation between sensation and watchfulness, and the watchfulness must not be a taskmaster's eye. Keats wrote to Bailey of 'another favorite Speculation of mine, that we shall enjoy ourselves here after by having what we called happiness on Earth repeated in a finer tone and so repeated—And yet such a fate can only befall those who delight in sensation rather than hunger as you do after Truth.'[4] But what Keats found that he hungered after was the relation of 'Truth' to 'delight in sensation', and this meant a recognition of the many ways in which what we feel about sensation (even when delightful it may not be ours) is not simply or solely delight. He gained the 'complex Mind' of which he spoke in this

[1] To Woodhouse, 22 Sept. 1819; ii. 174.
[2] Woodhouse to Taylor, 19–20 Sept. 1819; ii. 162.
[3] To Hessey, 8 Oct. 1818; i. 374.
[4] 22 Nov. 1817; i. 185.

same letter: 'one that is imaginative and at the same time careful
of its fruits—who would exist partly on sensation partly on thought.'

Keats's concern is the responsible lightening of responsibility.
Henry James, who can hardly be thought of as easy-going, objected
to Ruskin's unremittingness:

One may read a great many pages of Mr. Ruskin without getting
a hint of this delightful truth; a hint of the not unimportant fact
that art, after all, is made for us, and not we for art. This idea of the
value of a work of art being the amount of entertainment it yields
is conspicuous by its absence. And as for Mr. Ruskin's world of art
being a place where we may take life easily, woe to the luckless mortal
who enters it with any such disposition. Instead of a garden of delight,
he finds a sort of assize court, in perpetual session. Instead of a place
in which human responsibilities are lightened and suspended, he
finds a region governed by a kind of Draconic legislation.[1]

A consciousness of responsibilities suspended (not abolished or
ignored) animates Keats's garden of delight. This, and a sense that
there is truthful power in a recognition of uneasiness just where you
might have expected only a delight in the *physique* of our pleasures.
Henry James may well have been right to speak of a defect in
John Singer Sargent's 'El Jaleo', as a defect in this particular work,
but he is not right to base his judgement on an inexplicit and
unargued general principle that it could not ever be right for such a
work of art to make one feel (as part of one's response) vaguely
uneasy and even unhappy. James is confident that this feeling is an
'accident', but he does not give his reasons. The serenity which he
asks for (and which is to be unmixed) is to assuage the embarrassment at physicality evinced by the embarrassed jocosity of his
circling prose:

The merit of this production is that the air of reality is given in it
with remarkable breadth and boldness; its defect it is difficult to
express save by saying that it makes the spectator vaguely uneasy
and even unhappy—an accident the more to be regretted as a lithe,
inspired female figure, given up to the emotion of the dance, is not
intrinsically a displeasing object. 'El Jaleo' sins, in my opinion, in the

---

[1] *The Painter's Eye*, p. 21.

direction of ugliness, and independently of the fact that the heroine is circling round incommoded by her petticoats, has a want of serenity.[1]

Keats used to sit, rapt, by the Elgin Marbles. 'One afternoon, as he delighted to tell Severn, a man who apparently knew Keats strolled by and viewed the sculptures "condescendingly through an eye-glass", and at last said, "yes, I believe, Mr. Keats, we may admire these works safely".'[2] Much of our admiration for Keats is a matter of his being so incapable of granting that 'we may admire these works safely'; but part of our admiration for his poems is due to its not exactly being true that safely is how we may admire them.

Keats's delight in others' delight is not something which we should think easy. The creativity of the imagination draws him to the word 'conceive', and the essentially humanizing power of language draws him to the word 'volubility', when he has a characteristic flight of imagination at once grand and modest: 'He has affirmed that he can conceive of a billiard Ball that it may have a sense of delight from its own roundness, smoothness volubility. & the rapidity of its motion.'[3] Yet the magnanimity derives pleasure too from the very fact that others' pleasures can sometimes be inconceivable, as when he watches a country dance: 'I was extremely gratified to think, that if I had pleasures they knew nothing of. they had also some into which I could not possibly enter.'[4] The limits of the sympathetic imagination are deeply respected and valued by Keats's imagination.

We should not receive with consternation, nor should we be fixated upon, the fact that it is an achievement—and not just a reflex—to be happy in others' happiness.

> My heart aches, and a drowsy numbness pains
> My sense, as though of hemlock I had drunk,

---

[1] *The Painter's Eye*, p. 221.

[2] Walter Jackson Bate, *John Keats*, p. 247, quoting William Sharp's *Life and Letters of Joseph Severn* (1892).

[3] Woodhouse to Taylor, about 27 Oct. 1818; i. 389. Rollins quotes another version: 'He can conceive of a billiard Ball to be soothed & feel pleasure from a consciousness of its own smoothness—& the rapidy of its Motion.'

[4] To Tom Keats, 1 July 1818; i. 307.

> Or emptied some dull opiate to the drains
> One minute past, and Lethe-wards had sunk:
> 'Tis not through envy of thy happy lot,
> But being too happy in thine happiness,—
> ('Ode to a Nightingale')

So familiar is the poem that it is easy to be glazed to the way in which this opening is so surprising and yet so immediately acknowledged as a truth. Who, after all, would have assumed that the ache, the numbness, the pain was likely to have been caused by envy of the nightingale's happiness?[1] And yet, yes; the reflection is not a cynical one, and the repudiating of it is not any kind of indignation at a slander, but both a denial that it is true in this case and a reluctant admission that the human proclivity to envy should not amaze or shatter us.

Lionel Trilling has said:

> The lover in *Lamia* is generally taken to be an innocent youth, yet the most corrupt young man of Balzac's scenes of Parisian life would scarcely have spoken to his mistress or his fiancée as Lycius speaks to Lamia when he insists that she display her beauty in public for the enhancement of his prestige. Tocqueville said that envy was the characteristic emotion of plutocratic democracy, and it is envy of a particularly ugly kind that Lycius wishes to excite. 'Let my foes choke,' he says, 'and my friends shout afar, / While through the thronged streets your bridal car / Wheels round its dazzling spokes'.[2]

> What mortal hath a prize, that other men
> May be confounded and abash'd withal,

---

[1] 'Happy', 'happy', 'happiness': the sequence, with its strange possibility of aching, is achingly alive too in the 'Ode on a Grecian Urn', where we (as well as those on the urn, but in a different way) are excluded from happiness which imagination lets us entertain but not enter:

> Ah, happy, happy boughs! that cannot shed
> Your leaves, nor ever bid the Spring adieu;
> And, happy melodist, unwearied,
> For ever piping songs for ever new;
> More happy love! more happy, happy love!
> For ever warm and still to be enjoy'd . . .

[2] *Beyond Culture*, p. 65.

> But lets it sometimes pace abroad majestical,
> And triumph, as in thee I should rejoice
> Amid the hoarse alarm of Corinth's voice.
> Let my foes choke, and my friends shout afar . . .
>
> (*Lamia*, II. 57–62)

(The whole passage asks to be related to Lamia's earlier vision of Lycius 'Charioting foremost in the envious race'; I. 217.) But, way down, it could at least be said for Lycius that it was his foes and not his friends that he wished should choke with envy. Kingsley Amis has said of Christ: 'We may agree that to love our enemies is both important and difficult, but few of us have many enemies or many chances to love the ones we have. Loving our friends, behaving with love towards those we love, is just as important, and sometimes just as difficult.'[1] The relation of love to jealousy and to a blush is caught elsewhere in *Lamia*:

> Ah, what a world of love was at her feet!
> So Hermes thought, and a celestial heat
> Burnt from his winged heels to either ear,
> That from a whiteness, as the lily clear,
> Blush'd into roses 'mid his golden hair,
> Fallen in jealous curls about his shoulders bare,
>
> (I. 21–6)

How firmly jealousy is permitted to be a property of the curls alone; how sadly, seven lines later, we find that Hermes is himself 'full of painful jealousies'. The ruin of Lamia and Lycius comes when winged love itself grows jealous, and casts a glow which is not a heartening blush:

> Love, jealous grown of so complete a pair,
> Hover'd and buzz'd his wings, with fearful roar,
> Above the lintel of their chamber door,
> And down the passage cast a glow upon the floor.
>
> (II. 12–15)

The tribute which John Hamilton Reynolds paid in a letter to Keats is supreme: 'there is no one that I have more pleasure in communicating my own happiness to.'[2] It is good that Reynolds felt able

---

[1] *What Became of Jane Austen?* (1970), p. 220.   [2] 14 Oct. 1818; i. 377.

to communicate his pleasure in this fact itself so directly to Keats. Keats's tribute, in his turn, to his sister-in-law is a recognition of how extraordinarily grateful we should be that a happy person can be without complacency and that a 'delicate' person may in this sense 'want Imagination':

I had know[n] my sister in Law some time before she was my Sister and was very fond of her. I like her better and better—she is the most disinterrested woman I ever knew—that is to say she goes beyond degree in it—To see an entirely disinterrested Girl quite happy is the most pleasant and extraordinary thing in the world—it depends upon a thousand Circumstances—on my word 'tis extraordinary. Women must want Imagination and they may thank God for it— and so m[a]y we that a delicate being can feel happy without any sense of crime. It puzzles me and I have no sort of Logic to comfort me—I shall think it over.[1]

Nor are these considerations distinct from (though distinguish-able from) the challenge of contemplating with imagination the happiness of others; for it is precisely the vulnerability of intense happiness (especially of intense physicality) to the accusation that it is complacent, self-absorbed, indifferent to all the rest of us, which gives some cause for our being suspicious of it and so un-generous towards it. 'Very few men have ever arrived at a complete disinterestedness of Mind: very few have been influenced by a pure desire of the benefit of others—in the greater part of the Bene-factors to Humanity some meretricious motive has sullied their greatness—some melodramatic scenery has fascinated them—'[2]

To feel happy without any sense of crime: it was Keats's sense of the many ways in which sorrow is threatening which moved him to urge Reynolds to delight in his, Reynolds's, own happiness:

My dear Reynolds,
Believe me I have rather rejoiced in your happiness than fretted at your silence. Indeed I am grieved on your account that I am not at the same time happy—But I conjure you to think at Present of nothing but pleasure "Gather the rose &c" Gorge the honey of life. I pity you

¹ To Bailey, 10 June 1818; i. 293.
² To George and Georgiana Keats, 19 Mar. 1819; ii. 79.

as much that it cannot last for ever, as I do myself now drinking bitters.—Give yourself up to it—you cannot help it—and I have a Consolation in thinking so—I never was in love—Yet the voice and the shape of a woman[1] has haunted me these two days—at such a time when the relief, the feverous relief of Poetry seems a much less crime—This morning Poetry has conquered—I have relapsed into those abstractions which are my only life—I feel escaped from a new strange and threatening sorrow.—And I am thankful for it—There is an awful warmth about my heart like a load of Immortality.

Poor Tom—that woman—and Poetry were ringing changes in my senses—now I am in comparison happy—[2]

It was this same double sense of our duty to pleasure—our duty to gain it for ourselves, and our duty to delight in others' gaining it and at the same time to recognize a recalcitrance in doing so—which moved Keats to the embarrassing duty of telling Brown that he, Brown, had been too self-sacrificingly generous. Keats is embarrassed that he must embarrass Brown (not only by thanks for Brown's generosity but by remonstrating about this very generosity); the delicacy and directness of Keats's gratitude are embodied in the threefold application of 'duty':

And here I will take an opportunity of making a remark or two on our friendship, and all your good offices to me. I have a natural timidity of mind in these matters: liking better to take the feeling between us for granted, than to speak of it. But, good God! what a short while you have known me! I feel it a sort of duty thus to recapitulate, however unpleasant it may be to you. You have been living for others more than any man I know. This is a vexation to me; because it has been depriving you, in the very prime of your life, of pleasures which it was your duty to procure. As I am speaking in general terms this may appear nonsense; you perhaps will not understand it: but if you can go over, day by day, any month of the last year,—you will know what I mean. On the whole, however, this is a subject that I cannot express myself upon. I speculate upon it frequently; and, believe me, the end of my speculations is always an anxiety for your happiness. This anxiety will not be one of the least incitements to the plan I purpose pursuing. I had got into a habit of mind of looking towards you as a help in all difficulties. This very habit would be the parent of

---

[1] Jane Cox; see p. 46.   [2] 22 (?) Sept. 1818; i. 370.

idleness and difficulties. You will see it is a duty I owe myself to break the neck of it.[1]

The anguish of Keats's life, the anguish to which his very powers of sympathetic imagination made him so vulnerable, made him the more sanely insistent upon the duty of happiness. He wrote to his brother George about all their pain:

My dear George; There was a part in your Letter which gave me a great deal of pain, that where you lament not receiving Letters from England—I intended to have written immediately on my return from Scotland (which was two Months earlier than I had intended on account of my own as well as Tom's health) but then I was told by M[rs] W— that you had said you would not wish any one to write till we had heard from you. This I thought odd and now I see that it could not have been so; yet at the time I suffered my unreflecting head to be satisfied and went on in that sort of abstract careless and restless Life with which you are well acquainted. This sentence should it give you any uneasiness do not let it last for before I finish it will be explained away to your satisfaction—

I am g[r]ieved to say that I am not sorry you had not Letters at Philadelphia; you could have had no good news of Tom and I have been withheld on his account from beginning, these many days; I could not bring myself to say the truth, that he is no better, but much worse—However it must be told, and you must my dear Brother and Sister take example frome me and bear up against any Calamity for my sake as I do for your's. Our's are ties which independent of their own Sentiment are sent us by providence to prevent the deleterious effects of one great, solitary grief. I have Fanny[2] and I have you—three people whose Happiness to me is sacred—and it does annul that selfish sorrow which I should otherwise fall into, living as I do with poor Tom who looks upon me as his only comfort—the tears will come into your Eyes—let them—and embrace each other—thank heaven for what happiness you have and after thinking a moment or two that you suffer in common with all Mankind hold it not a sin to regain your cheerfulness—[3]

At which, Keats realizes that it would be something of a sin for a man to speak so and not to make the effort himself to regain his

---

[1] To Brown, 22 Sept. 1819; ii. 176–7.   [2] His sister.
[3] 14 Oct. 1818; i. 391–2.

cheerfulness; and so the letter moves into a few words about Georgiana's mother—'She was well, in good Spirits and I kept her laughing at my bad jokes'—and then into Keats's pleasure at the thought of George's pleasure: 'I should wish to give you a picture of our Lives here whenever by a touch I can do it; even as you must see by the last sentence our walk past Whitehall all in good health and spirits—this I am certain of, because I felt so much pleasure from the simple idea of your playing a game at Cricket—'

His watchfulness is continually noticing that he has momentarily fallen into the wrong tone of voice, a self-commiserating one perhaps; and then, with precisely his gift for accommodating rather than repudiating, he derives new energy of self-knowledge and invigoration:

I have pass'd my time in reading, writing and fretting—the last I intend to give up and stick to the other two. They are the only chances of benefit to us. Your wants will be a fresh spur to me. I assure you you shall more than share what I can get, whilst I am still young—the time may come when age will make me more selfish. I have not been well treated by the world—and yet I have capitally well—I do not know a Person to whom so many purse strings would fly open as to me—if I could possibly take advantage of them—which I cannot do for none of the owners of these purses are rich—[1]

How genially free from self-contempt is his rounding upon himself: 'I have not been well treated by the world—and yet I have capitally well'; how humorously 'capitally' becomes the 'purse strings'; and how equably the cliché is seen to be of not much practical use ('none of the owners of these purses are rich') but yet the gratitude to be true and deserved.

Though many kinds of hero, Keats was no kind of saint. When the sour Hodgkinson (partner of Keats's guardian, Richard Abbey) came to grief, Keats wrote to his sister Fanny: 'No one can regret Mr Hodgkinson's ill fortune: I must own illness has not made such a Saint of me as to prevent my rejoicing at his reverse.'[2] Yet his apprehension of life's pain was profound: 'However among the

---

[1] To George and Georgiana Keats, 17 Sept. 1819; ii. 185.
[2] 5 July 1820; ii. 305.

effects this breathing is father of is that tremendous one of sharpening one's vision into the heart and nature of Man—of convincing ones nerves that the World is full of Misery and Heartbreak, Pain, Sickness and oppression—'[1] It is 'convincing one's nerves' which is so authentically Keats; to convince one's reason, and to stir one's nerves, these are valuable enough, but the fusion in Keats's best poetry and letters, his essential ambition, was to convince one's nerves—his own and ours. Yet I think that his greatness as a man and as a writer has less to do with 'convincing ones nerves that the World is full of Misery and Heartbreak, Pain, Sickness and oppression', than with convincing one's nerves that the world is full of delight, health, and liberation—all of which are sometimes ours, and needing to be achieved rather than sure to drop into our hands, and all of which are other people's all around us. All this makes up the '*physique* of our pleasures', the pleasures being necessarily mostly others' and not ours (there being more others). To convince one's nerves of others' happiness, and then without perfunctoriness, embarrassment, cynicism, or dismay to rejoice at it, is Keats's central moral impulse and especial verbal power. Keats's most truly illuminating epithet for 'light' was 'generous': 'generous light' (*Endymion*, I. 154).

[1] To Reynolds, 3 May 1818; i. 281.

VII

CONCEPTIONS OF POEMS AND OF LETTERS

BLUSHES can be sexually attractive, and contagious like desire. It was long ago said of blushing that 'there is a "caught in the act" feeling about it', and the act called up might be a sexual one. In so far as a blush is the blood moving involuntarily and markedly, it can be a type of or metaphor for erection; in so far as it glows out and spends itself, a type of or metaphor for orgasm. For the poet, it can offer a glimpse, bizarre and even potentially fearful, of life stayed for ever in an eternal intensity of erect desire which is also an eternal intensity of sexual fulfilment:

> I'm giddy at that cheek so fair and smooth;
> O let it blush so ever! let it soothe
> My madness! let it mantle rosy-warm
> With the tinge of love, panting in safe alarm.
> (*Endymion*, IV. 311–14)

The 'safe alarm' is like that of art; and the eternal blush is at the other extreme from Moneta's eternal pallor: 'but bright blanch'd / By an immortal sickness which kills not.' Dr. Burgess in 1839 was moved by the thought of a fixed blush:

If the blush could be kept up for a given time, reasoning from analogy [with inflammation], we must infer, that structural derangement would eventually take place; thus showing us that nothing is ordained in the conformation of moral or physical man without some final object—some wise purpose; for, in blushing, were the efflorescence to be continued to any lengthened period, the great object for which it was designed would be altogether thwarted—in the first place, by rendering the phenomenon less striking to the observer in consequence of its *permanency*; and, in the second, by tending to produce a derangement in the functions of the parts. (p. 108)

The relating of blushing to erections is not the same sort of thing as seeing a high-heeled shoe as a phallic symbol. There is a real multiplicity of relation, even if we were to dismiss—as we cannot afford to do—the imagination of the psycho-analysts[1] as utterly remote from our imagination or from Keats's. For it is a physiological fact that in both cases blood rushes visibly to a part of the body, and that there are not many other ways in which this happens. Dr. Burgess thought it quite natural to quote from Dr. Macartney: '*heat* and *redness* are produced in the skin by a merely excited state of circulation, as may be observed in *blushing*, and in the turgid state of various erectile tissues, as the genital organs, the skin about the turkey-cock's neck, and many other similar structures'; and likewise he quoted from Dr. Muller a paragraph which brings together 'the reproductive organs when excited' and 'the act of blushing'.[2] Then blushing and sexual excitement often are intimately related; and an erection, like blushing itself, can be both the product and the producer of embarrassment—indeed, erections are implicated in innumerable kinds of embarrassment, whether they arise when they should not:

> Down, wanton, down! Have you no shame
> That at the whisper of Love's name,
> Or Beauty's, presto! up you raise
> Your angry head and stand at gaze?
> (Robert Graves, 'Down, Wanton, Down!')

or fail to when they should:

> Yet like as if cold hemlock I had drunk,
> It mockèd me, hung down the head, and sunk.
> Like a dull cipher or rude block I lay,
> Or shade or body was I, who can say?
> What will my age do, age I cannot shun,
> When in my prime my force is spent and done?

---

[1] On erections and blushing, see Therese Benedek, 'Notes from the Analysis of a Case of Ereuthophobia', *International Journal of Psycho-Analysis*, vi (1925); Edoardo Weiss, 'A Recovery from the Fear of Blushing', *Psychoanalytic Quarterly*, ii (1933); Edmund Bergler, 'A New Approach to the Therapy of Erythrophobia', *Psychoanalytic Quarterly*, xiii (1944); and Sandor Feldman, 'Blushing, Fear of Blushing, and Shame', *Journal of the American Psychoanalytic Association*, x (1962).

[2] pp. 107, 112–13.

I blush, that being youthful, hot and lusty,
I prove neither youth nor man, but old and rusty.
              (Christopher Marlowe, *Ovid's Elegies*, III. vi)[1]

Love dissolves all such throbbing embarrassments—'throbbing star', and 'solution sweet'.

> Beyond a mortal man impassion'd far
> At these voluptuous accents, he arose,
> Ethereal, flush'd, and like a throbbing star
> Seen mid the sapphire heaven's deep repose
> Into her dream he melted, as the rose
> Blendeth its odour with the violet,—
> Solution sweet: meantime the frost-wind blows
> Like Love's alarum pattering the sharp sleet
> Against the window-panes; St. Agnes' moon hath set.
>   ('The Eve of St. Agnes', XXXVI)

At such a moment, there is no room, even with mixed feelings, for any potentiality of the grotesque, such as there is in the variant passage because of 'flows / Into her burning ear' (compare the earlier stanza: 'and then / More pleasure followed in a dizzy stream / Palpable almost'):

> For on the midnight came a tempest fell
> More sooth for that his close [quick] rejoinder flows
> Into her burning ear;—

The dying into life of Apollo at the end of *Hyperion* is famously an unconsummated orgasm:

> Soon wild commotions shook him, and made flush
> All the immortal fairness of his limbs;
>   . . .
>   —At length
> Apollo shriek'd; and lo! from all his limbs
> Celestial   *   *   *

Admittedly I find this wild and approximate; as so often, Keats is

---

[1] Mrs. Allott, incidentally, cites the first line of this passage for 'as though of hemlock I had drunk' ('Ode to a Nightingale').

more humanly precise when he is writing of an animate life that is
neither divine nor human:

> A butterfly, with golden wings broad parted,
> Nestling a rose, convuls'd as though it smarted
> With over pleasure—
>
> ('Sleep and Poetry', 343-5)

William Howitt wrote of Keats in 1847: 'The worldly and the
worldly wise could not comprehend him, could not sympathize
with him. To them his vivid orgasm of the intellect was madness.'[1]
Madness, or embarrassment? It is quite natural for Erving Goffman
to speak of embarrassment in these terms: 'Some occasions of
embarrassment seems to have an abrupt orgasmic character; a sudden introduction of the disturbing event is followed by an immediate
peak in the experience of embarrassment and then by a slow return
to the preceding ease, all phases being encompassed in the same
encounter.'[2]

Keats has a poor sonnet which makes manifest the implications of
the eternal flush and the eternal pant:

> O that a week could be an age, and we
>   Felt parting and warm meeting every week,
> Then one poor year a thousand years would be,
>   The flush of welcome ever on the cheek:
> So could we live long life in little space,
>   So time itself would be annihilate,
> So a day's journey in oblivious haze
>   To serve our joys would lengthen and dilate.
> O to arrive each Monday morn from Ind!
>   To land each Tuesday from the rich Levant!

---

[1] *Keats: The Critical Heritage*, p. 311.
  No doubt Howitt meant the nineteenth-century sense of orgasm, 'paroxysm of
excitement'; yet though the *O.E.D.* also gives 1806 and 1875 instances for the non-
physiological sense, of its physiological instances those of 1684 and 1771 are not
specifically sexual whereas those of 1802 and 1899 are. By Howitt's time, 1847, the
word was perhaps foolhardy if it was not brave. Compare Burgess on blushing, the
corpora cavernosa, and the cheek: 'it proves that the latter as well as the former
possesses the characteristics and properties of an *erectile tissue*, and that both are liable
to become injected with blood from the same mental emotion. I firmly believe, that
the orgasm of this structure is produced solely by the influence of the organic nerves
in this instance' (p. 176).
[2] *Interaction Ritual*, p. 100.

> In little time a host of joys to bind,
> And keep our souls in one eternal pant!
> This morn, my friend, and yester evening taught
> Me how to harbour such a happy thought.

This is at once flat and preposterous, just because it reduces to an unequivocally happy thought what cannot for Keats be a simply pleasurable prospect; the simply pleasurable is never a prospect for him, and it is this fact which both makes us delight in such extremities of fantasy and also gives us a protection against them: the protection of not simply desiring them. Keats always comes to a truer sense of these relationships when he makes reading and writing themselves part of the complex of feelings. He does so in the verse epistle to Charles Cowden Clarke:

> Spenserian vowels that elope with ease,
> And float along like birds o'er summer seas;
> Miltonian storms, and more, Miltonian tenderness;
> Michael in arms, and more, meek Eve's fair slenderness.
> Who read for me the sonnet swelling loudly
> Up to its climax and then dying proudly?
>
> (56–61)

Likewise there is the movement from

> warm desires
> To see the sun o'er peep the eastern dimness,
> (85–6)

through

> When Cynthia smiles upon a summer's night,
> And peers among the cloudlet's jet and white,
> As though she were reclining in a bed
> (93–5)

to this:

> When many lines I'd written,
> Though with their grace I was not oversmitten,
> Yet, as my hand was warm, I thought I'd better
> Trust to my feelings, and write you a letter.

Such an attempt required an inspiration
Of peculiar sort,—a consummation;—
Which, had I felt, these scribblings might have been
Verses from which the soul would never wean:

                                                    (101–8)

It is a modest account of a poem not written, but the feelings which
it trusts are those about which Keats was most acutely in earnest.

'A displacement from below upward phallicizes the face', said
Dr. Bergler about the blush.[1] This may seem to belong rather to the
world of David Levine's caricature of John Updike (the unembarrassable John Updike) than to the world of John Keats. But Keats's
sense of the nature of creativity continually found it natural to
speak in such terms. 'The faint conceptions I have of Poems to
come brings the blood frequently into my forehead':[2] to take the
force of 'conceptions' there ('I shall certainly breed'[3]) we need to
think of *The Fall of Hyperion*, I. 275–7:

> So at the view of sad Moneta's brow,
> I ached to see what things the hollow brain
> Behind enwombed:

and to think of a more ancient myth than Moneta:

> Thou, Jove-like, struck'dst thy forehead,
> And from the teeming marrow of thy brain
> I spring complete Minerva!
>   (*Otho the Great*, I. i. 93–5)

We need also to think of three passages which Keats marked in his
Shakespeare:

> And in my heart the strong and swelling evil
> Of my conception.
>   (*Measure for Measure*, II. iv. 6–7)

> Why does my blood thus muster to my heart,
>   (Ibid., 20)

> I have a young conception in my brain.
>   (*Troilus and Cressida*, I. iii. 312)

---

[1] *Psychoanalytic Quarterly*, xiii (1944).
[2] To Woodhouse, 27 Oct. 1818; i. 387–8.   [3] See p. 127.

But the hot forehead relates embarrassment to creativity and to writing: 'the while I request the loan of a £20 and a £10—which if you would enclose to me I would acknowledge and save myself a hot forehead.'[1]

John Jones remarked upon the frequent foreheads:

As with eyes, so with foreheads: from the tiresome reiterations of the 1817 volume ('He bares his forehead to the cool blue sky', 'With forehead to the soothing breezes bare'), through some weird occurrences, again not good but characterful, in which the forehead is endowed with a kind of sensitiveness foreign to its ordinary self but proper to an organ of feel ('Holding his forehead, to keep off the burr / Of smothering fancies'), through open indulgencies of feel like 'more near against the marble cold / He had touch'd his forehead' and masked ones like 'with forehead 'gainst the window-pane', to the famous things in mature Keats: 'Nor suffer thy pale forehead to be kiss'd' in *Melancholy*, and 'A burning forehead and a parching tongue' in the *Grecian Urn*.[2]

This is warm and discriminating as far as the physical sensations and the bodily dispersal go, but I think it leaves the forehead too unrelated to head and heart, that it does not consider the dimensions of creativity and embarrassment which come together for Keats in the hot forehead. Embarrassment, erotic feeling, and poetic creativity fertilize each other.

> These wonders strange he sees, and many more,
> Whose head is pregnant with poetic lore,
> Should he upon an evening ramble fare
> With forehead to the soothing breezes bare,
> Would he naught see but the dark, silent blue
> With all its diamonds trembling through and through?
> Or the coy moon, when in the waviness
> Of whitest clouds she does her beauty dress,
> And staidly paces higher up, and higher,
> Like a sweet nun in holy-day attire?
> ('To My Brother George', 53–62)

---

[1] See p. 31.   [2] *John Keats's Dream of Truth*, p. 13.

So the hymn to Pan moves naturally from

> . . . With leaves about their brows!
>   Be still the unimaginable lodge
> For solitary thinkings; such as dodge
> Conception to the very bourne of heaven,
>   Then leave the naked brain:

to 'a new birth' and to

>   we humbly screen
> With uplift hands our foreheads . . .
>   (*Endymion*, I. 292–303)

In 'Lines on Seeing a Lock of Milton's Hair', a creativity from the past comes suddenly to reassert itself as a newly possible creativity; but the shock of recognition is like a sharp moment of love (as when in Sappho the loved one's name is suddenly vibrant), and is alive with embarrassment at youthfulness and at emulation all but preposterous.

> For many years my offerings must be hush'd;
>   When I do speak, I'll think upon this hour,
> Because I feel my forehead hot and flush'd,[1]
>   Even at the simplest vassal of thy power,—
>   A lock of thy bright hair,—
>   Sudden it came,
> And I was startled, when I caught thy name
>   Coupled so unaware;
>   Yet, at the moment, temperate was my blood.
> I thought I had beheld it from the flood.

So that when, in 'The Eve of St. Agnes', Porphyro (whose name is at home with his 'purple riot') suddenly conceives his stratagem of love, the conception is at once erect and flushed (and had, at one manuscript stage, been explicitly a blush):

> Sudden a thought came like a full-blown rose,
> Flushing his brow, and in his pained heart[2]

---

[1] Compare 'My temples with hot jealous pulses beat', 'Ode to Fanny', manuscript variant.

[2] Variants of these two lines:

> Sudden a rosy (rosy *added above*) thought [more rosy than the rose]
> Heated his brow *over* [Flush'd his young Cheek].

> Made purple riot: then doth he propose
> A stratagem, that makes the beldame start:
> (XVI)

Porphyro's creative imagination which here suddenly conceives its loving plan, is itself akin to the final enjoyment of its success in the plan, and so includes within itself again Keats's sense of the imagination as a nobly self-fulfilling prophecy. 'That which is creative must create itself.'[1] Coleridge described 'the primary imagination' as 'a repetition in the finite mind of the eternal act of creation in the infinite I AM' (*Biographia Literaria*, Chapter XIII); Keats located the essential repetition or parallel as that of the human imagination and the human act of creation. This is why

> Sudden a thought came like a full-blown rose,
> Flushing his brow,

soon finds itself taken up within the moment when this 'thought' passes through stratagem to achieved joy:

> Ethereal, flush'd, and like a throbbing star
> Seen mid the sapphire heaven's deep repose
> Into her dream he melted, as the rose
> Blendeth its odour with the violet,—
> (XXXVI)

It is because a blush, or an intense erotic flush, can be so naturally a type both of erection and of orgasm that the blush is so important to a poet like Keats, whose sense of imaginative and of erotic creation is so strongly proleptic, so akin to the self-fulfilling erotic prophecy of Adam: 'The Imagination may be compared to Adam's dream—he awoke and found it truth.'[2] Finding the imagination truth meant for Adam (and for Milton and Keats) immediately consummating the truth and proving it upon love's pulses; this is what Adam and Eve immediately do.

> To the Nuptial Bowre
> I led her blushing like the Morn:
> (*Paradise Lost*, VIII. 510–11)

---

[1] To Hessey, 8 Oct. 1818; i. 374.   [2] To Bailey, 22 Nov. 1817; i. 184–5.

Keats found embarrassability and unembarrassability to be humanly very revealing. His magnanimity made him especially good at describing ridiculous people vividly yet without scorn; partly this is a matter of his sense of how richly creative their muddle is (a similar delight warms Dickens's evocation of Flora Finching), and partly of Keats's spontaneous sense of a truthful juxtaposition with something from his own life.

Yesterday we dinned with a Traveller—We were talking about Kean—He said he had seen him at Glasgow 'in Othello in the Jew, I mean er, er, er, the Jew in Shylock' He got bother'd completely in vague ideas of the Jew in Othello, Shylock in the Jew, Shylock in Othello, Othello in Shylock, the Jew in Othello &c &c &c he left himself in a mess at last—Still satisfied with himself he went to the Window and gave an abortive whistle of some tune or other—it might have been Handel. There is no end to these Mistakes—he'll go and tell people how he has seen 'Malvolio in the Countess' 'Twehth night in 'Midsummer nights dream—Bottom in much ado about Nothing—Viola in Barrymore—Antony in Cleopatra—Falstaff in the mouse Trap.—July 14 We enterd Glasgow last Evening under the most oppressive Stare a body could feel—When we had crossed the Bridge Brown look'd back and said its whole population had turned to wonder at us—we came on till a drunken Man came up to me—I put him off with my Arm—he returned all up in Arms saying aloud that, 'he had seen all foreigners bu-u-u t he never saw the like o' me—I was obliged to mention the word Officer and Police before he would desist—[1]

'Still satisfied with himself': Keats has a reluctant admiration. 'Under the most oppressive Stare a body could feel': Keats in the very next bit of chronicling puts himself in the position of the one scrutinized.

Yet there was to be no sanctimonious colluding with false susceptibilities; Keats and his friends did not desist from enjoying themselves just because somebody was embarrassed by it all. As Haydon records,

Keats, Bewick, & I dined together, Keats brought some friend of his, a noodle. After dinner to his horror when he expected we should all

---

[1] To Tom Keats, 13–14 July 1818; i. 332.

be discussing Milton & Raphael &c., we burst into the most bois-
terous merriment. We had all been working dreadfully hard the
whole week. I proposed to strike up a concert. Keats was the bassoon,
Bewick the flagellet, & I was the organ & so on. We went on imitating
the sounds of these instruments till we were ready to burst with
laughing. Then I took a piano forte & they something else, and so on
we went, while the Wise acre sat by without saying a word, blushing
& sipping his wine as if we meant to insult him.[1]

Keats was sufficiently in favour of embarrassment, as humanizing,
and as humanly revealing, to think it permissible sometimes deliberately to inflict it. The practical joke is the deliberate infliction
of embarrassment, either as cruel malice or as affectionate therapy.
For Keats, it is the latter; not vengeful or public, but richly aware
of the affinities of such a creative imaginative stratagem to the
creative imagination of art itself. For the nineteenth century, the
practical joke did indeed gain the status of a minor art-form;
immense imagination, time, concern, and wit went to its making,
animated by the ripe gratuitousness and uselessness of art.[2]

Keats's telling of his tale begins in the comic world of Sterne,[3]
in its elaboration of physical posture, in its punctuational dashes
and quirks, and in its surprising rescinding of what it has just said:
and then it ends in the comic world of Chaucer and of the fabliau
and its 'dramatis personae'. Again the delicacy is a matter of the
two jokes forming a diptych; the joke on Brown shows the embarrassment of the practical joke; the joke on himself shows the
embarrassments of the over-active imagination itself:

If you would prefer a joke or two to any thing else I have too for you
fresh hatchd. just ris as the Baker's wives say by the rolls. The first
I play'd off at Brown—the second I play'd *on* on myself. Brown when
he left me "Keats! says he "my good fellow (staggering upon his left
heel, and fetching an irregular pirouette with his right) Keats says he

---

[1] 11 May 1818; *Diary*, ii. 198–9.
[2] See in particular the life of Theodore Hook, by R. H. D. Barham (1849). Hook
was the master practical-joker of Keats's age; a witticism involving his name is
recorded in Keats's letters (p. 217 below); and it is right that it should be under
unblushing that *O.E.D.* should preserve his name: 'Bold and unblushing comes
Theodore Hook. . . .'
[3] Sterne appears at i. 160, 245; ii. 245.

(depressing his left eyebrow and elevating his right one ((tho by the way, at the moment, I did not know which was the right one)) Keats says he (still in the same posture but forthermore both his hands in his waistcoat pockets and jutting out his stomach) "Keats —my—g-o-o-ood fell o-o-o-ooh! says he (interlarding his exclamation with certain ventriloquial parentheses)—no this is all a lie—He was as sober as a Judge when a judge happens to be sober; and said "Keats, if any Letters come for me—Do not forward them, but open them and give me the marrow of them in few words. At the time when I wrote my first to him no Letters had arrived—I thought I would invent one, and as I had not time to manufacture a long one I dabbed off a short one—and that was the reason of the joke succeeding beyond my expectations. Brown let his house to a Mr Benjamin a Jew. Now the water which furnishes the house is in a tank sided with a composition of lime and the lime imp[r]egnates the water unpleasantly—Taking advantage of this circumstance I pretended that Mr Benjamin had written the following short note—"Sir. By drinking your damn'd tank water I have got the gravel—what reparation can you make to me and my family? Nathan Benjamin" By a fortunate hit, I hit upon his right hethen name—his right Pronomen. Brown in consequence it appears wrote to the surprised Mr Benjamin the following "Sir, I cannot offer you any remuneration until your gravel shall have formed itself into a Stone when I will cut you with Pleasure. C. Brown" This of Browns Mr Benjamin has answered insisting on an explatinon of this singular circumstance. B. says "when I read your Letter and his following I roared, and in came Mr Snook who on reading them seem'd likely to burst the hoops of his fat sides—so the Joke has told well— Now for the one I played on myself—I must first give you the scene and the dramatis Personae—There are an old Mjor and his youngish wife live in the next apartments to me—His bed room door opens at an angle with my sitting room door. Yesterday I was reading as demurely as a Parish Clerk when I heard a rap at the door—I got up and opened it—no one was to be seen—I listened and heard some one in the Major's room—Not content with this I went up stairs and down look'd in the cubboards—and watch'd—At last I set myself to read again not quite so demurely—when there came a louder rap— I arose determin'd to find out who it was—I look out the Stair cases were all silent—"This must be the Major's wife said I—at all events I will see the truth" so I rapt me at the Major's door and went in to the utter surprise and confusion of the Lady who was in reality there—

after a little explanation, which I can no more describe than fly, I made my retreat from her convinced of my mistake. She is to all appearance a silly body and is really surprised about it—She must have been—for I have discoverd that a little girl in the house was the Rappee—I assure you she has nearly make me sneeze. If the Lady tells tits I shall put a very grave and moral face on the matter with the old Gentleman, and make his little Boy a present of a humming top.—[1]

The affinities of Keats's practical joke to art, to literature, are plain enough, right down to the special felicities of art, things falling happily: the guess as to Benjamin's first name, and the luck that not having time to concoct a long letter he dabbed off a short one—and this was all the better. Brown's climactic pun on 'cut' ('until your gravel shall have formed itself into a Stone when I will cut you with Pleasure') takes its place easily enough within the world, at once altogether ordinary and distinctly literary, of the practical joke. So does Keats's own climactic pun on 'Rappee'—as Hyder Rollins points out, 'a coarse kind of snuff'. As for the joke which Keats's erotic imagination played on himself, thus embarrassing him and embarrassing the Major's wife: this is a fabliau—old Major, young wife—and it is alive with a sense of the relation between reading and the activity, including the over-activity, of imagination. ('At last I set myself to read again not quite so demurely—.') The exuberance and good humour of it all have a truly Chaucerian freedom from misgiving; had Keats lived to bring more of this full world which is the world of his letters within the orbit of his poems, I should like to think that it would have been as a great heir to Chaucer—and not to Shakespeare, Milton, or Wordsworth—that he might have set forward. 'This Evening I go to Cantrerbury . . . I hope the Remembrance of Chaucer will set me forward like a Billiard-Ball.'[2]

It is characteristic of Keats that in telling Haydon of his practical joke his rueful tone should at once evaporate into a nimble progression from the word 'wild fire' to 'the portentous Book' of which the title was in fact *A Desultory Exposition of an Anti-British System of*

---

[1] To George and Georgiana Keats, 25 Sept. 1819; ii. 215–16.
[2] To Taylor and Hessey, 16 May 1817; i. 146–7.

Incendiary Publication:[1] 'I am sorry to say that since I saw you I have been guilty of—a practical Joke upon Brown which has had all the success of an innocent Wild fire among people—Some day in the next week you shall hear it from me by word of Mouth—I have not seen the portentous Book which was scimmer'd at you just as I left town.'[2]

It is characteristic, too, that Keats's practical joke should be one from which he makes himself vanish, the embarrassment and quasi-quarrelling all being between Brown and Benjamin; whereas the best practical joke which Byron ever created (a literary feat, in its way) equally characteristically kept himself in the forefront of attention. The following letter was sent to his friend Hobhouse as from Byron's valet:

Venice, June, 1818

SIR,—With great grief I inform you of the death of my late dear Master, my Lord, who died this morning at ten of the Clock of a rapid decline and slow fever, caused by anxiety, sea-bathing, women, and riding in the Sun against my advice.

He is a dreadful loss to every body, mostly to me, who have lost a master and a place—also, I hope you, Sir, will give me a charakter.

I saved in his service as you know several hundred pounds. God knows how, for I don't, nor my late master neither; and if my wage was not always paid to the day, still it was or is to be paid some-time and somehow. You, Sir, who are his executioner won't see a poor Servant wronged of his little all.

My dear Master had several phisicians and a Priest: he died a Papish, but is to be buried among the Jews in the Jewish burying ground; for my part I don't see why—he could not abide them when living nor any other people, hating whores who asked him for money.

He suffered his illness with great patience, except that when in extremity he twice damned his friends and said they were selfish

[1] Compare the elegantly good-humoured relation of 'blade', 'flesh', 'carv'd some beef', and 'measured', in this casually triumphant prose (to George and Georgiana Keats, 20 Sept. 1819; ii. 206):

'Henry was a greater blade than ever I remember to have seen him. He had on a very nice coat, a becoming waistcoat and buff trowsers—I think his face has lost a little of the spanish-brown, but no flesh. He carv'd some beef exactly to suit my appetite, as if I had been measured for it.'

[2] To Haydon, 3 Oct. 1819; ii. 220.

rascals—you, Sir, particularly and Mr. Kinnaird, who had never answered his letters nor complied with his repeated requests. He also said he hoped that your new tragedy would be damned—God forgive him—I hope that my master won't be damned like the tragedy.

His nine whores are already provided for, and the other servants; but what is to become of me? I have got his Cloathes and Carriages, and Cash, and everything; but the Consul quite against law has clapt his seal and taken an inventary and swears that *he* must account to my Lord's heirs—who they are, I don't know—but they ought to consider poor Servants and above all his Vally de Sham.

My Lord never grudged me perquisites—my wage was the least I got by him; and if I did keep the Countess (she is, or ought to be, a Countess, although she is upon the town) Marietta Monetta Piretta, after passing my word to you and my Lord that I would not never no more—still he was an indulgent master, and only said I was a damned fool, and swore and forgot it again. What could I do? she said as how she should die, or kill herself if I did not go with her, and so I did—and kept her out of my Lord's washing and ironing—and nobody can deny that, although the charge was high, the linen was well got up.

Hope you are well, Sir—am, with tears in my eyes,
Yours faithfoolly to command, Wm FLETCHER

P.S.—If you know any Gentleman in want of a Wally—hope for a charakter. I saw your late Swiss Servant in the Galleys at Leghorn for robbing an Inn—he produced your recommendation at his trial.[1]

It is Keats's friendship for Brown which both sharpens and makes tender the trick upon him. So it is not surprising that Keats and Brown should together have concocted an apparent love-letter to Mrs. Dilke, and enclosed it in a letter to their friend Dilke; or that Keats, writing to Dilke on another occasion, should have said: 'I was in a little funk yesterday, for I sent an unseal'd note of sham abuse, until I recollected from what I had heard Charles say, that the servant could neither read nor write—not even to her Mother as Charles observed.'[2] Brown, on holiday in Scotland with Keats, urged the composition of a Scottish ballad that might take in Dilke;

[1] *Byron: A Self-Portrait*, ii. 428–30.   [2] 21 Sept. 1818; i. 369.

the comic situation resembles that which was malignantly tragic in
what is perhaps the best deploying in literature of the practical joke,
Kipling's appalling and appalled story 'Dayspring Mishandled',
about a Chaucerian forgery designed to humiliate a notable scholar.
Keats, despite his admiration for that gifted forger of medievalisms
Thomas Chatterton, was unable to come up with anything at all
convincing; he wrote to his brother Tom: 'The reason for my
writing these lines was that Brown wanted to impose a galloway
song upon dilke—but it wont do—The subject I got from meeting
a wedding just as we came down into this place—'[1] Yet though the
lines, 'Ah! ken ye what I met the day', are good neither as poetry
nor as spoof, they have their interest; for what is at the heart of
them is the cancelled line 'There was a blush upon her', and the
sense of the reciprocity of lovers' embarrassment:

> Her cheek was flush wi timid blood
>   Twixt growth and waning
> . . .
> Young Tam came up an eyed me quick
>   With reddened cheek . . .

It was Keats's delight in the practical joke as embarrassment's
comedy that made him so deeply vulnerable to the practical joke
as embarrassment's cruel humiliation. In the whole of his life the
thing which morally outraged and hurt him most was the practical
joke played by his friend Charles Wells—played not upon Keats
himself (there his robustness would have gained him ease) but
upon his brother Tom. By the time Keats discovered the details
of it, Tom was already dead after long suffering and after Keats's
gentle nursing; indeed, Keats discovered the practical joke when
engaged in the inevitably painful experience of going through
Tom's effects. Keats was moved by anger and impotence of hatred
to what is for him little short of insanity (given his extraordinary
sanity and self-command in the face of the most appalling pains,
anxieties, and rebuffs). It is true that by this date (April 1819)
Keats's health was already imperilled; true too that the fictitious
love-letters which Wells concocted, love-letters to Tom from one

[1] 10 July 1818; i. 327–8.

'Amena Bellefila', include parodic adaptations of bits of Keats's early poetry and that this too will have hurt him.[1] But even in conjunction these do not account for Keats's especial bitterness and laceration; we need to recognize the proximity—so like and yet so unlike in spirit—of Wells's practical-joke letters to Keats's own practical-joke letters. Of course the hurt to Tom (was Keats right to think that Tom *was* hurt and his health damaged? We shall never know) and the demeaning of Tom were the most important constituents of Keats's bitter anger; but the medium of this anger was a sense of how centrally important to life embarrassment could be, and how the inflicting of embarrassment did not have to be an inflicting of pain but could be affectionately liberating. There is nothing inherently trivial about suggesting that it mattered to Keats that Wells demeaned the practical joke and demeaned the encompassing friendship within which such jokes could flourish as warm and enhancing.

Moreover, the surviving letter from 'Amena' was a demeaning of two things about which Keats always felt strongly because of their relation to loving sympathy and to himself:

Oh you modest youth I think I must name you bashful Tom Steel Keep your Temper thats all dont let me compliment before I know whether you deserve as for hurting my Modesty tis nonsense you know what a Jade I am I am the Amazon who is to meet you with open Arms & give you an hundred Kisses remember that & think if I can blush you think me more modest than I really am & yet you shall find me innocent spotless as your own or Chas[s]. heart

Charles here says my distinction of Character does not do me credit or I should never have chosen for a companion such a little vagabond as himself did you ever hear it seems impossible to break him of it I am tired to hear it he is a good and a noble fellow & in my opinion

---

[1] Robert Gittings, *John Keats: The Living Year* (1954; 1962 edn.), p. 120: 'From the one surviving letter, it seems impossible that he meant it as a genuine full-blooded hoax; it is a joke so obvious that it seems certain it was meant to be found out. The major part of the letter sets out to be only one thing—a parody of the romantic mock-Spenserian language used by the Keats boys and their circle. What is more, it is a parody of the style and subject-matter of Keats's own early poetry.' The letter is printed as an appendix to the fourth edition (1952) of M. B. Forman's edition of Keats's letters.

is all the better for being little I am but little myself & I am determined to have a little Husband if I ever have any.

Keats found it very difficult to tell his brother George of all this:

I have been to Mrs Bentley's this morning and put all the Letters two
and from you and poor Tom and me—I have found some of the correspondence between him and that degraded Wells and Amena—It is a
wretched business. I do not know the rights of it—but what I do
know would I am sure affect you so much that I am in two Minds
whether I will tell you any thing about it—And yet I do not see why
—for any thing tho' it be unpleasant, that calls to mind those we still
love, has a compensation in itself for the pain it occasions—so very
likely tomorrow I may set about coppying thee whole of what I have
about it: with no sort of a Richardson self satisfaction—I hate it to a
sickness—[1]

The sickness does seem to have infected Keats here; later in the
same letter to George, he expresses a vengeful violence which
becomes slaked only by his imagining the torments of Hell—the
sequence of thinking and feeling is a striking one:

I have been looking over the correspondence of the pretended Amena
and Wells this evening—I now see the whole cruel deception—
I think Wells must have had an accomplice in it—Amena's Letters
are in a Man's language, and in a Man's hand imitating a woman's—
The instigations to this diabolical scheme were vanity, and the love
of intrigue. It was no thoughtless hoax—but a cruel deception on a
sanguine Temperament, with every show of friendship. I do not think
death too bad for the villain—The world would look upon it in a
differrent light should I expose it—they would call it a frolic—so I
must be wary—but I consider it my duty to be prudently revengeful.
I will hang over his head like a sword by a hair. I will be opium to his
vanity—if I cannot injure his interests—He is a rat and he shall have
ratsbane to his vanity—I will harm him all I possibly can—I have
no doubt I shall be able to do so—Let us leave him to his misery alone
except when we can throw in a little more—The fifth canto of Dante
pleases me more and more—it is that one in which he meets with Paulo
and Francesca—I had passed many days in rather a low state of mind
and in the midst of them I dreamt of being in that region of Hell. The

[1] 15 Apr. 1819; ii. 82–3. Compare Keats's remark: 'Wells should have brothers
and sicker than I even had' (Robert Gittings, *John Keats*, p. 360).

dream was one of the most delightful enjoyments I ever had in my life—[1]

The natural medium for the practical joke was the letter (as in Hook's great Berners St. practical joke, for which he sent out 4,000 letters), and it is the intimate link of letters with friendship which either redeems the joke into affection's liberties or else poisons the joke into betrayal. It was natural not only that Keats's practical joke on Brown should involve Brown's request about his letters and Keats's creation of a fictitious letter, but should also involve Keats's telling his brother about it so vividly and so humanely in a letter. For the creation of a practical joke by means of a letter brings home the singleness of all imaginative creation, and this is particularly true of Keats whose artistic achievement as a letter-writer is not less than as a poet. So some part of Keats's bitterness at the 'Amena Bellefila' episode will have been precipitated by the feeling that Wells had degraded letters too. Keats was very alive to letters and to their implications, and a great deal of his emotional and intellectual life was more than merely transmitted by, it was created by, letters. There are the jokes—wonderfully aware of an embarrassing thought that might rise in the mind of any of his correspondents—about his letters being published.[2] There is the scruple which made him decide not to send the letter to Dilke which would have put Dilke in a disabling embarrassing position.[3] He will have appreciated the candour (itself evaporating all embarrassment) of his friend Woodhouse apropos embarrassments financial and otherwise: 'Upon subjects like those in this letter, it is to me always more pleasant to write than to speak.—It gave me much pleasure to learn from Taylor that you are leaving us tolerably easy as to money matters'[4]—and so into a truly gentlemanly offer to Keats of money in the future.

Keats's sensitivity about letters could sometimes become too exacerbated, as when he decided that 'some curious body has detained my Letters—I am sure of it. They know not what to make of me—not an acquaintance in the Place—what can I be about? so

---

[1] 16 Apr. 1819; ii. 90–1.
[2] To George and Georgiana Keats, 28 June 1818, i. 305; to Fanny Brawne, Mar. (?) 1820, ii. 282.   [3] See p. 128.   [4] 16 Sept. 1820; ii. 336.

they open my Letters.'[1] Or when, desperately ill it is true, he met with a very unfortunate contretemps at Leigh Hunt's: 'An accident of an unpleasant nature occured at Mr Hunt's and prevented me from answering you, that is to say made me nervous. That you may not suppose it worse I will mention that some one of Mr Hunt's household opened a Letter of mine—upon which I immediately left Mortimer Terrace, with the intention of taking to Mrs Bentley's again';[2] on which Hyder Rollins noted:

Maria Gisborne in her Journal for Sunday, August 20 (pp. 44 f.), observes: 'Yesterday . . . Mrs. Hunt came in to tea; she called to apologize for herself and Mr. Hunt, for not having kept their appointment on the Saturday before; they were prevented by an unpleasant circumstance that happened to Keats. While we were there on Thursday a note was brought for him after he had retired to his room to repose himself; Mrs. Hunt being occupied with the child desired her upper servant to take it to him, and thought no more about it. On Friday the servant left her, and on Saturday Thornton produced this note open (which contained not a word of the least consequence), telling his mother that the servant had given it to him before she left the house with injunctions not to shew it to his mother till the following day. Poor Keats was affected by this inconceivable circumstance beyond what can be imagined; he wept for several hours, and resolved, notwithstanding Hunt's intreaties, to leave the house; he went to Hampstead that same evening.'

But the other side of this forgivable heart-breaking hypersensitivity, to which Keats came in the end, was a spirited normality. I know of nobody whose letters are so truly alive to the rich commonplaceness which clogs and embarrasses so many letters: the necessity for either concealing or tricking out the fact that one has been a neglectful correspondent. Keats's moral temperament and choice make him naturally the author of an immediate concession such as is not merely disarming:

My dear Brothers
    When once a man delays a letter beyond the proper time, he delays it longer for one or two reasons; first because he must begin in a very

---

[1] To Woodhouse, 22 Sept. 1819; ii. 173–4.
[2] To Fanny Keats, 13 Aug. 1820; ii. 313.

commonplace style, that is to say, with an excuse; & secondly things & circumstances become so jumbled in his mind, that he knows not what, or what not, he has said in his last—I shall visit you as soon as I have copied my poem all out. . . .[1]

My dear Bailey,

When a poor devil is drowning, it is said he comes thrice to the surface, ere he makes his final sink if however, even at the third rise, he can manage to catch hold of a piece of weed or rock, he stands a fair chance,—as I hope I do now, of being saved. I have sunk twice in our Correspondence, have risen twice and been too idle, or something worse, to extricate myself—I have sunk the third time and just now risen again at this two of the Clock P.M. and saved myself from utter perdition—by beginning this, all drench'd as I am and fresh from the Water—and I would rather endure the present inconvenience of a Wet Jacket, than you should keep a laced one in store for me. Why did I not stop at Oxford in my Way?—How can you ask such a Question? Why did I not promise to do so? Did I not in a Letter to you make a promise to do so? Then how can you be so unreasonable as to ask me why I did not? This is the thing—(for I have been rubbing up my invention; trying several sleights—I first polish'd a cold, felt it in my fingers tried it on the table, but could not pocket it: I tried Chilblains, Rheumatism, Gout, tight Boots, nothing of that sort would do, so this is, as I was going to say, the thing.—I had a Letter from Tom saying how much better he had got, and thinking he had better stop —I went down to prevent his coming up—Will not this do? Turn it which way you like—it is selvaged all round—I have used it these three last days to keep out the abominable Devonshire Weather—by the by you may say what you will of devonshire:[2]

The very fervour of Keats's imaginative attention to his own delinquency as a correspondent is the high compliment which he pays his correspondent. Two months earlier he had paid Bailey an explicit compliment of a different kind but from this same world of moral feeling: 'Your tearing, my dear friend, a spiritless and gloomy Letter up to rewrite to me is what I shall never forget—it was to me a real thing.'[3] Bailey's true considerateness, and Keats's highly

[1] To George and Tom Keats, 14 (?) Feb. 1818; i. 226.
[2] 13 Mar. 1818; i. 240–1.
[3] 23 Jan. 1818; i. 209.

considering it, come together not only in his greatly valued word
'real' but also in the turn, 'is what I shall never forget'. How this
turn itself is unforgettable: 'an old woman in a dog-kennel Sedan
with a pipe in her Mouth, is what I can never forget.'

The desperate sadness of Keats's love for Fanny Brawne, as it
developed through illness, loneliness, torrid violence of emotion,
and suspicion, is that Keats was unable to maintain for ever the
dear dryness which could keep a letter like this altogether true:

My dearest Fanny,
    I had a better night last night than I have had since my attack,
and this morning I am the same as when you saw me. I have been
turning over two volumes of Letters written between Rosseau and
two Ladies in the perplexed strain of mingled finesse and sentiment
in which the Ladies and gentlemen of those days were so clever, and
which is still prevalent among Ladies of this Country who live in a
state of resoning romance. The Likeness however only extends to the
mannerism not to the dexterity. What would Rousseau have said at
seeing our little correspondence! What would his Ladies have said!
I don't care much—I would sooner have Shakspeare's opinion about
the matter. The common gossiping of washerwomen must be less
disgusting than the continual and eternal fence and attack of Rousseau and these sublime Petticoats. One calls herself Clara and her
friend Julia two of Rosseau's Heroines—they all the same time
christen poor Jean Jacques St Preux—who is the pure cavalier of his
famous novel. Thank God I am born in England with our own great
Men before my eyes—Thank god that you are fair and can love me
without being Letter-written and sentimentaliz'd into it—Mr Barry
Cornwall has sent me another Book, his first, with a polite note—I
must do what I can to make him sensible of the esteem I have for his
kindness. If this north east would take a turn it would be so much
the better for me. Good bye, my love, my dear love, my beauty—
    love me for ever—

                                                    J— K—[1]

Six months later there is the pathos in the sheer ordinariness of the
stratagem (known to any lover who has ever needed to write a

[1] 27 (?) Feb. 1820; ii. 266-7.

letter where he has no privacy) by which Keats does not fill in his letter's superscription till the very last minute:

> I do not write this till the last, that no eye may catch it.

My dearest Girl,
I wish you could invent some means to make me at all happy without you. Every hour I am more and more concentrated in you; every thing else tastes like chaff in my Mouth. . . .[1]

So begins the last surviving letter to Fanny Brawne, probably the last which Keats ever wrote to her. It is characteristic of Keats that even at such a time the ordinary social embarrassment should still be important to him, and not neurasthenically so. It is characteristic, too, that when he lay in Italy on the sick-bed that was so quickly becoming a death-bed, he set aside unopened the letters which included one from Fanny Brawne. In doing so, he was properly protecting himself against useless anguish ('they tear him to pieces', said Severn),[2] and at the same time—with that concurrence of what is truly considerate to oneself and to others which is so central to Keats's freedom from self-punishment and from selfishness—protecting Fanny against the inevitable injustice which he would now be likely to do to a letter of hers.

[1] Aug. (?) 1820; ii. 311. [2] *The Keats Circle*, i. 92.

VIII

SOMEBODY READING

'EVERY hour I am more and more concentrated in you; every thing else tastes like chaff in my Mouth.' For Keats, eating was a natural metaphor not only for love but also for reading: 'I should not like to be Pages in your way when in a tolerable hungry mood—you have no Mercy—your teeth are the Rock tarpeian down which you capsise Epic Poems like Mad—'[1] Cowden Clarke said of Keats that 'he devoured rather than read'.[2] Perhaps it is a coincidence that Bergler's ereutophobe reduced the same metaphor to its cliché: 'From a cheerful, friendly child she turned into a "shy, unfriendly, retiring stay-at-home" who very soon found only one joy—reading. "I swallowed books, nothing else interested me at this time".'[3] But consider the relation between embarrassment and the other arts. Music may give the special relief and release which it does partly because the medium is one in which so many considerations that are embarrassing in life simply cannot arise; it is hard to imagine how music as an art could make use of embarrassment— indeed, the attempt to lever open the traditional sense of music to the point at which it has either greatly widened or simply split apart has been to some extent an attempt to make embarrassment imaginable and invigorating: that John Cage can create embarrass- ment for his audience is clearer than that what he creates is music. Again, it must be a real question whether sculpture can tell of a blush unless it paints itself; one of the reasons why nude sculpture in marble, for instance, has been found unperturbing and un- embarrassing by societies—Victorian England, for one—easily made uneasy by nudes in paint is perhaps that the nude sculpture is on these terms unembarrassable and so unable to pass on a contagious embarrassment; such a nude can express modesty but cannot blush

[1] To Bailey, 30 Oct. 1817; i. 175.   [2] *The Keats Circle*, ii. 148.
[3] *Psychoanalytic Quarterly*, xiii (1944).

—and this itself is an effect of art which we can value and be assisted by just because in life having the one without the other is not often clean cut. Again, the painter's art is one which can distinguish between a blush and a flush only by showing a situation or even a story from which we deduce it to be the one or the other; in this respect, it is freed from both the powers and the constraints which go with language's ability to *say* that it was the one or the other. In 'My Last Duchess', the Duke tellingly repeats the neutral phraseology of 'that spot of joy', encompassed by which he can speak of a 'half-flush' that—as if his medium were Fra Pandolf's paint rather than words—is pointedly not conceded to be a blush:

> Sir, 'twas not
> Her husband's presence only, called that spot
> Of joy into the Duchess' cheek: perhaps
> Frà Pandolf chanced to say 'Her mantle laps
> Over my lady's wrist too much', or 'Paint
> Must never hope to reproduce the faint
> Half-flush that dies along her throat:' such stuff
> Was courtesy, she thought, and cause enough
> For calling up that spot of joy.

It was Browning's distinction as a poet to know and care enough about the visual arts to be able to divine with great acuteness just what words could do which paint, say, could not. The same is true of Henry James, whose art-criticism is altogether apt to Keats and yet asks to be re-angled because of the differences of medium. So John Bayley's wish to bring the word 'vulgarity' into relation with Keats may recall James's formulation about Rubens and yet would need to inaugurate an inquiry into why vulgarity is a different thing in an art whose medium is words: 'He belongs, certainly, to the small group of the world's greatest painters, but he is, in a certain way, the vulgarest of the group.' A full paragraph by James about Rubens trembles both with commitment and with irony, and again is a counterpart, yet not altogether so, to what is a widespread and true response to Keats:

Was Rubens lawfully married to Nature, or did he merely keep up the most unregulated of flirtations? Three or four of his great carnal cataracts ornament the walls of the Pitti. If the union was really solemnized it must be said that the ménage was at best a stormy one. He is a strangely irresponsible jumble of the true and the false. He paints a full flesh surface that radiates and palpitates with illusion, and into the midst of it he thrusts a mouth, a nose, an eye, which you would call your latest-born a blockhead for perpetrating.

The admiration is patent yet puzzled, as it is when James moves from Burne-Jones's *The Tree of Forgiveness* to Rubens, rather as if he is sustained by a deep sense of what *rubens* really means: 'The mass of almond blossom introduces a great deal of fresh and moist-looking white; the flesh-tones are wan and bloodless, as befits the complexion of people whom we see through the medium of a certain incredulity. It would never do for Phyllis and Demophoön to present themselves with the impudence of, say, Rubens's flesh and blood'.[1] Yet in Keats the impudence has its own *pudor*, and this is effected because language has both its own palpitating power of illusion and its own recognition of a proper incredulity: we are being told of things which we know not to have happened, and this is a different matter from our being shown a picture of things which we know not to have happened.

I have already argued that there cannot be a visual *equivalent* to the effect of the word 'nipple', or—for different reasons—of the word 'pout'.[2] This bears on 'Sleep and Poetry':

> —and the swift bound
> Of Bacchus from his chariot, when his eye
> Made Ariadne's cheek look blushingly.
>
> (334–6)

Ian Jack[3] points out that this derives from or alludes to Titian's 'Bacchus and Ariadne'; but what then matters is the essentially different relation to the blush which the different artistic media have. For the picture shows Ariadne flushing or blushing, and the act of interpreting the picture is in this respect different from that of interpreting Keats's lines. But not only does the picture not say anything equivalent to 'made Ariadne blush', it could not begin

[1] *The Painter's Eye*, pp. 119, 20, 207.   [2] See pp. 14, 107.
[2] *Keats and the Mirror of Art*, p. 130.

to say anything equivalent to 'Made Ariadne's cheek look blushingly'—a different thing from blushing or from looking blushing. What *look* does there is mingle observer and observed into the reciprocity of embarrassment, of desire, and of love. Behind this is the linguistic fact that at first blush a blush was a look: *O.E.D.* 2, 'To cast a glance, glance with the eye, give a look'. I do not mean that no comparable effect is attainable in the sister art; simply that any such attaining would have to be by very different means, and that then in art a difference of means necessarily creates a difference of effect—the effect then being comparable, not equivalent. That these considerations are not imperceptible to Keats is clear, I think, from the swift bound which his own verse then takes, into what at first might seem scarcely to the point:

> and the swift bound
> Of Bacchus from his chariot, when his eye
> Made Ariadne's cheek look blushingly.
> Thus I remember all the pleasant flow
> Of words at opening a portfolio.

It is 'flow' that connects the blush and the words; it is the words and the portfolio which enforce a recognition of the invigorating and subtle differences between the sister arts.

Drama has an oddly equivocal relation to the blush, for the reason of which Darwin reminds us: 'Seneca remarks "that the Roman players hang down their heads, fix their eyes on the ground and keep them lowered, but are unable to blush in acting shame".'[1] In other words, they act shame rather than embarrassment. Even more than the flow of tears, and perhaps even more than the equivocation about erections in *Oh! Calcutta!*, the flow of blood to the face is a test case for the actor, since the art cannot simply call upon it and yet the art is of such an explicitly encompassing kind that it can hardly exclude from its entire purview the blush. The blush in drama therefore focuses a traditional doubt about drama[2] and about its ministering to the willed, the cunning, and the

---

[1] *The Expression of the Emotions in Man and Animals*, p. 323.
[2] See Jonas A. Barish, 'Exhibitionism and the Antitheatrical Prejudice' (*ELH*, xxxvii, 1969), and 'Antitheatrical Prejudice in the Nineteenth-Century' (*University of Toronto Quarterly*, xl, 1971).

histrionic and not to the spontaneous. Shakespeare's subtlety in the matter is clear enough from several passages which select themselves in that Keats marked them in his Shakespeare. There is Cleopatra's taunt:

> As I am Egypt's Queen,
> Thou blushest, Antony, and that blood of thine
> Is Caesar's homager: else so thy cheek pays shame
> When shrill-tongued Fulvia scolds.
>
> (I. i. 29–32)

The force of this is inherently dramatic, inherently of the dramatic medium, in that Cleopatra's animus is so strong that we have no way of telling whether Antony has indeed blushed or whether she is dextrously making it up; an intense and significant dramatic effect is in either case possible but markedly different in what it tells us. Similarly with Lucio's address to Isabella:

> Hail, virgin, if you be, as those cheek-roses
> Proclaim you are no less.
>
> (*Measure for Measure*, I. iv. 16–17)

The flush or the blush of maidenhood? Or is Lucio's compliment at once fervent and false? Again, there is the blush in *Romeo and Juliet*:

> There stays a husband to make you a wife.
> Now comes the wanton blood up in your cheeks:
> They'll be in scarlet straight at any news.
>
> (II. v. 68–71; Keats marked the last line)

Or take the blush in *Troilus and Cressida*, with Pandarus urging Troilus: 'You must be witty now. She does so blush . . .' (III. ii. 29)—(this leads into the word a moment later when Pandarus brings her to Troilus with 'Come, come, what need you blush?') Another passage marked by Keats manifestly replaces the essentially dramatic (a character blushing or not, on the stage) by the poetic and even epic style that gives *Troilus and Cressida* at many points a curiously Miltonic ring ('blushing like the Morn'):

> a blush
> Modest as morning when she coldly eyes
> The youthful Phoebus . . .
>
> (I. iii. 228–30)

The most immediately obvious correspondence between blushing and the arts is the central equivocation or paradox of private and public, the belief that both blushing and the arts are at once intensely public and intensely private, in some way public expressions of privacy. There is a close analogy between the traditional problems about whether an art cannot be conceived of as existing until it is apprehended, and the equally traditional ones about whether there can be—either on linguistic, philosophical, or psychological grounds—such a thing as private embarrassment. What creates the problems is the status of imagining, as with the old questions about blushing alone or in the dark, or about the blushes of the blind.[1] Erving Goffman speaks of 'the real or imagined presence of others';[2] but one would think that the embarrassment in the one case will not be of the same kind as in the other. 'The figure the individual cuts before others felt to be there at the time': but there is a difference between knowing-and-feeling that others are there, and just feeling it (while perhaps knowing that they either are not really there or cannot really observe—for example, the presence in some sense of the man talking from the television screen). The strength and strangeness of art, and in particular of literature since its medium is the medium of daily human relationship, derive from our feeling that we both are and are not in the presence of another human being; there is a voice which we can hear but which cannot hear us, a presence that can be passionately felt to the point of an ennobling superstition, rather as Keats felt Shakespeare to be his 'presider', but which does not need to be mystical. In some way, any great work of literature which touches and changes us is a presence and a presider. 'Required both to be present and to not be present': Goffman's core of embarrassment is a core of literature. 'Because of possessing multiple selves the individual may find he is required both to be present and to not be present on certain occasions. Embarrassment ensues: the individual finds himself being torn apart, however gently. Corresponding to the oscillation of his conduct is the oscillation of his

---

[1] See Feldman, *Journal of the American Psychoanalytic Association*, x (1962). Also Modigliani, *Journal of Personality and Social Psychology*, xvii (1971); but of course embarrassment due to failure (at anagram solving, in this case) is a very different thing from other forms of embarrassment.　　　　[2] *Interaction Ritual*, p. 98.

self.'[1] Part of such an oscillation is between the sense in which the role of a reader is truly passive (Wordsworth's 'wise passiveness' is attuned to books as to nature) and the sense in which the role of a reader is truly active. Some people find this duality more than they can take, and are fretful or embarrassed by not knowing what they are supposed to *do* as a reader; it is not just their attention to the book, but the book's attention to them, which discomposes and even threatens them. Again embarrassment is such a discomposure:

In other cases the source of threat is not so obvious, though we would argue it is always present. Consider, for example, the case of being embarrassed by sheer volume of attention as when one is being introduced to an unfamiliar audience, or is the focal point of 'Happy Birthday to You.' We suggest that the threatening element in such situations arises from the passive nature of one's role.[2]

What Goffman says of 'composure' in relation to games and sports, and of 'style', could be said of the composure and composition[3] in the arts, especially in the art for which the word 'style' is least a manner of speaking:

. . . a capacity to maintain composure. Nor should it come as a surprise that many of our games and sports commemorate the themes of composure and embarrassment: in poker, a dubious claim may win money for the player who can present it calmly; in judo, the maintenance and loss of composure are specifically fought over; in cricket, self-command or 'style' is supposed to be kept up under tension.[4]

A blush is an act of communication. There are Tennyson's lines in *Maud*:

> Pass and blush the news
>   Over glowing ships;
> Over blowing seas,
>   Over seas at rest,
> Pass the happy news,
>   Blush it through the West . . .
>
>   (I. xvii)

[1] *Interaction Ritual*, p. 110.   [2] Modigliani, *Sociometry*, xxxi (1968).
[3] On composing as composure and as composition, Wordsworth is especially fine; see my essay on Wordsworth, *Essays in Criticism*, xxi (1971).
[4] *Interaction Ritual*, p. 104.

Behind this, there is the exchange between Camillo and Perdita in *The Winter's Tale*:

> '... Prosperity's the very bond of love,
> Whose fresh complexion and whose heart together
> Affliction alters.'
>
>   'One of these is true.
> I think affliction may subdue the cheek,
> But not take in the mind.'
>
>   (IV. iv. 566–70)

This leads, by a beautiful reversal of the impulse (back from 'affliction' to 'prosperity'), to Perdita's communicating in words of her communicative blush:

>   For this
>   I'll blush you thanks.

Goffman aptly cites Dr. Johnson's *Rambler*, No. 159 (24 September 1751) to remind us that embarrassment has its positive part to play:

It generally happens that assurance keeps an even pace with ability, and the fear of miscarriage, which hinders our first attempts, is gradually dissipated as our skill advances towards certainty of success. That bashfulness therefore which prevents disgrace, that short and temporary shame, which secures us from the danger of lasting reproach, cannot be properly counted among our misfortunes.

Yet the interesting thing about Johnson's main argument is the way this piece of writing needs to avert its eyes from writing and the motives to writing. For Johnson's consolatory adjuration to the bashful is to assure them that it is not true that everybody is looking at them—nobody is looking at them. 'But the truth is, that no man is much regarded by the rest of the world. He that considers how little he dwells upon the condition of others, will learn how little the attention of others is attracted by himself.' Yet this truth, or this compensatory and humane counter-exaggeration, is patently and inherently unhelpful to a writer.

Bashfulness, however it may incommode for a moment, scarcely ever produces evils of long continuance; it may flush the cheek, flutter in the heart, deject the eyes, and enchain the tongue, but its mischiefs soon pass off without remembrance. It may sometimes exclude pleasure, but seldom opens any avenue to sorrow or remorse. It is observed somewhere, that 'few have repented of having forborn to speak.'

But with these very words Johnson is necessarily not forbearing to speak; and Johnson's magnificent peroration gains some of its pathos and humanity from its implicit recognition that a writer must stand differently to time from other men, and must indeed be conscious of 'the test of time':

No cause more frequently produces bashfulness than too high an opinion of our own importance. He that imagines an assembly filled with his merit, panting with expectation, and hushed with attention, easily terrifies himself with the dread of disappointing them, and strains his imagination in pursuit of something that may vindicate the veracity of fame, and shew that his reputation was not gained by chance. He considers, that what he shall say or do will never be forgotten; that renown or infamy are suspended upon every syllable, and that nothing ought to fall from him which will not bear the test of time.

For the fact is that no artist—no writer, one would particularly say, given the terms Johnson uses—could accept with equanimity the concluding admonition with which Johnson properly seals for us what could not properly be so sealed for him:

While we see multitudes passing before us, of whom perhaps not one appears to deserve our notice, or excites our sympathy, we should remember, that we likewise are lost in the same throng, that the eye which happens to glance upon us is turned in a moment on him that follows us, and that the utmost which we can reasonably hope or fear is to fill a vacant hour with prattle, and be forgotten.

We can come at a further relation of literature to embarrassment if we compare a remark by Trilling about Keats—'we express our high esteem for such a work by supposing that it judges us'—with what happened elsewhere when Trilling expanded and elaborated 'W. H. Auden's remark that a real book reads us':

I have been read by Eliot's poems and by *Ulysses* and by *Remembrance of Things Past* and by *The Castle* for a good many years now, since early youth. Some of these books at first rejected me; I bored them. But as I grew older and they knew me better, they came to have more sympathy with me and to understand my hidden meanings. Their nature is such that our relationship has been very intimate. No literature has ever been so shockingly personal as that of our time—it asks every question that is forbidden in polite society.[1]

This is wittier than I could do, but nevertheless as it contemplates the embarrassingness of modern literature it does itself become a bit embarrassed. The signs of this are the way in which the elaboration from Auden starts to become whimsical (whimsy is inherently a protection against embarrassment), and the way in which the prose can only jump, not pass, into the last sentence above, a sentence which simply is not at home with the earlier tone.[2] For although it is indeed true that we judge a book and that a book judges us, it is importantly not true (importantly, because our valuation of and gratitude to art are intimately involved with the fact) that we can shame or embarrass a book although a book can shame or embarrass us. 'No literature has ever been so shockingly personal as that of our time': agreed, but what Trilling's serious sustained joke-by-inversion needed to be able to say was not 'shockingly' but 'shockably'. It is a crucial fact about the genuine mutuality and reciprocity, and indeed intimacy, of our relation to books that there is no mutuality or reciprocity of embarrassment.

When Leigh Hunt sent some books to Charles Cowden Clarke, he apologized both for the delay in sending them and for their having been inadvertently bound in red: 'You must fancy the books are blushing for having been so long before they came.'[3] That such a joke is at one with the ways of the imagination for Keats comes out from the lines about Ariadne's blush which I have already mentioned; to quote at greater length from 'Sleep and Poetry' (319–40)

---

[1] *Beyond Culture*, pp. 71, 8.

[2] The right home for it is the context of a unified tone which Trilling has since created: 'The paradox to be discerned in the position begins, of course, in the extent to which the work of the great modern masters is preoccupied with personal concerns, with the self and with the difficulties of being true to it. If I may quote a characterization of the classic literature of the early century that I once had occasion to make, "No literature has ever been so shockingly personal— . . ." ' (*Sincerity and Authenticity*, 1972, p. 7).

[3] Cowden Clarke, *Recollections of Writers*, pp. 193–4.

is to make clear that the blush is encompassed by such thoughts and
is not just succeeded by them:

> The hearty grasp that sends a pleasant sonnet
> Into the brain ere one can think upon it;
> The silence when some rhymes are coming out;
> And when they're come, the very pleasant rout:
> The message certain to be done to-morrow—
> 'Tis perhaps as well that it should be to borrow
> Some precious book from out its snug retreat,
> To cluster round it when we next shall meet.
> Scarce can I scribble on; for lovely airs
> Are fluttering round the room like doves in pairs;
> Many delights of that glad day recalling,
> When first my senses caught their tender falling.
> And with these airs come forms of elegance
> Stooping their shoulders o'er a horse's prance,
> Careless, and grand—fingers soft and round
> Parting luxuriant curls;—and the swift bound
> Of Bacchus from his chariot, when his eye
> Made Ariadne's cheek look blushingly.
> Thus I remember all the pleasant flow
> Of words at opening a portfolio.
>
> Things such as these are ever harbingers
> To trains of peaceful images . . .

In the same realm of relations there is the hot flush and the name
of Milton in 'Lines on Seeing a Lock of Milton's Hair'; or the
'fever'd' and the 'temperate blood', the 'leaves of his life's book' and
the 'maidenhood', of the sonnet 'On Fame'. Or there is the sudden
and bizarre arrival of writing in 'Sleep and Poetry':

> Most awfully intent
> The driver of those steeds is forward bent,
> And seems to listen: O that I might know
> All that he writes with such a hurrying glow.
>
> (151–4)

John Jones is right to find this preposterous: ' "All that he writes"
has come completely out of the blue, with no mention of a pen in

his hand or of any material to write on. By occupying his charioteer thus strangely—and dangerously, since he is busy driving—Keats falls into the same violent and irrational oscillation between life and literature as in the earlier passage.'[1] But though the oscillation is indeed 'irrational', the link of thought and feeling that led to 'he writes' is not so, or not only so; 'All that he writes with such a hurrying glow' had its glow for Keats partly because the previous verse-sentence had included

> Some with upholden hand and mouth severe;
> Some with their faces muffled to the ear
> Between their arms . . .

More importantly, it is this sense, that the deep and true consolations of art are made possible by a relationship that is indeed not mutual or reciprocal as are the deep and true consolations of human relationships, which animates one of the greatest passages that Keats ever wrote:

> But for her eyes I should have fled away.
> They held me back, with a benignant light,
> Soft-mitigated by divinest lids
> Half closed, and visionless entire they seem'd
> Of all external things—they saw me not,
> But in blank splendor beam'd like the mild moon,
> Who comforts those she sees not, who knows not
> What eyes are upward cast.
>   (*The Fall of Hyperion*, I. 264–71)

The blank splendour of the moon is a type of the blank (not empty) splendour of art, which comforts those she sees not, and knows not what eyes are upward cast. The consolation which Keats here imagines, he at the same time provides; he comforts those he sees not, and this is of the essence of art. That the night-sky could epitomize and precipitate such feelings in Keats is clear from a sequence elsewhere:

> When I have fears that I may cease to be
> Before my pen has glean'd my teeming brain,

---

[1] *John Keats's Dream of Truth*, p. 46.

Before high-piled books, in charact'ry,
    Hold like rich garners the full-ripen'd grain;
When I behold, upon the night's starr'd face,
    Huge cloudy symbols of a high romance . . .

The high romance of Keats's love for Fanny Brawne demanded
that the relation between life and literature should not be a confusion of the two; it was for this that he loved her:

You say you are affraid I shall think you do not love me—in saying
this you make me ache the more to be near you. I am at the diligent
use of my faculties here, I do not pass a day without sprawling some
blank verse or tagging some rhymes; and here I must confess, that,
(since I am on that subject,) I love you the more in that I believe
you have liked me for my own sake and for nothing else—I have met
with women whom I really think would like to be married to a Poem
and to be given away by a Novel.[1]

It was his confidence of the distinction between life and literature
which released his fantasy to be so untimorous, and which made
him fond both of imagined vistas that involve reading and writing
(as if by the graphic skill and wit of a Steinberg) and of attempts to
imagine a person's real postures. For the imagined—with Hazlitt
taken up into the world of the play he was writing about—
there is the note which Keats made at the end of Hazlitt's chapter
on *The Tempest* in *Characters of Shakespeare's Plays*: 'I cannot help seeing
Hazlitt like Ferdinand—"in an odd angle of the Isle sitting"—his
arms in this sad knot.'[2] Or there is the sweetly affectionate circu-
larity with which he writes to his young sister Fanny:

Tell me also if you want any particular Book; or Pencils, or drawing
paper—any thing but live Stock—Though I will not now be very
severe on it, remembring how fond I used to be of Goldfinches,
Tomtits, Minnows, Mice, Ticklebacks, Dace, Cock salmons and all
the whole tribe of the Bushes and the Brooks: but verily they are
better in the Trees and the water—though I must confess even now
a partiality for a handsome Globe of goldfish—then I would have it
hold 10 pails of water and be fed continually fresh through a cool pipe

---

[1] 8 July 1819; ii. 127.   [2] Robert Gittings, *John Keats*, p. 174.

with another pipe to let through the floor—well ventilated they would preserve all their beautiful silver and Crimson—Then I would put it before a handsome painted window and shade it all round with myrtles and Japonicas. I should like the window to open onto the Lake of Geneva—and there I'd sit and read all day like the picture of somebody reading.—[1]

To be acutely aware of the difference between the real and the imagined is not necessarily to be less at the mercy of the imagined; Keats's crisp ritual sets forward to woo the muse as if she were a girl: 'I feel I can bear real ills better than imaginary ones. Whenever I find myself growing vapourish, I rouse myself, wash and put on a clean shirt brush my hair and clothes, tie my shoestrings neatly and in fact adonize as I were going out—then all clean and comfortable I sit down to write. This I find the greatest relief—'[2] 'I sit down to write': it was a preoccupation of Keats's, to attempt to imagine those whom he loved or admired in this posture and activity particularly. It is thus that he writes to his brother George and his sister-in-law, as in the most disinterestedly painful letter he ever had to write, that which tells them of Tom's death and then moves through his own writing to an imagined reading in common:

My dear Brother and Sister,

You will have been prepared, before this reaches you for the worst news you could have, nay if Haslam's letter arrives in proper time, I have a consolation in thinking the first shock will be past before you receive this. The last days of poor Tom were of the most distressing nature; but his last moments were not so painful, and his very last was without a pang—I will not enter into any parsonic comments on death—yet the common observations of the commonest people on death are as true as their proverbs. I have scarce a doubt of immortality of some nature of [or] other—neither had Tom. My friends have been exceedingly kind to me every one of them—Brown detained me at his House. I suppose no one could have had their time made smoother than mine has been. During poor Tom's illness I was not able to write and since his death the task of beginning has been a hindrance to me. Within this last Week I have been every where—and I will tell you as nearly as possible how all go on—With Dilke

[1] 13 Mar. 1819; ii. 46.
[2] To George and Georgiana Keats, 17 Sept. 1819; ii. 186.

and Brown I am quite thick—with Brown indeed I am going to
domesticate—that is we shall keep house together—I Shall have the
front parlour and he the back one—by which I shall avoid the noise
of Bentley's Children—and be the better able to go on with my
Studies—which ave been greatly interrupted lately, so that I have
not the Shadow of an idea of a book in my head, and my pen seems
to have grown too goutty for verse. How are you going on now?
The going[s] on of the world make me dizzy—there you are with
Birkbeck—here I am with brown—sometimes I fancy an immense
separation, and sometimes, as at present, a direct communication of
spirit with you. That will be one of the grandeurs of immortality—
there will be no space and consequently the only commerce between
spirits will be by their intelligence of each other—when they will
completely understand each other—while we in this world merely
comp[r]ehend each other in different degrees—the higher the degree
of good so higher is our Love and friendship—I have been so little
used to writing lately that I am affraid you will not smoke my meaning
so I will give an example—Suppose Brown or Haslam or any one
whom I understand in the nether degree to what I do you, were in
America, they would be so much the farther from me in proportion
as their identity was less impressed upon me. Now the reason why
I do not feel at the present moment so far from you is that I remember
your Ways and Manners and actions; I known [know] you manner of
thinking, you manner of feeling: I know what shape your joy or your
sorrow would take, I know the manner of you walking, standing,
sauntering, sitting down, laughing, punning, and evey action so truly
that you seem near to me. You will remember me in the same manner
—and the more when I tell you that I shall read a passage of Shakspeare every Sunday at ten o Clock—you read one at the same time
and we shall be as near each other as blind bodies can be in the same
room—[1]

It was imagining *this*, somebody reading or somebody writing,
which was to Keats so important a type case for the imaginative
energy of love and art.

This is the sort of feu de joie he [Hazlitt] keeps up—there is another
extract or two—one especially which I will copy tomorrow—for the
candles are burnt down and I am using the wax taper—which has a

---

[1] 16 Dec. 1818; ii. 4–5.

long snuff on it—the fire is at its last click—I am sitting with my back
to it with one foot rather askew upon the rug and the other with the
heel a little elevated from the carpet—I am writing this on the Maid's
tragedy which I have read since tea with Great pleasure—Besides this
volume of Beaumont & Fletcher—there are on the tabl[e] two
volumes of chaucer and a new work of Tom Moores call'd 'Tom
Cribb's memorial to Congress—nothing in it—These are trifles—
but I require nothing so much of you as that you will give me a like
description of yourselves, however it may be when you are writing
to me—Could I see the same thing done of any great Man long since
dead it would be a great delight: as to know in what position Shakspeare sat when he began 'To be or not to be "—such thing[s] become
interesting from distance of time or place. I hope you are both now
in that sweet sleep which no two beings deserve more that [than]
you do—I must fancy you so—and please myself in the fancy of
speaking a prayer and a blessing over you and your lives—God bless
you—I whisper good night in your ears and you will dream of me—[1]

Writing has this disadvan[ta]ge of speaking. one cannot write a wink,
or a nod, or a grin, or a purse of the Lips, or a *smile—O law*! One
can-[not] put ones fingers to one's nose, or yerk ye in the ribs, or lay
hold of your button in writing—but in all the most lively and titterly
parts of my Letter you must not fail to imagine me as the epic poets
say—now here, now there, now with one foot pointed at the ceiling,
now with another—now with my pen on my ear, now with my elbow
in my mouth—O my friends you loose the action—and attitude is
every thing as Fusili said when he took up his leg like a Musket
to shoot a Swallow just darting behind his shoulder. And yet does
not the word mum! go for ones finger beside the nose—I hope it does.
I have to make use of the word Mum! before I tell you that Severn
has got a little Baby—all his own let us hope—he told Brown he had
given up painting and had tu[r]n'd modeller. I hope sincerely tis not
a party concern; that no M^r— or **** us the real *Pinxit* and Severn
the poor *Sculpsit* to this work of art—You know he has long studied
in the Life-Academy.—[2]

Keats sets such store by the attempt to imagine a writer or a reader
because doing so will release reading and writing from the inevitable

---

[1] To George and Georgiana Keats, 12 Mar. 1819; ii. 73-4.
[2] Ibid., 20 Sept. 1819; ii. 205.

anxieties of solitude—narcissism, solipsism, lonely indulgent
fantasizing. It is for such reasons that many of us set such store by
the public discussion of literature. To write about literature, argue
about it, teach it: these, though they bring other anxieties, are
valued because they can help to restore a vital balance of private
and public in our relation with literature. Since the balance is delicate and since it should vary, it is easily upset into uneasiness.
I therefore think it odd of Dr. Sattler[1] to give the following as one
of the cited 'Unclassifiable' statements by his schizophrenics about
what they find embarrassing, while he notes that the Unclassifiable
category 'contains descriptions which were vague or nonmeaningful': 'It's embarrassing when listening or reading then have
crinkling of paper in other parts or rooms if they aren't studying.'
This does not seem to me 'vague or nonmeaningful'; moreover
I concur with it; it is alert to a disconcerting and embarrassing
aspect of reading in public: a lot of people doing separately and
publicly what it seems natural to do on one's own and privately,
and thus having neither the truly public sense of literature nor the
truly private. 'It's embarrassing . . .': the relation of reading in
public to embarrassment and to erotic anxiety was not sufficiently
attended to in its own right when Gross and Stone concentrated on
their 'stigmata' alone:

Ordinarily, persons will avoid recognizing such stigmata, turn their
eyes away, and pretend them out of existence, but on occasion stigmata will obtrude upon the situation causing embarrassment all
around. A case in point was a minor flirtation reported by one of our
students. Seated in a library a short distance from a beautiful girl,
the student began the requisite gestural invitation to a more intimate
conversation. The girl turned, smiling, to acknowledge the bid,
revealing an amputated left arm. Our student's gestural line was
brought to a crashing halt. Embarrassed, he abandoned the role he
was building even before the foundation was laid, pretending that his
inviting gestures were directed toward some imaginary audience
suggested by his reading. Such stigmata publicize body-maintenance
activities, and, when they are established in social transactions, inter-
fere with role performance.[2]

[1] *Genetic Psychology Monographs,* lxxi (1965).
[2] *American Journal of Sociology,* lxx (1964), 10–11.

It is not just the language of this (and all which that entails) but also its lack of imaginative interest in the relation of reading in a library to embarrassment and to erotic anxieties which make it so much less good at its own work than is Merrill Moore's sonnet 'Eyes in Libraries':

> I observe peculiarities
> In the movements of the human eyes
> Over desks of public libraries.
>
> Eyes there rove a bit more than is wise,
> Often show inquisitiveness or surprise,
> Notice gloves and shoes and socks and ties
> And even query *whose* and *whats* and *whys*.
>
> You can notice peculiarities
> In the motions of the people's eyes
> In and near to public libraries.
>
> Men and women go there to sit and read
> But they squirm and rove, survey each other
> Not as sister, quite, and not as brother,
> But more with nervous desire or anxious dread.

IX

THE TRUE, THE BLUSHFUL

ON the relation of Keats's sensuousness to his seriousness, Aubrey de Vere wrote excellently in 1849:

Perhaps we have had no other instance of a bodily constitution so poetical. With him all things were more or less sensational; his mental faculties being, as it were, extended throughout the sensitive part of his nature—as the sense of sight, according to the theory of the Mesmerists, is diffused throughout the body on some occasions of unusual excitement. His body seemed to think; and, on the other hand, he sometimes appears hardly to have known whether he possessed aught but body. His whole nature partook of a sensational character in this respect, namely, that every thought and sentiment came upon him with the suddenness, and appealed to him with the reality of a sensation. It is not the lowest only, but also the loftiest part of our being to which this character of unconsciousness and immediateness belongs. Intuitions and aspirations are spiritual sensations; while the physical perceptions and appetites are bodily intuitions.[1]

'His body seemed to think': when James Russell Lowell, five years later, spoke in such terms, he was explicit about their origins for him; of the idea of a separation of the bodily from the mental, Lowell wrote: 'But poets are not built on this plan, and especially poets like Keats, in whom the moral seems to have so perfectly interfused the physical man, that you might almost say he could feel sorrow with his hands, so truly did his body, like that of Donne's mistress, think and remember and forebode.'[2]

> She, of whose soul if we may say, 'twas gold,
> Her body was th' electrum, and did hold
> Many degrees of that; we understood
> Her by her sight, her pure and eloquent blood

[1] *Keats: The Critical Heritage*, p. 343. [2] Ibid., p. 360.

Spoke in her cheeks, and so distinctly wrought,
That one might almost say, her body thought.
('Second Anniversary', 241–6)

Donne's lines do not speak explicitly of a blush, nor are they to
be limited to that particular way in which blood speaks in our
cheeks and in which our body thinks, but the suggestion is distinctly there, warmed as it is by the 'degrees' of heat. Dr. Burgess's
book on blushing (1839) found it natural to use this very phrase
'eloquent blood':

What picture can be more interesting than the virgin cheek in the act
of blushing? The eloquent blood sympathizing with every mental
emotion, rising and spreading over the cheek—

'——— giving WARMTH as it flies,
From the lips to the cheek, from the cheek to the eyes,'

affords a beautiful example of that 'harmonie poetique' which exists
between the mental emotions and sympathetic system in man. (p. 9)

Elsewhere, Burgess's sense of the physical alliance between 'vitality'
and 'susceptibility' in a blush expands in the creative 'genial
warmth' of a quotation from Shakespeare to a fuller feeling for
vitality and susceptibility: 'The blood, the source of all heat, must
traverse through "gates and alleys," where it was not required
before, to diffuse its genial warmth, convey increased vitality, and
its natural consequence, susceptibility, to the part concerned'
(p. 126). To a contemporary reviewer in 1820, *Endymion* was 'not *a*
poem at all. It is an ecstatic dream of poetry—a flush—a fever.'[1] To
Thomas de Quincey in 1846 the challenge of Keats was simply a
mixture of the good and bad, not an inextricability of principled
pleasure and principled displeasure such as de Quincey's concluding choice of metaphor might rather have suggested:

It is in relation to literature, and to the boundless questions as to the
true and the false arising out of literature and poetry, that Keats
challenges a fluctuating interest; sometimes an interest of strong
disgust, sometimes of deep admiration. There is not, I believe, a case

---

[1] Ibid., p. 136.

on record throughout European literature, where feelings so repulsive of each other have centred in the same individual. The very mid-summer madness of affectation, of false vapoury sentiment, and of fantastic effeminacy, seemed to me combined in Keats's *Endymion,* when I first saw it near the close of 1821. The Italian poet Marino had been reputed the greatest master of gossamery affectation in Europe. But *his* conceits showed the palest of rosy blushes by the side of Keats's bloody crimson.[1]

That Keats believed that ordinary life demanded that one should be a good-humoured discriminator of blushes is clear from a letter to Reynolds:

My Dear Reynolds
I have parcelld out this day for Letter Writing—more resolved thereon because your Letter will come as a refreshment and will have (sic parvis &c) the same effect as a Kiss in certain situations where people become over-generous. I have read this first sentence over, and think it savours rather; however an inward innocence is like a nested dove; or as the old song says.

1

O blush not so, O blush not so
    or I shall think ye knowing;
And if ye smile, the blushing while
    Then Maidenheads are going.

2

There's a blush for want, and a blush for shan't
    And a blush for having done it,
There's a blush for thought, and a blush for naught
    And a blush for just begun it.

3

O sigh not so, O sigh not so
    For it sounds of Eve's sweet Pipin
By those loosen'd hips, you have tasted the pips
    And fought in an amorous nipping.

[1] *Keats: The Critical Heritage,* pp. 308–9.

4

Will ye play once more, at nice cut core
For it only will last our youth out,
And we have the prime, of the Kissing time
We have not one sweet tooth out.

5

There's a sigh for yes, and a sigh for no,
And a sigh for "I can't bear it"—
O what can be done, shall we stay or run
O cut the sweet apple and share it?[1]

Yet the deepest truest blushes in Keats are those within a pathetic
fallacy, known to be a tender fiction; this most human of bodily
sensations and communications is for a moment thought of as a
property of the non-human, and we are to ponder the human truths
and assurances which may come from imagining so. What the
pathetic fallacy does is spare our blushes. So Keats adapts Potter's
Antiquities, 'The bride was usually conducted in a chariot from her
father's house to her husband's in the evening, that time being
chosen to conceal her blushes'; Keats does not conceal her blushes
but he spares them by imaginatively and coolly transferring them
to the unembarrassable evening:

It was the custom then to bring away
The bride from home at blushing shut of day.
(*Lamia*, II. 106–7)

O for a beaker full of the warm South,
Full of the true, the blushful Hippocrene,
With beaded bubbles winking at the brim,
And purple-stained mouth;
('Ode to a Nightingale')

Why is the water of Hippocrene 'blushful'? The fundamental point,
clearly, is to intimate a relation between the delights of wine and
the delights of poetry, Hippocrene being the spring on Mount
Helicon sacred to the muses. So that the true, the real Hippocrene—

[1] 31 Jan. 1818; i. 219–20.

moving men to creative delight—is the real wine, not the imagined water. But the force of 'blushful' is not limited to this; the phrasing, 'the true, the blushful Hippocrene', asks us to think of relations between truth and blushing as well as between wine and the poetic imagination. Mrs. Allott aptly cites Crashaw in noting that 'Wine as blushing water has its origin in seventeenth-century allusions to the changing of wine into water at Cana.' *Nympha pudica Deum vidit et erubuit*—Crashaw's own translation, 'The conscious water saw its God, and blushed', harshly excludes the water-nymph. Yet the Biblical miracle is there in Keats not in order to lessen the miraculousness of ordinary wine and of the poetic imagination, but to give a sense of the ways in which they too are miraculous. The water of Hippocrene, like any water or any wine, cannot be said to blush —except by a conscious figure of speech—any more than a poem can; the relief and release of this are like the relief and release of wine and of poetry themselves. What Keats values in poetry is its strange true kind of blushfulness; that it can both create a composed embarrassment and free us from the discomposures of embarrassment.

Wine, too, stands oddly to blushfulness; it makes us less inhibited, less immediately liable to blush—but then more liable to flush and more liable, if altogether unrestrained, to be precipitated into situations for which we do indeed blush now or later. It is for these involuted contrarieties that wine can truly be called 'blushful'. Empson's note to his poem 'Bacchus' says: 'The notion is that life involves maintaining oneself between contradictions that can't be solved by analysis. . . . Drink is taken as typical of this power because it makes you more outgoing and unself-critical, able to do it more heartily—e.g. both more witty and more sentimental.' Both more and less embarrassable? The blush is both diffused and defused. Empson's Bacchus may call up Keats's:

> Now, when the wine has done its rosy deed,
> And every soul from human trammels freed,
> No more so strange; for merry wine, sweet wine,
> Will make Elysian shades not too fair, too divine.
> Such was God Bacchus at meridian height;
> Flush'd were their cheeks, and bright eyes double bright:
> (*Lamia*, II. 209–14)

It is a beautifully true paradox, then, that speaks of the wine which does its rosy deed and frees every soul from human trammels (embarrassments—'for I am everlastingly getting my mind into such like painful trammels')[1] as 'the true, the blushful Hippocrene'. To comprehend the full range and point of the paradox is to be aware of an important aspect of the richly ordinary reasons for which we estimate art.

Another of Keats's famous blushes within a pathetic fallacy is placed by him as a climax:

> A casement high and triple-arch'd there was,
> All garlanded with carven imag'ries
> Of fruits, and flowers, and bunches of knot-grass,
> And diamonded with panes of quaint device,
> Innumerable of stains and splendid dyes,
> As are the tiger-moth's deep-damask'd wings;
> And in the midst, 'mong thousand heraldries,
> And twilight saints, and dim emblazonings,
> A shielded scutcheon blush'd with blood of queens and kings.
> ('The Eve of St. Agnes', XXIV)[2]

Mrs. Allott's note provides exactly the right inauguration: 'A coat-of-arms. It "blushed with blood" because it was "on a field gules" and also showed the quarterings of the family and their royal connection.' John Bayley feels the word's amplitude: '*Blush'd* has a typically Keatsian weight; it universalizes the erotic not only among the living but back into the past, calling up the fears and desires that once warmed the dead.' Yet the amplitude, like the fears, is not limited to the erotic; the blood of queens and kings is not only their lineage and that which might rise even to their grand cheeks, but also that which is shed by queens and kings.

---

[1] See p. 42.
[2] Compare the cancelled opening:

> A Casement [ach'd] triplle archd and diamonded
> With many coloured glass fronted the moon
> In midst [of which] (wereof *above*) a shilded scutcheon shed
> High blushing gules: [upon she kneeled saintly down]
> And inly prayed for grace and heavenly boon
> The blood-red gules fell on her silver cross
> And [her] whitest (st *squeezed in*) hands devout

so colourfully and famously. For Porphyro—whose name is blood's purple—is risking his life, and we must let 'blush'd with blood' be suffused by blood which is shed. The first example in *O.E.D.* of a transferred sense of 'blush' is 'If our streets . . . should blush with the blood of Massacred Protestants' (1679); under 1866 it has 'The streets . . . Blushed with their children's gore'; and under 1747, 'But where the Saviour's flowing Vein Had blush'd it with a sanguine Stain'. 'A shielded scutcheon blush'd with blood of queens and kings': its pain and pathos are now the lovely consolatory dignity of art. Then Madeline herself is treated with the cool clarity of a pathetic fallacy, since though as a human being she could indeed blush, she is only appearing to do so:

> Full on this casement shone the wintry moon,
> And threw warm gules on Madeline's fair breast,
> As down she knelt for heaven's grace and boon;
> Rose-bloom fell on her hands, together prest,
> And on her silver cross soft amethyst,
> And on her hair a glory, like a saint:
> She seem'd a splendid angel, newly drest,
> Save wings, for heaven:—Porphyro grew faint:
> She knelt, so pure a thing, so free from mortal taint.

An angel, she does and does not blush; her breast, her very hands, blush by the gentle solicitude of a pathetic fallacy lavished upon a person. The unheated blush is not that of a lover's heated imagination; since the gules are indeed warm but only in colour (they are the gift of the wintry moon), the coolness of this pathetic fallacy—alive not upon a thing but upon a person—characterizes rather the quizzical affection which contemplates the love enjoyed by others.

M. R. Ridley is right to praise the change from 'And threw red gules on Madeline's fair face' but wrong to be so little interested in the blush, and to be so determined to sound unembarrassable:

Red is redundant and becomes first *warm* and then *rich* (carried over from the deletion in the last stanza); *face* suffers from all possible disabilities; it suggests no feasible rhyme except *grace* which cannot be deferred till the fourth line; it is feebly Leigh Huntian; and in any case we do not want the heroine red in the face, even though by the operation of lunar cosmetics; so alter it to *breast*. . . .[1]

This is too negative, and too much sees the imagination's choices as splendidly *faute de mieux* ('*face* suffers from all possible disabilities . . . so alter it to *breast*'); what is needed is a more generous conception of imagination's generosity, as in Leigh Hunt's praise of a moment in early Keats as 'a fancy founded, as all beautiful fancies are, on a strong sense of what really exists or occurs'.[2] Faces do blush; breasts do perhaps or sometimes; hands apparently do not.

The intimate mingling of a consolatory fancy with a chastened recognition of what really exists and occurs is at work in the most famous pathetic fallacy in English poetry involving blushing, where the blush is consolatory both as a benign fantasy about life and as a stoical recognition of the nature of life.

> Full many a gem of purest ray serene
> The dark unfathomed caves of ocean bear:
> Full many a flower is born to blush unseen
> And waste its sweetness on the desert air.
> (Gray, 'Elegy Written in a Country Churchyard', 53–6)

Dr. Burgess in his book on blushing (1839),[3] with true sensibility stationed Gray's lines in the opening paragraph of a chapter on 'Sensibility of Plants':

In the vegetable kingdom we can find an abundance of poetic allusions to the subject under consideration, in the name, for instance, of the *Blush rose*, of the *Carnation*, *Rubens uva*, &c., and who is not familiar with the following beautiful lines—

> 'Full many a flower is born to BLUSH unseen,
> And waste its fragrance on the desert air'?

A comparable poignancy, for many readers of Keats, is to be found in the deep pain and deep serenity of 'To Autumn'. A relation of the chaste to the chastened is implicit in Keats's letter to

---

[1] *Keats' Craftsmanship*, p. 152.   [2] *Keats: The Critical Heritage*, p. 59.
[3] p. 12.

Reynolds, with Keats delighting in the odd congruity of 'chaste' and 'warm':

How beautiful the season is now—How fine the air. A temperate sharpness about it. Really, without joking, chaste weather—Dian skies—I never lik'd stubble fields so much as now—Aye better than the chilly green of the spring. Somehow a stubble plain looks warm— in the same way that some pictures look warm—this struck me so much in my sunday's walk that I composed upon it. I hope you are better employed than in gaping after weather. I have been at different times so happy as not to know what weather it was—No I will not copy a parcel of verses.[1]

But to Woodhouse that same day he did copy the verses; and how strangely yet aptly he leads up to them, through warmth, and eating, and embarrassment, and social curtseys which are erotic courtesy:

Dear Woodhouse,
    If you see what I have said to Reynolds before you come to your own dose you will put it between the bars unread; provided they have begun fires in Bath—I should like a bit of fire to night—one likes a bit of fire—How glorious the Blacksmiths' shops look now—I stood to night before one till I was verry near listing for one. Yes I should like a bit of fire—at a distance about 4 feet 'not quite hob nob'—as words-worth says—The fact was I left Town on Wednesday—determined to be in a hurry—You don't eat travelling—you're wrong—beef— beef—I like the look of a sign—The Coachman's face says eat eat, eat—I never feel more contemptible than when I am sitting by a good looking coachman—One is nothing—Perhaps I eat to persuade myself I am somebody. You must be when slice after slice—but it wont do—the Coachman nibbles a bit of bread—he's favour'd—he's had a Call—a Hercules Methodist—Does he live by bread alone? O that I were a Stage Manager—perhaps that's as old as 'doubling the Cape'—"How are ye old 'un? hey! why dont'e speak?' O that I had so sweet a Breast to sing as the Coachman hath! I'd give a penny for his Whistle—and bow to the Girls on the road—Bow—nonsense— 't is a nameless graceful slang action—Its effect on the women suited to it must be delightful. It touches 'em in the ribs—en passant—very

[1] 21 Sept. 1819; ii. 167.

off hand—very fine—Sed thongum formosa vale vale inquit Heigh
ho la! You like Poetry better—so you shall have some I was going to
give Reynolds—

> Season of Mists and mellow fruitfulness,
> Close bosom friend of the maturing sun . . .[1]

The whole poem asks to be quoted:

1

Season of mists and mellow fruitfulness,
  Close bosom-friend of the maturing sun;
Conspiring with him how to load and bless
  With fruit the vines that round the thatch-eves run;
To bend with apples the moss'd cottage-trees,
  And fill all fruit with ripeness to the core;
    To swell the gourd, and plump the hazel shells
With a sweet kernel; to set budding more,
  And still more, later flowers for the bees,
  Until they think warm days will never cease,
    For Summer has o'er-brimm'd their clammy cells.

2

Who hath not seen thee oft amid thy store?
  Sometimes whoever seeks abroad may find
Thee sitting careless on a granary floor,
  Thy hair soft-lifted by the winnowing wind;
Or on a half-reap'd furrow sound asleep,
  Drows'd with the fume of poppies, while thy hook
    Spares the next swath and all its twined flowers:
And sometimes like a gleaner thou dost keep
  Steady thy laden head across a brook;
  Or by a cyder-press, with patient look,
    Thou watchest the last oozings hours by hours.

3

Where are the songs of Spring? Ay, where are they?
  Think not of them, thou hast thy music too,—
While barred clouds bloom the soft-dying day,
  And touch the stubble-plains with rosy hue;

[1] 21 Sept. 1819; ii. 169–70.

> Then in a wailful choir the small gnats mourn
>   Among the river sallows, borne aloft
>   Or sinking as the light wind lives or dies;
> And full-grown lambs loud bleat from hilly bourn;
>   Hedge-crickets sing; and now with treble soft
> The red-breast whistles from a garden-croft;
>   And gathering swallows twitter in the skies.

So compact, masterful, and yet gentle a poem is great in many
ways, and in suggesting that the poem suits my book I am not
saying that it is great because it suits my book. Nevertheless, I
concur with those who find this markedly the greatest of Keats's
odes, and there is no coincidence in its being also the one which most
naturally, subtly, and unmisgivingly accommodates the ambivalence of feeling which I consider characteristic of Keats's truest
imagination. For the conclusive climax of the single sentence which
comprises the first stanza, a sentence which swells and buds and
runs round the stanza's eaves, and which brims, is this:

> For Summer has o'erbrimm'd their clammy cells.

And the conclusive climax of the second stanza is this:

> Thou watchest the last oozings hours by hours.

Our delight in the hive and in the cyder-press is tempered by
'clammy' and by 'oozings'[1]—not lessened, but strengthened to
include a recognition of the way in which the delights of physical
sensation cannot but have a distasteful possibility which we must
magnanimously concede even in the moment of delighting in them.
Pressure: the ambivalence of physical sensation is another of the
strange, truthful, and bracing pressures which give poignant life
to 'To Autumn'—pressure downwards, loading and bending the
trees; pressure inwards, filling all fruit with ripeness to the core;
pressure outwards, swelling the gourd and plumping the hazel
shells; the pressure of poise and movement, as the gleaner steps
across the brook and yet keeps steady her laden head; the pressure
of sleep and of opiate; the pressure of the wind; the direct and

---

[1] It had been in manuscript 'oozing', which works differently upon us.

patient pressure of the cyder-press. And at one with all these, the pressure of futurity and of approaching winter. Then in the final stanza we have the pressure of Keats's greatest blush, again within the pathetic fallacy but to be apprehended—since it is not made explicit—by a sensibility as humanely apprehensive as the poet's:

> While barred clouds bloom the soft-dying day,
> And touch the stubble-plains with rosy hue;

So gently, so unembarrassingly, is this done that it may be argued that I am simply imagining a blush. But think of the blush of evening elsewhere in Keats:

> There blush'd no summer eve but I would steer
> My skiff . . .
> (Endymion, III. 357–8)

> The good-night blush of eve was waning slow . . .
> (Endymion, IV. 484)

> . . . at blushing shut of day . . .
> (Lamia, II. 106)

Think, too, of the association of autumn and blushing:

> The creeper, mellowing for an autumn blush . . .
> The creeper, blushing deep at Autumn's blush . . .
> (Endymion, II. 416)

—and of the fruit and mists for this season of mists and mellow fruitfulness:

> Autumn's red-lipp'd fruitage too,
> Blushing through the mist and dew . . .[1]
> ('Fancy', 13–14)

'And touch the stubble-plains with rosy hue': 'Somehow a stubble plain looks warm': is it far-fetched to quote from the manuscript of *Hyperion* 'Let a warm rosy hue distain', and to point out, not only that a line later there is 'And the corn-haunting poppy', but that

---

[1] Compare Byron, *Don Juan*, XIII. 76: 'An English autumn, though it hath no vines, / Blushing with bacchant coronals.'

these variants belong within this passage which is about a universal blush, the blush of evening clouds and of love, and about the power of the god who fathers all poetry?

> For lo! 'tis for the Father of all verse.
> Flush every thing that hath a vermeil hue,
> Let the rose glow intense and warm the air,
> And let the clouds of even and of morn
> Float in voluptuous fleeces o'er the hills;
> Let the red wine within the goblet boil,
> Cold as a bubbling well; let faint-lipp'd shells,
> On sands, or in great deeps, vermilion turn
> Through all their labyrinths; and let the maid
> Blush keenly, as with some warm kiss surpris'd.
> (*Hyperion*, III.13–22)

I think that the warmth and breadth of the last stanza of 'To Autumn' are directly involved in its tacit humanizing blush; just as at sunset the day is 'soft-dying', without pain, so it blushes without shame or displeasure. One might apply Empson's words about Shelley: 'It looks as though the race of man needs a feeling of being accepted by the universe, such as is immensely conveyed by Shelley, if it is to live with mental health or perhaps survive at all in the world presented by modern science.'[1] To be at one with the otherness of nature is the arching complement to that other impulse, to be at one with the otherness of other people. The erotic life of nature, like that of other people, is both warming and chastening to contemplate. Keats welcomes what would in any case insist upon making its presence felt, this large intimation of a parallel (at one with, but not one) between human and non-human life, taking part in each other's existence.

You perhaps at one time thought there was such a thing as Worldly Happiness to be arrived at, at certain periods of time marked out— you have of necessity from your disposition been thus led away— I scarcely remember counting upon any Happiness—I look not for it if it be not in the present hour—nothing startles me beyond the Moment. The setting sun will always set me to rights—or if a

---

[1] *Critical Quarterly*, v (1963), 270.

Sparrow come before my Window I take part in its existince and pick about the Gravel.[1]

'The setting sun will always set me to rights': how composed and unselfconscious is that progression from 'setting' to 'set'. 'Its [Poetry's] touches of Beauty should never be half way therby making the reader breathless instead of content: the rise, the progress, the setting of imagery should like the Sun come natural natural too him—shine over him and set soberly although in magnificence leaving him in the Luxury of twilight—'[2]

[1] To Bailey, 22 Nov. 1817; i. 186.   [2] To Taylor, 27 Feb. 1818; i. 238.

X

TAKING LEAVE

'To Autumn'—and it is this which makes its calm poise a thing
of such dignity—is a poem of parting: the parting of the day, the
parting of the swallows, the parting of Autumn, the parting from
life. Partings moved Keats to special sympathy, tact, and pleasure.
He relished the various affiliations of parting to embarrassment;
his practical joke on Brown with the fictitious letter depended
upon the parting from Brown which he renders so vividly, and the
embarrassment which Dilke deliberately let play upon Brown after
the flattery of the old ladies depended upon Brown's parting, pro-
tracted by Dilke's finding more than one window from which to
call after him.

For Keats it was a type case for the variety, poignancy, and
humour of human solicitude. So in one letter he quotes in full
Katherine Philips's poem 'to her friend Mrs M. A. at parting';[1] in
another, writing to his young sister he hatches from his own poem
a delicate departure:

> Two or three dove's eggs
> To hatch into sonnets—

Good bye I've an appoantment—can't stop pon word—good bye—
now dont get up—open the door myself—go-o-o d bye—see ye
Monday

J— K—[2]

Friendship was among other things an art of parting, without hurry,
embarrassment, or constraint. His friend Charles Cowden Clarke
records a crucial moment:

Keats met me; and, turning, accompanied me back part of the way.
At the last field-gate, when taking leave, he gave me the sonnet

---

[1] To Reynolds, 21 Sept. 1817; i. 163.
[2] 1 May (?) 1819; ii. 57.

entitled, 'Written on the day that Mr. Leigh Hunt left Prison'. This I felt to be the first proof I had received of his having committed himself in verse; and how clearly do I recall the conscious look and hesitation with which he offered it![1]

So it is apt, and again an illustration of the affinity between the creative imagination and the daily one, that Keats should have decided that the right way in which to part from his poem to Cowden Clarke was to live again his gradual parting:

> Since I have walk'd with you through shady lanes
> That freshly terminate in open plains,
> And revel'd in a chat that ceased not
> When at night-fall among your books we got:
> No, nor when supper came, nor after that,—
> Nor when reluctantly I took my hat;
> No, nor till cordially you shook my hand
> Mid-way between our homes:—your accents bland
> Still sounded in my ears, when I no more
> Could hear your footsteps touch the grav'ly floor.
> Sometimes I lost them, and then found again;
> You chang'd the footpath for the grassy plain.
> In those still moments I have wish'd you joys
> That well you know to honour:—"Life's very toys
> "With him," said I, "will take a pleasant charm;
> "It cannot be that ought will work him harm."
> These thoughts now come o'er me with all their might:—
> Again I shake your hand,—friend Charles, good night.

It is apt, too, that Cowden Clarke should be our witness to the poignancy with which imagined partings told upon Keats:

Once when reading the 'Cymbeline' aloud, I saw his eyes fill with tears, and his voice faltered when he came to the departure of Posthumus, and Imogen saying she would have watched him—

> Till the diminution
> Of space had pointed him sharp as my needle;
> Nay follow'd him till he had *melted from*

---

[1] *Recollections of Writers* (1878), p. 127

The smallness of a gnat to air; and then
Have turn'd mine eye and wept.[1]

The man who so much values that piece of writing is also the man
who knows why we so much value the ordinary writing of daily
life; to his sister Fanny, on the eve of his sick-bed journey to Italy,
he writes: 'It will give me great Pleasure to see you here, if you
can contrive it; though I confess I should have written instead of
calling upon you before I set out on my journey, from the wish of
avoiding unpleasant partings.'[2]

The most lacerating parting of all was from Fanny Brawne: 'The
persuasion that I shall see her no more will kill me. I cannot q——.'
'He could not', records Brown, 'go on with this sentence, nor even
write the word "quit",—as I suppose.'[3] There is a terrible irony in
the fact that Keats had written to Fanny Brawne: 'I shall never be
able to bid you an entire farewell.'[4] The vision of her which finally
haunted him had all the sharp misery and yet none of the merciful
finality of a parting from her: 'The thought of leaving Miss Brawne
is beyond every thing horrible—the sense of darkness coming over
me—I eternally see her figure eternally vanishing.'[5]

> And Joy, whose hand is ever at his lips
> Bidding adieu . . .
>   ('Ode on Melancholy')

But there are partings where the unpleasantness is not tragic
loss but commonplace embarrassment. One of the extracts which

---

[1] *Recollections of Writers*, p. 126. Compare the letter to Fanny Brawne (May (?)
1820; ii. 291): 'Perhaps then I may see you at a greater distance, I may not be
able to appropriate you so closely to myself. Were you to loose a favorite bird
from the cage, how would your eyes ache after it as long as it was in sight; when
out of sight you would recover a little.' The passage from *Cymbeline* is behind
Endymion, II. 579–84:

>   At these words up flew
> The impatient doves, up rose the floating car,
> Up went the hum celestial. High afar
> The Latmian saw them minish into nought;
> And, when all were clear vanish'd, still he caught
> A vivid lightning from that dreadful bow.

[2] 23 Aug. 1820; ii. 329.   [3] To Brown, 1 Nov. 1820; ii. 351.
[4] June (?) 1820; ii. 293.   [5] To Brown, 30 Sept. 1820; ii. 345.

Keats copied out from Horace Smith's 'Nehemiah Muggs' was
this:

> But in their hurry to proceed
> Each reached the door at the same minute
> Where as they scuffled for the lead
> Both struggling stuck together in it[1]

Such a social contretemps was always of interest to Keats because
he saw that it challenged human sympathy in an ordinary yet
taxing way—what *is* a fully imaginative and creative reaction to such
a social embarrassment?

> I must tell you a good thing Reynolds *did*: 't was the best thing he
> ever *said*. You know at taking leave of a party at a door way, some-
> times a Man dallies and foolishes and gets awkward, and does not
> know how to make off to advantage—Good bye—well—good-bye—
> and yet he does not—go—good bye and so on—well—good bless you
> —You know what I mean. Now Reynolds was in this predicament
> and got out of it in a very witty way. He was leaving us at Hamp-
> stead. He delay'd, and we were joking at him and even said, 'be off'—
> at which he put the tails of his coat between his legs, and sneak'd off
> as nigh like a spanial as could be. He went with flying colours:[2]

How beautifully this catches the importance of a daily triviality:
that people become embarrassed and embarrassing when they
cannot see the easy proper way to leave, and that how we then treat
them, and how they then treat us, may be an index of a true
humanity. How imaginatively (alive with its own tact) does Keats's
coinage *foolishes* ('a Man dallies and foolishes') bring together the
right cluster of things without the censoriousness or condescension
that would come from saying *becomes foolish* or *behaves foolishly* or *looks
foolish* or *lingers foolishly*. (And I do not think that the last 'good
bless you' should be tidied into 'god bless you'; it catches an
embarrassed trammelled muddle.) How rightly they decided that
the proper way out of the embarrassment was explicitly to maximize it—'be off'; and how rightly Reynolds, with modest but creative
imagination, saw that the proper way out of *that* momentary
doubt (would he be offended?) was again to maximize it; if they
spoke to him as if he were a dog, he would rise to the occasion: 'at

[1] i. 229.   [2] To George and Georgiana Keats, 20 Sept. 1819; ii. 207–8.

which he put the tails of his coat between his legs, and sneak'd off as nigh like a spanial as could be.' Then how affectionately Keats adds his own further punning tribute, not capping Reynold's enacted witticism but taking off from it: 'He went with flying colours.'

There is in this small anecdote even more which calls up Keats's subtle humanity, that 'widest heart' of his ('Indeed I think a real Love is enough to occupy the widest heart').[1] 'I must tell you a good thing Reynolds *did*: 't was the best thing he ever *said*.' For Keats's respect for words is at one with a respect for all which is not words, and for all those occasions when the best thing to say is to do something. What is here a comic delight can elsewhere underlie a tragic recognition:

> only his lips
> Trembled amid the white curls of his beard.
> They told the truth, though, round, the snowy locks
> Hung nobly . . .
>
> (*The Fall of Hyperion*, I. 450–3)

A touching combination of the tragic and the comic enlivens the anecdote told by Severn of the first days in Rome with the dying Keats:

On our arrival in Rome we were sadly servd with dinners and as the price was great Keats determined to set it right.—Neither of us could speak Italian sufficiently to do it, but Keats told me he had found an effectual way of doing it without words—When the dinner came in the basket as usual, he went & opend it & finding it bad as usual, he opened the window & calmly & collectedly emptyd out each dish into the Street & then pointed to the Porter to take the basket away —Keats was right, in a quarter the man returned with an excellent dinner nor did we ever have a bad one again.—We were not charged for the condemned one.[2]

For the 'effectual way of doing it without words' is clearly incomparably more effectual than any words could have been: ''t was the best thing he ever *said*.' A living imagination can seize from apparent disadvantage—as art can—the best thing to do.

Then, from the opposite viewpoint, it is characteristic too that he should go on from Reynolds's silent witticism (the tails of his

---

[1] To Fanny Brawne, May (?) 1820; ii. 290.   [2] *The Keats Circle*, ii. 135.

coat between his legs) to pay tribute to a witticism of Reynolds's and of another; the point, after all, is the better in that Reynolds might have been expected to reach for words:

He went with flying colours: this is very clever—I must, being upon the subject, tell you another good thing of him; He began, for the service it might be of to him in the law, to learn french. He had Lessons at the cheap rate of 2·6 per fag. and observed to Brown Gad says he, the man sells his Lessons so cheap he must have stolen 'em.' You have heard of Hook the farce writer. Horace Smith said to one who ask'd him if he knew Hook "Oh yes' Hook and I are very intimate." Theres a page of Wit for you—

Keats's special right to that last joke (Keats as the best of friends, with the best of friends) is the true complementarity of his friendships, like a hook and an eye: "Oh yes' Hook and I are very intimate."

Yet the complex of feelings, so warmly and comically affectionate in that anecdote of Reynolds's departure, is to me alive in the last letter which he ever wrote. Perhaps it is merely a coincidence, though a rather extraordinary one, that the earlier sequence should have been this: 'There was indeed a buzz about her and her mother's being at old M^rs So and So's *who was like to die*—as the jews say— but I dare say, keeping up their dialect, *she was not like to die*. I must tell you a good thing Reynolds *did*: 't was the best thing he ever *said* . . .' But consider Keats's last letter, that to Brown on 30 November 1820. What makes it so difficult for him to write is not only the pain and terror of his anguish and imminent death, but also the sheer embarrassment of it. How do you tell a friend that you are about to die, without the embarrassments of true fear or the embarrassments of false stoicism? True to the last, Keats makes his very last words ones which directly raise to Brown's and to his own attention this awful awkwardness:

Rome. 30 November 1820.
My dear Brown,
'Tis the most difficult thing in the world to me to write a letter. My stomach continues so bad, that I feel it worse on opening any book,—yet I am much better than I was in Quarantine. Then I am afraid to encounter the proing and conning of any thing interesting

to me in England. I have an habitual feeling of my real life having past, and that I am leading a posthumous existence. God knows how it would have been—but it appears to me—however, I will not speak of that subject. I must have been at Bedhampton nearly at the time you were writing to me from Chichester—how unfortunate—and to pass on the river too! There was my star predominant! I cannot answer any thing in your letter, which followed me from Naples to Rome, because I am afraid to look it over again. I am so weak (in mind) that I cannot bear the sight of any hand writing of a friend I love so much as I do you. Yet I ride the little horse,—and, at my worst, even in Quarantine, summoned up more puns, in a sort of desperation, in one week than in any year of my life. There is one thought enough to kill me—I have been well, healthy, alert &c, walking with her—and now—the knowledge of contrast, feeling for light and shade, all that information (primitive sense) necessary for a poem are great enemies to the recovery of the stomach. There, you rogue, I put you to the torture,—but you must bring your philo- sophy to bear—as I do mine, really—or how should I be able to live? Dʳ Clarke is very attentive to me; he says, there is very little the matter with my lungs, but my stomach, he says, is very bad. I am well disappointed in hearing good news from George,—for it runs in my head we shall all die young. I have not written to xxxxx [Haslam?] yet, which he must think very neglectful; being anxious to send him a good account of my health, I have delayed it from week to week. If I recover, I will do all in my power to correct the mistakes made during sickness; and if I should not, all my faults will be forgiven. I shall write to xxx [Dilke?] to-morrow, or next day. I will write to xxxxx [Woodhouse?] in the middle of next week. Severn is very well, though he leads so dull a life with me. Remember me to all friends, and tell xxxx [Reynolds?] I should not have left London without taking leave of him, but from being so low in body and mind. Write to George as soon as you receive this, and tell him how I am, as far as you can guess;—and also a note to my sister—who walks about my imagination like a ghost—she is so like Tom. I can scarcely bid you good bye even in a letter. I always made an awkward bow.

God bless you!
John Keats[1]

'I can scarcely bid you good bye even in a letter. I always made an awkward bow. God bless you!' Behind those words, with terrible

[1] 30 Nov. 1820; ii. 359–60.

pathos, there are the words of the aspiring young poet who had said: 'In a great nation, the work of an individual is of so little importance; his pleadings and excuses are so uninteresting; his "way of life" such a nothing; that a preface seems a sort of impertinent bow to strangers who care nothing about it.'[1] Even more poignantly there are the words of humane embarrassability: 'You know at taking leave of a party at a door way, sometimes a Man dallies and foolishes and gets awkward, and does not know how to make off to advantage—Good bye—well—good-bye—and yet he does not—go—good bye and so on—well—good bless you.' How staunch and imaginative it is of Keats that at the moment when he is indeed taking leave he can so perfectly accommodate his undisguisedly tragic suffering to a rich and simple solicitude for the embarrassment of others. 'I always made an awkward bow. God bless you!' It must be the least awkward bow ever made, and this for the saddest, fearful final bow. There is no more to say of it than that it brings tears to the eyes. 'The tears will come into your Eyes—let them.'[2]

It is better to end, however, not with the tragic solicitude of Keats's dying but with the solicitous comedy of his daily life. His delicate gratitude for others' delicacy is clear in one of the most tender passages in his letters, in its way a rueful tribute to a parting. It tells of how he met Isabella Jones again, and of the fineness with which she forgave him for embarrassing her and at the same time released him from embarrassment. The whole description is alive with a sense that it is 'taste'—not as a tremulous or self-important thing—which knows about our strongest appetites and our finest discriminations.

On thursday I walked with Hazlitt as far as covent Garden: he was going to play Rackets—I think Tom has been rather better these few last days—he has been less nervous. I expect Reynolds tomorrow Since I wrote thus far I have met with that same Lady again, whom I saw at Hastings and whom I met when we were going to the English Opera. It was in a street which goes from Bedford Row to Lamb's Conduit Street—I passed her and turned back—she seemed glad of it;

---

[1] Draft preface to *Endymion*.
[2] To George and Georgiana Keats, 14 Oct. 1818; i. 391.

glad to see me and not offended at my passing her before We walked
on towards Islington where we called on a friend of her's who keeps
a Boarding School. She has always been an enigma to me—she has
been in a Room with you and with Reynolds and wishes we should
be acquainted without any of our common acquaintance knowing it.
As we went along, some times through shabby, sometimes through
decent Street[s] I had my guessing at work, not knowing what it
would be and prepared to meet any surprise—First it ended at this
House at Islington: on parting from which I pressed to attend her home.
She consented and then again my thoughts were at work what it might
lead to, tho' now they had received a sort of genteel hint from the Boarding School. Our Walk ended in 34 Gloucester Street Queen Square—not
exactly so for we went up stairs into her sitting room—a very tasty sort
of place with Books, Pictures a bronze statue of Buonoparte, Music,
æolian Harp; a Parrot a Linnet—A Case of choice Liquers &c &c &.
she behaved in the kindest manner—made me take home a Grouse
for Tom's dinner—Asked for my address for the purpose of sending
more game—As I had warmed with her before and kissed her—I
though[t] it would be living backwards not to do so again—she had
a better taste: she perceived how much a thing of course it was and
shrunk from it—not in a prudish way but in as I say a good taste—
She cont[r]ived to disappoint me in a way which made me feel more
pleasure than a simple kiss could do—she said I should please her
much more if I would only press her hand and go away. Whether she
was in a different disposition when I saw her before—or whether I
have in fancy wrong'd her I cannot tell—I expect to pass some pleasant hours with her now and then: in which I feel I shall be of service
to her in matters of knowledge and taste: if I can I will—I have no
libidinous thought about her—she and your George are the only
women à peu près de mon age whom I would be content to know for
their mind and friendship alone—[1]

The self-possession with which Keats sets all this down, so entirely
without self-abasement or self-congratulation, is itself a tribute to
Isabella Jones. His erotic imagination and her affectionate imagination are both seen as intimately related to the deep multifariousness
of art and of embarrassment. There is the enigmatic relation of
public to private: 'and wishes we should be acquainted without
any of our common acquaintance knowing it'. There is the erotic

[1] To George and Georgiana Keats, 24 Oct. 1818; i. 402–3.

fertility of thought: 'I had my guessing at work, not knowing what
it would be and prepared to meet any surprise'—such fertility is
akin to the paradox of creativity (prepared to meet surprise) and to
a reader's attentive vigilance. ('And then again my thoughts were
at work what it might lead to.') Then there is the relation of the books
to the 'choice Liquers'; and the spring from 'sending more game'
to 'As I had warmed with her before', where the erotic sense of
game¹ warms into kissing her, and this warmth leads into an
embarrassment averted by her true courtesy as soon as kindled.
'She had a better taste'—how responsible yet unpriggish is Keats's
understanding of all the word should mean. Her intuitive resource-
fulness is like that of art: 'She contrived to disappoint me in a way
which made me feel more pleasure than a simple kiss could do.' Art,
and especially erotic literature, contrives to disappoint us in a way
which makes us feel more pleasure than a simple kiss could do—
and this without cramping or falsifying the occasions when it is a
simple kiss, and not art, that we rightly want. Yet the delicate
humanity of the letter comes out of embarrassment; to meet her
again and *not* kiss would be to be living backward, and might after
all embarrass her; but once Keats has made his mistake he is at once
freed from all self-reproach about it by her unembarrassable and
unembarrassing magnanimity. His appreciating her for it is one of
the things for which we greatly appreciate him, and it is especially
with regard to all such embarrassments as might otherwise make
us shrink, or blush, or be glassy, that Keats is of service to us too in
matters of knowledge and taste.

---

¹ Keats marked in his Shakespeare:

Fie, fie upon her!

There's language in her eye, her cheek, her lip;
Nay, her foot speaks. Her wanton spirits look out
At every joint and motion of her body.
O, these encounterers, so glib of tongue,
That give a coasting welcome ere it comes,
And wide unclasp the tables of their thoughts
To every tickling reader, set them down,
For sluttish spoils of opportunity
And daughters of the game.

(*Troilus and Cressida*, IV. v. 54–63)

The language in her cheek may be an exploited blush; and the metaphor of the
'reader' is to me profoundly acute about what unifies our imaginings.

INDEX